A Choice
of Poets

Editor: Dr David Edwards

NEW EDITION

Thomas Nelson & Sons Ltd
Delta Place
27 Bath Road
Cheltenham GL53 7TH
United Kingdom

© David Edwards 1999

First published by Thomas Nelson & Sons Ltd 1999
ISBN 0 17 432607 6
9 8 7 6 5 4 3 2
04 03 02 01

Author's Acknowledgements
I would like to thank everyone who has given me advice, support and
encouragement in the preparation of this book. Amongst my family and
friends, especial thanks are due to Brangwyn Edwards, Jenny and
Catherine Pinder, Roger Adams, George Macdonald, Paul Dongha, and my
wife Llinos. The staff at Nelson, particularly Sarah Mitchell, were
unfailingly helpful, and the pupils and staff of Hellenic College have been
a constant source of inspiration. Finally I would like to pay tribute to my
predecessor as editor of A Choice of Poets, R.P. Hewett. His edition has
been in print for over 30 years, and while I welcome this opportunity to
update the selection, I am aware of how popular and influential his
choice has been.

Designed and typeset by Moondisks Ltd, Cambridge
Printed in China by L. Rex

CONTENTS

Foreword   v

Introduction   1

How to Use this Anthology   2

**The Renaissance and Beyond
(1520–1780)**   5

Sir Thomas Wyatt   12
  Remembrance   12
William Shakespeare   14
  Sonnet 17   14
  Sonnet 116   15
Christopher Marlowe   16
  The Passionate Shepherd
    to His Love   16
Sir Walter Raleigh   18
  The Nymph's Reply to the Shepherd   18
John Donne   20
  The Bait   20
  The Flea   22
  The Sun Rising   24
  Song   26
  The Good-Morrow   28
  The Apparition   30
  Death Be Not Proud   31
  Holy Sonnet   32
  A Hymn to God the Father   34
George Herbert   36
  The Collar   36
Andrew Marvell   39
  To His Coy Mistress   39
John Milton   42
  Paradise Lost (extract)   42
Alexander Pope   44
  Essay on Criticism (extract)   44

The Romantic Era (1780–1830)   47

William Blake   54
  Holy Thursday   54
  A Poison Tree   57
  Nurse's Song   58
  On Another's Sorrow   60
  The Sick Rose   62
  The Garden of Love   63
  The Tyger   64
  London   66

William Wordsworth   68
  Expostulation and Reply   68
  The Tables Turned; An Evening
    Scene, on the Same Subject   70
  The Prelude (extract)   72
  Nutting   76
  My Heart Leaps Up   79
  Composed upon
    Westminster Bridge   80
  The World is Too Much With Us   81
  The Solitary Reaper   82
Percy Shelley   84
  Ozymandias   84
  The Mask of Anarchy   86
John Keats   90
  On First Looking into
    Chapman's Homer   90
  O thou whose face hath felt the
    Winter's wind   92
  Hyperion (extract)   94
  La Belle Dame Sans Merci   96
  This Living Hand, now Warm
    and Capable   99
  Ode to a Nightingale   100
  Ode on Melancholy   104
  To Autumn   106

The Victorian Age (1830–1900)   111

Alfred Lord Tennyson   116
  Mariana   116
  Song – The Owl   120
  The Kraken   121
  The Eagle (fragment)   122
  Ulysses   123
  Break, break, break   126
  The Charge of the Light Brigade   127
  Crossing the Bar   130
Robert Browning   132
  Porphyria's Lover   132
  My Last Duchess   135
Emily Brontë   138
  High waving heather, 'neath
    stormy blasts bending   138
  A little while, a little while   140
  Riches I hold in light esteem   143
  To Imagination   144
  Cold in the earth, and the
    deep snow piled above thee!   146

Contents

Star	148
Stanzas	150
No coward soul is mine	152
Matthew Arnold	154
Dover Beach	154
Gerard Manley Hopkins	156
God's Grandeur	156
Heaven-Haven	158
Pied Beauty	159
Inversnaid	160
Thou art indeed just, Lord	162

The First World War and Beyond (1900–1939) 165

Thomas Hardy	172
The Darkling Thrush	172
In Time of 'The Breaking of Nations'	174
Rupert Brooke	176
The Soldier	176
Siegfried Sassoon	178
The General	178
Wilfred Owen	180
The Send-Off	180
Dulce et Decorum Est	182
Strange Meeting	185
The Dead-Beat	188
Mental Cases	190
Anthem for Doomed Youth	192
Inspection	194
W.B. Yeats	196
The Lake Isle of Innisfree	196
An Irish Airman Foresees His Death	198
Edward Thomas	200
As the Team's Head-brass	200
T.S. Eliot	202
The Love Song of J. Alfred Prufrock (extract)	202
Robert Frost	205
Mowing	205
Mending Wall	206
After Apple-Picking	208
Two Look at Two	210
Tree at My Window	212
An Old Man's Winter Night	214
The Silken Tent	216
D.H. Lawrence	218
Piano	218
Last Lesson of the Afternoon	220
Intimates	222
Snake	223
The Mosquito	227

The Mosquito Knows	231
Think - !	232
Let us be Men -	233
W. H. Auden	234
Epitaph on a Tyrant	234

The Modern Age: After the Second World War (1939–1999) 237

Philip Larkin	244
Toads	244
Ted Hughes	248
The Jaguar	248
The Thought-Fox	250
Sylvia Plath	252
Medallion	252
Mushrooms	254
You're	256
Morning Song	258
Wuthering Heights	260
Blackberrying	262
Mirror	264
Among the Narcissi	266
Seamus Heaney	268
Mid-term Break	268
Digging	270
Follower	272
Blackberry-Picking	274
Old Smoothing Iron	276
Punishment	278
R.S. Thomas	282
The Evacuee	282
Farm Child	284
Cynddylan	285
Children's Song	286
A Blackbird Singing	287
Lore	288
The Window	290
Moorland	292
Derek Walcott	293
A Country Club Romance	293
Tales of the Islands	296
Midsummer, Tobago	301
The Virgins	302
The Bright Field	304
Grace Nichols	307
Those Women	307
Tropical Death	308

Glossary of Literary Terms 310

FOREWORD

A new edition of *A Choice of Poets* is particularly welcome because this text has long been one of the most useful collections for able GCSE students or those beginning A level. The collection has been extended to include additional modern and earlier poets, so that the student using the anthology can appreciate more of the main figures in the history of English poetry. The collection is helpful because it includes sufficient poems by an individual poet to give a flavour of the work and because it places the poet in the context of period and style. It dispels the notion that there is something distinct about 'pre-twentieth century' poets, that category so strangely and arbitrarily introduced into so many of our modern assessment systems in English and English Literature; instead it allows students to trace poets' uses of form and structure, as well as themes and ideas, across time.

At GCSE, as at AS and A Level, candidates are asked particularly to respond to literary texts in terms of their social, cultural and historical background and the literary contexts in which they were written and understood. The introductions to periods and poets in this collection, and the notes and suggested activities, help them to do this effectively, providing them with sufficient information to enable them to contextualise – but not so much that they are swamped by information about the poems and poets included.

We develop our own tastes and preferences by reading widely and by comparing the newest thing we come across with what we remember of what we have read before. Interested students may well be asked to study some of these poems and poets in depth, but I would also like to encourage them to dip into the rest of this collection and to read whatever sparks their interest. Poetry, after all, is not just meant to be studied. Much enjoyment can come from studying poetry in detail, but pleasure can also be gained from single readings and from dipping into an anthology. Because many poems are short they can be read and savoured in a relatively short time; this collection allows students to read in terms of historical context if they wish, but also allows them to read for ideas, feelings and uses of language as well as form and structure.

Earlier editions of this anthology gave me great pleasure both when I was a student and when I was a teacher. I hope that the present collection will continue to interest and engage new readers who, through their study of literature in school or college, will become independent readers of poetry.

Dr PETER BUCKROYD
Chief Examiner, GCSE English and English Literature,
and A level English Literature, for the NEAB

INTRODUCTION

Amongst the thousands of great poems to be written in the English langauge it is difficult to pick out the greatest. Even to pick out the greatest poets presents problems. This volume is a choice of poets and it will always be possible to dispute that choice. I have tried to represent some of the greatest poetry written at various stages of the development of literature. In each section there is always at least one poet, sometimes three or four, represented more thoroughly than others. This is so that, in keeping with the first edition of this title, there is the scope for some in-depth study of a range of work by the same author. However, I have also included several other poems written in the same era, chosen both on their own merits and in so far as they shed light on the poetry of the main poets I have chosen. There is not meant to be any value judgement implied: I am not suggesting that Lawrence and Frost are greater poets than Yeats and Hardy. However, I have found a body of work by the former which is sufficiently challenging, accessible and coherent both in its own terms and in terms of the light it sheds on (and often the contribution it makes to) the spirit of the age.

That spirit of the age is an important underlying theme in the edition. I have tried, in both the notes and the general introductions to the age, to give a historical context to each work so that it takes its place alongside other thinkers and poets, other events and trends. No poet writes in a cultural vacuum. As well as a biographical context there is always a wider one and to ignore that background is to risk failing to appreciate and enjoy many aspects of the poem. This should not replace close reading of a poem, but simply provide a frame for such close attention to nuances of meaning, and the effects of structure and rhythm, sound and sense, thought and emotion. The notes are meant to guide the reader to an appreciation of these local effects at least as much as to the larger context.

It is also true to say that some poems reach out not only to others written in the same era but also to different eras in the great tradition of the literary heritage. This is sometimes in the form of deliberate allusions to earlier work, often in the shape of unconscious echoes, but most frequently it is because poets, like all artists, respond not only to current and contemporary dilemmas, but also to the eternal human issues of love, struggle and happiness, birth and death, change and stability and our relations with our environment. The differing responses are always relevant, since these issues continue to define our humanity and to ignore what some of the wisest people have had to say on these matters is to impoverish ourselves.

Finally, it is always worthwhile remembering Robert Frost's opinion that a poem should 'begin in delight and end in wisdom'. There are many wise words in this choice of some of the great poets – but also the sheer delight in the magic of words and the wonder of shared ideas and impressions should never be forgotten. I can only hope that the notes help make the appreciation of these poems more, not less, full of delight.

How to Use this Anthology

Having read the introduction to each section it may be useful, before reading the poems, to look at those questions marked ☼ in the notes. These are designed to introduce you to the themes of the poem by making them personal and thus increase the possibility of involvement in the poem. The questions may be used as the basis for class discussion, written notes, the beginning of a creative piece of your own, or simply the subject of a moment's thought before confronting what the poet has to offer. It may be helpful to return to one's own thoughts after having discussed and analysed the poem. Did the poem surprise you or confirm your own thoughts? Consider any differences in history, class, background, gender or race which may have helped making the poet's response distinct from your own. It is often such personal insights which help us avoid mere parrot-fashion responses to literature. They help in a personal engagement with the text.

The commentary is generally brief and, though informed by research into what other critics have said, is naturally biased by my own stance on literature. It is meant as a useful guide but will often be the cause of debate about interpretation. Avoid quoting it at length in essays, particularly without attribution, as if these were your own ideas; instead ask yourself to what extent you agree with what I say. If a particular phrase seems to sum up a poem well, quote it and say who wrote it originally. I have never avoided using those phrases which form the specialist terminology of the literary critic. Many of them will already be familiar to you, but there is a useful reminder of their definitions in the Glossary section at the back of the book. When focusing on your own personal response to a text there is a danger that you might forget to include specialist terms like 'metaphor' or 'alliteration'. Such specialist vocabulary is not only invaluable in terms of describing the author's effects but shows an understanding on your part of the 'mechanics' of literature. I have deliberately tried to challenge the reader, believing that the dangers of condescension are greater than those of pitching too high. The inquisitive reader can always find out what I mean from a teacher or dictionary. I have tried to give clear contexts for difficult terms so that the general gist of what I mean will be clear from the rest of the sentence.

The questions I include are to persuade you to engage with particular effects within the poem, some of which may be obvious, others less so. Once again I use specialist terms wherever appropriate. Again the answers may be noted individually, written out in full, form the basis for class or group discussion or merely the subject of reflection by individual readers.

The longer questions (marked ✍) are geared towards essays or perhaps coursework and often involve comparison with similar (or dissimilar) poems within this volume. Obviously for an extended piece of coursework more research could be done, but the backgrounds to the poets and their eras should be borne in mind as well as the commentary and the answers to both the questions marked ☼ and those marked ✐ . You will find more essay-style (✍) questions at the end of the sections for each poet.

The Renaissance and Beyond *(1520–1780)*

The term Renaissance Man was made for such figures as Wyatt, Milton, Raleigh and Donne, all of whom occupied important posts in church or government as well as being amongst the great poets of a great age. Such all-round ability – these were men of action as well as thinkers – is one of the factors which led a great critic of our own century to claim that, in this era, 'thought and feeling' were united. T.S. Eliot was referring specifically to the work of the Metaphysical poets, the chief of whom was John Donne. Donne's poetry fuses together the rational and logical with the emotional and passionate to form a very human combination. The logic is never foolproof – but at the same time the emotions are always tempered by a witty and occasionally cruel intellect.

The poems are often a response to the massive insecurity of an age of political favours, fashions and intrigue in which an important courtier like Raleigh or Wyatt and lesser figures like Donne and Marlowe would attach themselves to great patrons (Essex, Leicester, Thomas Cromwell or the Earl of Southampton) to whose fortunes their own were then tied. Great successes were followed by terrible failures as reflected in Donne's obsession with figures of power. Death also formed an unsettling ever-present backdrop to the poets' lives, with the very real threat of execution being added to those of the plague and countless other diseases fuelled by the lack of hygiene in the era. It is scarcely surprising that the poets turned as often as they did both to God and to thoughts of poetic immortality. Preserving something of yourself – whether it be your soul or your poetry – for posterity became something of an obsession of this fragile age. Religious conviction was of course virtually universal at this time, but the form it might take varied. Catholics, persecuted throughout Elizabeth's reign (partly in revenge for the Protestants persecuted under her Catholic sister and predecessor, Mary) were denied any chance of advancement in the careers (law, the court, etc.) which really mattered. Many, like Donne, denied their early faith to become members of the Church of England in the hopes of advancement. It is certain, however, that faith was a very important part of everyday lives.

It was a combination of religious fervour (Charles I seemed to favour the gradual reintroduction of what seemed to be more Catholic practices into the Church of England) and the insecurity of living under the arbitrary power of the monarch which eventually led to the English Civil War of the 1640s, in which the parliamentary powers under Oliver Cromwell eventually defeated and beheaded Charles I. In the light of these insecurities it may seem odd to trace the huge outgoing confidence of this era. However, a young nation experiencing an extended period of peace under the Tudors and growing in power on the world stage afforded numerous opportunities for the young and adventurous, not merely in the court world but also in that of the new colonies. The imagery of maps and gold, sailing and adventure certainly finds its way into the poetry of the time. With it came the confidence in an era when anything seemed possible. Wit and poetry went hand in hand as demonstrations of poetic skill formed a way of impressing one's acquaintances.

Because of Britain's limited poetic heritage (since the days of Chaucer the language itself had changed) there were wonderful opportunities to create. Little seemed to have been done before so that the freedom was enormous. However, the lack of role models meant that the English poets turned to examples from continental Europe and, more importantly, classical Greece and Rome. It was a renaissance, a rebirth of culture after the dark ages of medieval times. The tradition of great literature, sustained throughout Europe in the study of the classics, suddenly seemed accessible enough to emulate. Thus the myth of Arcadia – a poetic paradise in hilly Greece – finds its way into Marlowe's work; the Italian form of the sonnet was reinvented for Elizabethan audiences, and references to classical mythology fill the works of the poets.

Conventions of comparing your love to roses and lilies, conventions inherited from the great Italian poet Petrarch, became widespread. It was partly in rebellion against this that Donne set himself. For with the new-found confidence of having the Elizabethan tradition behind him, Donne felt he might do without some of the classical models and rely on ingenuity and wit instead of age-old conventions. His love poetry assumes a sophisticated audience and a sophisticated lover to read it. His religious poetry is full of unexpected impudence as well as unexpected comparisons. Daring is the word one might best use to describe it and he was followed in this by other Metaphysical writers such as Herbert, Marvell and Vaughan. Following on from the great poetic dramas of the day (written by such great playwrights as Marlowe and Shakespeare), Donne and his followers introduced drama into poetry, as there is often either an ongoing situation described in the poetry or a huge sense of dramatic conflict as the poet attempts to persuade an unwilling reader to acknowledge the power of his arguments. Whether the poet himself is as convinced by these arguments as his sure tone suggests is another question.

BIOGRAPHICAL NOTES

Sir Thomas Wyatt (1503–42)

A diplomat who travelled widely on the continent, Wyatt translated and imitated the poetry of the Italian Petrarch. He was associated with Thomas Cromwell, who was eventually executed by Henry VIII. After this time (1540), Wyatt's fortunes turned. He eventually died of a fever after one last diplomatic venture for the king.

William Shakespeare (1564–1616)

The son of a Stratford glover, Shakespeare did not forget his roots and returned to buy property in the area after a hugely successful career. Initially an actor with various London theatre companies, Shakespeare went on to write many of the world's most famous plays. These plays contain some of the greatest poetry in the language, but Shakespeare also wrote and published poems. His sonnets, the most famous of his non-dramatic works, appeared unofficially in 1609. Probably written in the 1590s, they have become more celebrated than their great predecessors, the sonnet sequences of Sidney and Spenser. All of these use a variation of the sonnet form known as the Elizabethan or Shakespearian; all deal primarily with love.

Christopher Marlowe (1564–93)

Like Shakespeare, Marlowe came from fairly humble family, being the son of a Canterbury shoemaker; unlike him, Marlowe went to university. However, Marlowe remained associated with the low-life of London, being involved in various fights and brawls in a number of which men (including finally Marlowe himself) were killed. Almost certainly a spy, Marlowe's was a life necessarily clouded in mystery. However, he was widely celebrated for his plays and his poems after his untimely death, his plays in particular being a model for Shakespeare's own. Shakespeare paid tribute to Marlowe in his play *As You Like It*, referring to him as the 'dead shepherd'.

Walter Raleigh (1554–1618)

Born in South Devon, Raleigh became, after a brief spell at Oxford University, one of the most famous colonisers and explorers in an age of colony and exploration. He enjoyed Queen Elizabeth's favour intermittently throughout the latter years of the queen's reign, despite a marriage to one of her maids of honour, Elizabeth Throckmorton. A great friend of Marlowe, Raleigh was at times a soldier, an influential courtier and a very accomplished poet – a typical Renaissance Man. One of his most successful long poems ('The Ocean to Scinthia') was about the somewhat fickle favour of the queen. But it was the next monarch, James I, who had him tried and eventually executed on spurious charges of treason.

John Donne (1572–1631)

Born into a prominent and devout Catholic family, Donne went at a young age to Hart Hall, Oxford (favoured by Catholics because it had no chapel), but because of his religion he could take no degree. He studied law at Lincoln's Inn, London from 1592 and renounced his Catholic faith. This might have been due to ambition, or sheer fear for his life; his brother had died in prison after being arrested for sheltering a Catholic priest. He went on two of the anti-Spanish voyages of the 1590s, the second of which was with Raleigh to the Azores to hunt Spanish treasure ships. On this voyage he gained the patronage of Sir Thomas Egerton and became Member of Parliament for Brackley in Northamptonshire in 1601 due to Egerton's influence. However when he secretly married Ann More, Egerton's niece, he was dismissed from Egerton's service and then spent many years in the political wilderness searching for employment. In 1621, he gained the favour of James I's favourite, the Duke of Buckingham, who acquired for him the influential Church of England post of the Dean of St Paul's. He became one of the great preachers of the age. His wife, to whom one may presume at least some of his love poetry was addressed, had died in 1617 at the age of 33 while giving birth to their twelfth child. Dating Donne's poetry is difficult but it seems that much of the love poetry belongs to the end of the 1590s and the beginning of the 1600s, whilst the Holy Sonnets were written in about 1610–1611.

George Herbert (1593–1633)

One of Donne's many powerful patrons was Lady Magdalen Herbert of Montgomery. Her fifth son, George, was heavily influenced by Donne's poetry. He was at first an extremely ambitious and proud man, having pursued a successful career at Cambridge University before becoming a Member of Parliament. However he became disenchanted with the world of advancement and political power and became a relatively humble parish priest at Bemerton, near Salisbury. He decided to 'lose himself in an humble way', devoting himself to God, and performed his duties in his brief time as rector with unusual compassion, energy and humility, especially considering his grand family background. He died of consumption (tuberculosis) shortly after his fortieth birthday. All his poetry was religious and often deals with the priest's struggles with his faith.

Andrew Marvell (1621–78)

One of the great political survivors of a turbulent age of politics, Marvell was the son of a Yorkshire vicar who grew up in Hull before studying in Cambridge. He spent the Civil War years on the continent and had friends who were Royalist as well as others who were Parliamentarians. With Parliament's victory he became strongly pro-Cromwell and a Member of Parliament for Hull – a seat he retained until his death. He continued to favour the interests of non-conformist Protestants, even after the restoration of the monarchy in 1660, and was instrumental in Milton's release from prison. His lyric poetry has only recently (since the writings of T.S. Eliot) really been fully valued.

John Milton (1608–74)

One of the greatest English literary figures, Milton had already written many great works by 1637. After this date he wrote virtually no English poetry for twenty years, being heavily involved in the politics of the time. He was a hugely influential thinker and writer for the cause of Parliament, becoming Latin secretary to the Council of State, an important position from which he wrote numerous pamphlets and treatises about the morality and politics of the time. Partly because of his growing blindness, he was assisted in this post at one time by Andrew Marvell. After the restoration of Charles II, Milton retired from public life (after a brief time under arrest) and began work on his greatest poems, 'Paradise Lost', 'Paradise Regained' and 'Samson Agonistes'.

Alexander Pope (1688–1744)

The greatest and most influential of the Augustan poets of the eighteenth century, Pope was largely self-taught and his early work *Essay on Man* made him known to the literary circle of the day. His reputation during the Romantic period fell dramatically as he was considered too artificial, but he has again been appreciated during our own century as not only one of the wittiest of our poets but one of the wisest. He championed the causes of the Enlightenment, believing that through rational common sense as opposed to wild uncontrolled fancies human beings might achieve the heights of excellence. This is not to say that his work lacked imagination, but such imagination was always under the control of an intelligent and reasonable mind.

Sir Thomas Wyatt

Remembrance

They flee from me, that sometime did me seek
With naked foot, stalking in my chamber.
I have seen them gentle, tame, and meek,
That now are wild, and do not remember
That sometime they put themselves in danger   5
To take bread at my hand; and now they range
Busily seeking with a continual change.

Thanked be fortune it hath been otherwise
Twenty times better; but once, in special,
In thin array, after a pleasant guise,   10
When her loose gown from her shoulders
     did fall,
And she me caught in her arms long and
     small,
Therewith all sweetly did me kiss
And softly said, 'Dear heart, how like you this?'

It was no dream; I lay broad waking: 15
But all is turned, thorough my gentleness,
Into a strange fashion of forsaking;
And I have leave to go of her goodness,
And she also to use newfangleness.
But since that I so kindly am served,   20
I would fain know what she hath deserved.

This famous lyric of the early sixteenth century captures the mood of the era precisely. Wyatt was not only a great poet but a courtier, an ambassador and a professional politician in the court of Henry VIII. What seems like a love poem therefore becomes a metaphor for favours, political fashions and the loss of power, as fortune, or Fate, traditionally characterised as a woman, turns against people. Wyatt knew exactly what it was to be in political danger, having confessed to the king that Anne Boleyn (Henry's second wife) had been his mistress. The loss of favour in politics was of course not unconnected with loss of favour in love. Few women of the time would connect themselves with a man in political danger, although many did not have the option. Why would former lovers have *put themselves in danger* by entering Wyatt's *chamber* with *naked foot*? Explore the terms which make these women seem like creatures in the wild. In the second stanza Wyatt looks at one particular incident, a typical example of one *small* (petite or slim) woman granting her favours after a *guise* (a masquerade, or dance with masks and disguises). In what sense does the masquerade continue in the bedroom scene? In the final stanza Wyatt looks at the turnaround in fortunes by which she now gives him permission to go. What does she do in the meanwhile? Explain the final couplet referring to the sarcastic tone. Comment on the title of the poem.

WILLIAM SHAKESPEARE

*S*onnet 17

Shall I compare thee to a summer's day?
Thou art more lovely and more temperate:
Rough winds do shake the darling buds of May,
And summer's lease hath all too short a date:
Sometime too hot the eye of heaven shines,   5
And often is his gold complexion dimmed;
And every fair from fair sometime declines,
By chance, or nature's changing course untrimmed;
But thy eternal summer shall not fade,
Nor lose possession of that fair thou owest,   10
Nor shall Death brag thou wanderest in his shade,
When in eternal lines to time thou growest;
So long as men can breathe, or eyes can see,
So long lives this, and this gives life to thee.

This is the seventeenth in the sequence of 154 sonnets
which were originally published in 1609 but written in the
1590s. Why, according to the poet, is the person addressed
more lovely than a *summer's day*? Give as many reasons as
you can. To *lease* is to rent something temporarily; bearing
this in mind explain the fourth line. How will nature's
untrimmed, or wild and unpredictable, *course* ensure that
every beautiful person will *decline* from beauty? Why is the
expression of the idea both clever and succinct? Summarise
the argument after the volta. How can a person *owe* beauty
to the world? Death cannot *brag* that the beloved is in his
shade or shadowy realm, but the poet can brag about the
power of his *lines*. Explain the boast he makes in the final
couplet. Was he justified in the boast?

Sonnet 116

Let me not to the marriage of true minds
Admit impediments. Love is not love
Which alters when it alteration finds,
Or bends with the remover to remove.
O, no! it is an ever-fixèd mark,   5
That looks on tempests and is never shaken;
It is the star to every wandering bark,
Whose worth's unknown, although his height be taken.
Love's not Time's fool, though rosy lips and cheeks
Within his bending sickle's compass come;   10
Love alters not with his brief hours and weeks,
But bears it out even to the edge of doom.
If this be error, and upon me proved,
I never writ, nor no man ever loved.

What are *impediments* to love? What does the poet mean
when he says he does not want to *admit* such impediments.
In what three ways can the first four lines be said to be a
unit? Explain the next quatrain (5–8) in general terms
(bearing in mind that a *bark* is a ship) and how it forms a
change of direction from the first. Why would the metaphor
be a very relevant one in Shakespeare's day (discuss the
taking of the *height* of the star)? What would the *tempests*
represent in terms of love? How should love respond to such
tempests? Why would the *worth* (or size) of the star not be
known? A *fool* could be an entertainer, or a foolish person.
Explain the personification of Time as having a *bending
sickle*. Why would *lips and cheeks* come within the range
(or *compass*) of this sickle and yet Love would not? Why
does the poet use the adjective *brief* for Time? With what is
this contrasted on the next line?

How does the poet achieve a tone of absolute certainty in the
sonnet? Trace the stages of his argument. Are you convinced?

CHRISTOPHER MARLOWE

The Passionate Shepherd to His Love

Come live with me and be my love,
And we will all the pleasures prove,
That hills and valleys, dales and fields,
And all the craggy mountains yields.

There we will sit upon the rocks,   5
And see the shepherds feed their flocks,
By shallow rivers to whose falls
Melodious birds sing madrigals.

And I will make thee beds of roses
With a thousand fragrant posies,   10
A cap of flowers, and a kirtle
Embroidered all with leaves of myrtle;

A gown made of the finest wool
Which from our pretty lambs we pull;
Fair linèd slippers for the cold,   15
With buckles of the purest gold;

A belt of straw and ivy buds,
With coral clasps and amber studs:
And if these pleasures may thee move,
Come live with me and be my love.   20

The shepherds' swains shall dance and sing
For thy delight each May morning:
If these delights thy mind may move,
Then live with me and be my love.

It was a tradition in classical love poetry to offer a woman the delights of the simple life, the pastoral life of hills and rural retreats. Often the poet himself would follow the early tradition of Arcadia (an area of Greece famous for poets, mountains, goats and sheep) and take on the role of the shepherd. This convention reaches its height in English poetry in this beautiful lyric by Marlowe, where the offers of pastoral beauty are enhanced by subtle touches of wealth and security which might have appealed more to the young Elizabethan beauty for whom the poem was meant.

List the pleasures which the poet invites his beloved to *prove* or try. How does he combine the simplistic and rural with the more sophisticated and materialistic? Look especially at expressions like *purest gold* and *madrigals* (which were complex love songs for several voices). How do the rhythm and rhyme schemes add to the simplicity?

Before looking at the next poem, try composing your own reply as if you were the *love* addressed by the shepherd. Decide at the outset whether you are impressed or sceptical about his offers and then refer closely to all that he proposes. Keep the same rhythm and rhyme scheme in your reply.

SIR WALTER RALEIGH

The Nymph's Reply to the Shepherd

If all the world and love were young,
And truth in every shepherd's tongue,
These pretty pleasures might me move
To live with thee and be thy love.

Time drives the flocks from field to fold,   5
When rivers rage and rocks grow cold,
And Philomel becometh dumb;
The rest complains of cares to come.

The flowers do fade, and wanton fields
To wayward winter reckoning yields;   10
A honey tongue, a heart of gall,
Is fancy's spring, but sorrow's fall.

Thy gowns, thy shoes, thy beds of roses,
Thy cap, thy kirtle, and thy posies
Soon break, soon wither, soon forgotten,   15
In folly ripe, in reason rotten.

Thy belt of straw and ivy buds,
Thy coral clasps and amber studs,
All these in me no means can move
To come to thee and be thy love.   20

But could youth last and loves still breed,
Had joys no date nor age no need,
Then these delights my mind might move
To live with thee and be thy love.

Raleigh, a friend of Marlowe, as well as being an accomplished explorer and coloniser, was a highly accomplished poet. Here he takes on the role of the *nymph*, unimpressed by Marlowe's shepherd. Obviously the poem should be looked at in close conjunction with Marlowe's. In what ways does realism break through in the reply? Explore the role of time in the arguments of the nymph. In what season would sheep be driven from the fields to the sheepfold or shelters? How have rivers and rocks changed their roles from one poem to the next? Explore how both poets use alliteration in very different ways in the second stanzas of their poems. In the third and fourth stanzas, Raleigh uses alliteration slightly differently to highlight his antithesis. Look closely at those lines which can be divided into two halves, the first representing what the shepherd appears to be offering and the second looking at the reality. Having utterly undermined the shepherd's offers, the nymph chooses to be more gentle in the final stanza. What kind of tone does she finish on?

JOHN DONNE

The Bait

Come live with me and be my love,
And we will some new pleasures prove
Of golden sands, and christall brooks,
With silken lines, and silver hooks.

There will the river whispering run   5
Warmed by thy eyes, more than the Sun.
And there th'inamored fish will stay,
Begging themselves they may betray.

When thou wilt swim in that live bath,
Each fish, which every channel hath,   10
Will amorously with thee swim,
Gladder to catch thee, than thou him.

If thou, to be so seen, beest loath,
By Sun, or Moon, thou darknest both,
And if my self have leave to see,   15
I need not their light, having thee.

Let others freeze with angling reeds,
And cut their legs, with shells and weeds,
Or treacherously poor fish beset,
With strangling snare, or windowie net: 20

Let coarse bold hands, from slimy nest
The bedded fish in banks out-wrest,
Or curious traitors, sleavesilke flies
Bewitch poor fishes wandring eyes.

For thee, thou needst no such deceit,   25
For thou thy selfe art thine own bait;
That fish, that is not catch'd thereby,
Alas, is wiser far than I.

This poem perfectly indicates the differences between Donne's Metaphysical style and that of the poets who had gone before. Not content with trying to improve on the offers of Marlowe's shepherd, Donne makes the proposal an excuse for demonstrating his wit in one long metaphysical conceit – a complex comparison between two things which seem to have little in common. Here he picks up on Marlowe's image of *shallow rivers*: how does he improve on them in the third line of the poem? The theme of riches is continued in the fourth line also: what kind of lifestyle does Donne seem to be promising? How does he achieve a poised balance in these lines? What is the most crucial amendment to Marlowe's second line? The flattery of the second stanza needs to be looked at in relation to 'The Sun Rising'. Explain why the fish behave as they do in the second and third stanzas. Why is this rather peculiar flattery? How would the nymph display her power in the fourth stanza? Explain the various ways which *others* employ to catch fish according to the fifth and sixth stanzas. How does Donne wittily tie up the conceit in the final stanza? Who is the fish and who is the *bait*? Look back to the fourth line of the poem and explain why the terms used are suddenly very appropriate for what will happen in the world the poet has created.

In what sense is the whole poem a *bait* for a more sophisticated woman than Marlowe's poem addresses?

Which of these three poems do you find the most effective and why?

*T*he *Flea*

Marke but this flea, and marke in this,
How little that which thou deny'st me is;
Me it suck'd first, and now sucks thee,
And in this flea, our two bloods mingled be;
Confess it, this cannot be said   5
A sinne, or shame, or losse of maidenhead,
   Yet this enjoys before it woo,
    And pamper'd swells with one blood made of two,
   And this, alas, is more than we would do.

Oh stay, three lives in one flea spare,   10
Where we almost, nay more than married are:
This flea is you and I, and this
Our marriage bed, and marriage temple is;
Though parents grudge, and you, w'are met,
And cloysterd in these living walls of Jet.   15
   Though use make thee apt to kill me,
   Let not to this, self murder added be,
   And sacrilege, three sinnes in killing three.

Cruel and sodaine, hast thou since
Purpled thy naile, in blood of innocence?   20
In what could this flea guilty be,
Except in that drop which it suckt from thee?
Yet thou triumph'st, and saist that thou
Find'st not thy self, nor me the weaker now;
   'Tis true, then learn how false fears be;   25
   Just so much honor, when thou yeeld'st to me,
   Will wast, as this flea's death took life from thee.

What images would you expect in a poem which tried to woo a lover?

Typical of Donne in that it argues with a distorted logic, this poem traces the poet's attempts to persuade his mistress to sleep with him. We are to imagine the two close together and with a dramatic situation unfolding as the poem progresses. Fleas were more common even in rich people's houses in the sixteenth and seventeenth centuries probably because of the horses and other animals which they kept. The poem begins dramatically with a command to the mistress to *marke* or notice the tiny flea. What do you think the woman is denying him? Why do you think he is saying it is such a *little* thing? How, because of the flea, have they already been joined together? In the seventh line, Donne complains that the flea does not have to *woo* the mistress and yet still *enjoys* her. Why does this so annoy him, to see the flea so *pamper'd*?

In the second stanza, Donne begs his mistress to *stay* or stop. What had she been about to do? How would this, metaphorically, have killed *three lives*? How can the flea be exaggeratedly referred to as the *marriage bed, and marriage temple* in which, despite all opposition, they are already *cloysterd*, or living holy lives? Explain the phrase *living walls of Jet*. Why would the poet say that the mistress is *apt to kill* him? Why would she metaphorically be committing suicide and also *sacrilege* (in this case destroying a holy place)? Explain why all these three killings are *sinnes*.

What sudden change has occurred between stanzas two and three? Explain the phrase *purpled thy naile*. Why would the woman *triumph* – why does she think she has proved him wrong? Explain carefully the sudden twist in the last three lines, bearing in mind just how much *life* the flea's death actually took from the lovers. This, says the poet, is the same amount as the *honor* she would lose. Explain the two applications of the phrase *false fears*.

Compare Lawrence's poems on mosquitoes.

The Sun Rising

Busy old fool, unruly Sun,
 Why dost thou thus,
Through windows and through curtains call on us?
Must to thy motions lovers seasons run?
 Saucy pedantique wretch, go chide   5
 Late school boys, and sour prentices,
 Go tell Court-huntsmen, that the King will ride,
 Call country ants to harvest offices;
Love, all alike, no season knows, nor clime,
Nor hours, days, months, which are the rags of time.   10

 Thy beams, so reverend, and strong
 Why shouldst thou think?
I could eclipse and cloud them with a wink,
But that I would not lose her sight so long:
 If her eyes have not blinded thine,   15
 Look, and tomorrow late, tell me,
 Whether both the'India's of spice and Mine
 Be where thou leftst them, or lie here with me.
Ask for those Kings whom thou saw'st yesterday,
And thou shalt hear, All here in one bed lay.   20

 She is all States, and all Princes, I,
 Nothing else is.
Princes do but play us; compar'd to this,
All honor's mimique; All wealth alchemy.
 Thou sun art half as happy'as we,   25
 In that the world's contracted thus;
 Thine age asks ease, and since thy duties be
 To warm the world, that's done in warming us.
Shine here to us, and thou art every where;
This bed thy center is, these walls, thy sphere.   30

Like 'The Flea', this poem is dramatic. However the drama here lies not in ongoing changes in action but a twist in the argument so that the poet contradicts what he said at the beginning of the poem. The poet uses wit and hyperbole to exaggerate the importance of two lovers who are disturbed by the sun's rays. Why might this be irritating to them? How does Donne simultaneously scold and criticise the sun in the first stanza? What does he imply the sun is good for? Why do you think he does this? In what lines does Donne imply that he is above the worlds of court and country life? It is as well to remember that Donne's own court ambitions were frustrated. The seeming arrogance of the poetry is an essential part of his response to his setbacks as he created his own spheres of influence in imaginary courts and colonies. Explain the last two lines of the first stanza relating them to Shakespeare's sonnets. How could a person *eclipse* the sun's rays by closing his eyes? What view of the world does this imply? In what sense can the *India's of spice* exist in this one room? Why might Donne be so obsessed with them? Examine the pun on *contracted* in the final stanza. In which line in the final stanza is there a patronising insult to the sun? How does Donne turn this into a triumphant tone for the close of the poem?

'In this era confidence was everything.' In the light of this remark, compare this poem with Wyatt's 'Remembrance'.

25

*S*ong

Sweetest love, I do not go,
    For weariness of thee,
Nor in hope the world can show
    A fitter Love for me;
        But since that I   5
Must die at last, 'tis best,
To use myself in jest
    Thus by fain'd deaths to die.

Yesternight the Sun went hence,
    And yet is here to day,   10
He hath no desire nor sense,
    Nor half so short a way:
        Then fear not me,
But believe that I shall make
Speedier journeys, since I take   15
    More wings and spurs than he.

O how feeble is man's power,
    That if good fortune fall,
Cannot add another hour,
    Nor a lost hour recall!   20
        But come bad chance,
And we join to it our strength,
And we teach it art and length,
    It self o'r us to'advance.

When thou sigh'st, thou sigh'st not wind,   25
    But sigh'st my soul away,
When thou weep'st, unkindly kind,
    My life's blood doth decay.
        It cannot be
        That thou lov'st me, as thou say'st,   30
If in thine my life thou waste,
    Thou art the best of me.

Let not thy divining heart
   Forethink me any ill,
Destiny may take thy part, 35
   And may thy fears fulfill;
    But think that we
Are but turn'd aside to sleep;
They who one another keep
   Alive, ne'er parted be. 40

Unlike many of Donne's rather twisted lyrics, which follow the rhythms of a strongly argued, if distorted, logic, this is a more flowing 'Song'. However, even here, Donne cannot simply express his love but must always be proving and arguing – here persuading his mistress that by complaining when he leaves, she is harming, not helping, their relationship.

In the opening quatrain, the poet gives two reasons the mistress may suspect that he is leaving. What are these? Donne's reply is typically witty: that he pretends to die so as to prepare her for his eventual death. Explain this.

As in the previous poem, Donne both personifies the sun and exaggerates his own importance in comparison. What is the purpose of the comparison in this poem? What are the two attitudes to time described in the third stanza? Why is the poet referring to them? What are the effects of the lady's sighs and tears, as described in stanza four? A *divining heart* is one which thinks it can predict the future. What does the phrase *forethink me any ill* mean and how might *destiny* her *fears fulfil*?

The Good-Morrow

I wonder by my troth what thou and I
Did, till we lov'd? were we not wean'd till then?
But suck'd on countrey pleasures, childishly?
Or snorted we i'the seven sleepers den?
'Twas so; But this, all pleasures fancies be.   5
If ever any beauty I did see,
Which I desir'd and got, 'twas but a dream of thee.

And now good morrow to our waking souls,
Which watch not one another out of fear;
For love, all love of other sights controls,   10
And makes one little room an every where.
Let sea-discoverers to new worlds have gone,
Let Maps to others, worlds on worlds have shown,
Let us possess our world, each hath one, and is one.

My face in thine eye, thine in mine appears,   15
And true plain hearts do in the faces rest,
Where can we find two better hemispheres
Without sharp North, without declining West?
What ever dies, was not mixt equally;
If our two lives be one, or, thou and I   20
Love so alike, that none do slacken, none can die.

To say *good morrow* is to say good morning or good day.
Here Donne uses the term to describe the waking up of a
person who is properly in love for the first time – as if he has
been asleep until love woke him.

How does Donne achieve an informal, conversational tone in
the opening lines? What is to be *wean'd* and how does this
connect with the images of the third line? Why might these
qualities be associated with the simple countryside rather
than the sophisticated town? The *seven sleepers* were
legendary figures who hid in a cave during a time of
persecution near Ephesus. According to legend they were
found alive over two centuries later. How does Donne use
the legend? In the next line Donne claims that except for
love all pleasures are merely *fancies*. What clever example
does he give of *fancies* in the remainder of the stanza?

What tense is the rest of the poem in and why is this
important? How can it be that love *controls* all desire of
other sights? How can a face appear in an eye? In what
sense are they *two better hemispheres* than those that make
up the real world? What do you suppose Donne means by a
love which was *not mixt equally*? The metaphor is taken
from chemistry and describes two substances (what today
we would call elements). In the final couplet Donne claims
that if their loves for each other are *one* (the same element),
or of elements which are compatible, then their love will not
wane and die but last forever.

The Apparition

When by thy scorn, O murdress, I am dead,
   And that thou thinkst thee free
From all solicitation from me,
Then shall my ghost come to thy bed,
And thee, fain'd vestal, in worse arms shall see;   5
Then thy sick taper will begin to wink,
And he, whose thou art then, being tir'd before,
Will, if thou stir, or pinch to wake him, think
   Thou call'st for more,
And in false sleep will from thee shrink,   10
And then poor Aspen wretch, neglected thou
Bath'd in a cold quicksilver sweat wilt lie
   A verier ghost than I;
What I will say, I will not tell thee now,
Lest that preserve thee; and since my love is spent,   15
I'had rather thou shouldst painfully repent,
Than by my threatenings rest still innocent.

What forms might revenge take in one who has been
rejected in love?

 In what sense is the woman addressed in the poem a
murdress? Where does the speaker plan to haunt her? A
fain'd vestal is one who has pretended to be pure. Why
would this be a terrible insult to a woman in Donne's day?
Describe in your own words the scene Donne imagines as
his ghost confronts the woman. Why might her *taper* or
candle *begin to wink*? Why would the new lover be *tir'd
before*? Explain the humour of the next lines and the insult
behind it.

An *aspen* is a tree which shakes easily in the wind. Why
would she be *a verier ghost* than the actual ghost? A
detailed warning of all he might say would preserve her
because she would have time to repent of what she had
done. What effect might the vagueness of the threat have on
her?

Death Be Not Proud

Death be not proud, though some have called thee
Mighty and dreadful, for, thou art not so,
For, those whom thou thinkst thou dost
    overthrow,
Die not, poor death, nor yet canst thou kill me;
From rest and sleep, which but thy pictures be,   5
Much pleasure, then from thee, much more must flow,
And soonest our best men with thee do go,
Rest of their bones, and soules delivery.
Thou art slave to Fate, chance, kings, and
    desperate men,
And dost with poison, war, and sickness dwell,   10
And poppy, or charms can make us sleep as well,
And better than thy stroke; why swell'st thou then?
One short sleep past, we wake eternally,
And death shall be no more. Death thou shalt die.

In an age of plagues, poor hygiene and massive infant
mortality, death was much more commonplace, immediate
and conspicuous than today. Five of Donne's twelve children
died in infancy. It is no wonder that the poet personifies
death as a figure that swells with pride, godlike and all-
powerful. This sonnet, one of a series entitled 'Holy Sonnets'
written in about 1609, sets out to undermine death just as
the sun was undermined in 'The Sun Rising'. Being a holy
sonnet, the final reason for death's powerlessness is a
religious one. Where does the poet patronise death in the
first four lines? In what sense are *rest and sleep* the *pictures*
of death?

*H*oly *Sonnet*

Batter my heart, three person'd God; for, you
As yet but knock, breathe, shine, and seek to mend;
That I may rise, and stand, o'erthrow me, and bend
Your force, to break, blow, burn and make me new.   5
I, like an usurpt town, to'another due,
Labour to'admit you, but Oh, to no end,
Reason your viceroy in me, me should defend,
But is captiv'd, and proves weak or untrue,
Yet dearly'I love you, and would be lov'd fain,
But am betroth'd unto your enemy,   10
Divorce me, 'untie, or break that knot again,
Take me to you, imprison me, for I
Except you'enthrall me, never shall be free,
Nor ever chast, except you ravish me.

List the ways a fortress or walled town might be defeated in Donne's day.

This poem is a series of paradoxes in which Donne the preacher asks God to take control of his soul once more as if it were a walled town which had been taken over by the enemy. What tactical mistake is God making in his efforts to win back the soul? How does God emphasise the power of what is necessary in lines 1 and 4? Look at the sounds of the words and their positioning in the line as well as their meaning. Who has *usurpt* or taken over the town unlawfully? Explain the personification of *reason* as God's *viceroy*; why has he let God down? This is itself paradoxical as Donne uses reason or logic as much as ever to persuade God to do something about this situation! Explain each of the paradoxes in the poem. The final sestet changes the imagery from one of war to love – yet Donne forces it back into violent, fairly shocking images at the end.

Compare this sonnet with one by Shakespeare. In what ways has Donne achieved something new?

A Hymn to God the Father

Wilt thou forgive that sin where I begun,
Which is my sin, though it were done before?
Wilt thou forgive those sins through which I run,
And do them still: though still I do deplore?
When thou hast done, thou hast not done,   5
    For, I have more.

Wilt thou forgive that sin by which I won
Others to sin? and, made my sin their door?
Wilt thou forgive that sin which I did shun
A year, or two: but wallowed in, a score?   10
When thou hast done, thou hast not done,
    For, I have more.

I have a sin of fear, that when I have spun
My last thread, I shall perish on the shore;
Swear by thy self, that at my death thy Sun   15
Shall shine as it shines now, and heretofore;
And, having done that, Thou hast done,
    I have no more.

Donne wrote this hymn during a serious illness in 1623 and later had it set to music. Unlike the rather hectoring tone of the two sonnets, there is a genuine (though typically ingenious) humility in the poem – a humility nicely reflected in the simple rhythmical device of the final lines of each stanza. Try to work out the characteristics of each of the sins which is described. Do you find that they become progressively worse – as though Donne is challenging God? The first sin is 'original sin' which means that (because of the first sin of Adam and Eve in the Garden of Eden) each of us is born a sinner, imperfect and needing God's forgiveness. There is a subtle pun on the word *done* here, implying that just as Donne inherited his name, so he inherited sin. Where else does the poet use the same pun in the poem? Explain the pun on *Sun* in the final stanza. Describe the structure of the poem, explaining why it would suit music.

Does Donne display the same qualities in his religious poetry that he employs in his love poetry?

A later poet, John Dryden, complained that Donne 'affects the metaphysics', perplexing the minds of women with 'speculations of philosophy'. Is Donne's style too complex to make proper love poetry?

The eighteenth century critic Dr Johnson criticised the Metaphysicals for their conceits, which he described as 'heterogenous ideas yoked by violence together'. Explore two or three Metaphysical poems which use unexpected conjunctions of ideas. Do you find the 'violence' of the comparisons justified in the contexts, or too far-fetched?

GEORGE HERBERT

The Collar

I struck the board, and cried, 'No more!
　　　　　I will abroad.
　　What? shall I ever sigh and pine?
My lines and life are free; free as the road,
　　Loose as the wind, as large as store. 　　　　5
　　　　　Shall I be still in suit?
　　Have I no harvest but a thorn
　　To let me blood, and not restore
What I have lost with cordial fruit?
　　　　　Sure there was wine 　　　　10
Before my sighs did dry it: there was corn
　　　Before my tears did drown it.
　　Is the year only lost to me?
　　　Have I no bays to crown it?
No flowers, no garlands gay? all blasted? 　　15
　　　　　All wasted?
　　Not so, my heart: but there is fruit,
　　　　And thou hast hands.
　　Recover all thy sigh-blown age
On double pleasures: leave thy cold dispute 　　20
　　Of what is fit, and not. Forsake thy cage,
　　　　　Thy rope of sands,
Which petty thoughts have made, and made to thee
　　Good cable, to enforce and draw,
　　　　　And be thy law, 　　　　25
While thou didst wink and wouldst not see.
　　　　　Away; take heed:
　　　　　I will abroad.
Call in thy death's head there: tie up thy fears.
　　　　He that forbears 　　　　30
　　　To suit and serve his need,
　　　　　Deserves his load.'

But as I raved and grew more fierce and wild
At every word,
Methoughts I heard one calling, 'Child!'   35
And I replied, 'My Lord'.

This poem deals with the hard and narrow life of the priest, resisting all temptation. The central metaphor is the white collar of the priest and how this can symbolise those restrictions, as if the vicar were a prisoner. We are to imagine him sitting at a table, or *board* (perhaps a writing desk where he would have composed sermons), wishing to go *abroad* or out into town. The poem is an unusual example of the *carpe diem* mode, in which poets urge themselves or others to seize the day, to make the most of life on earth instead of trusting to the afterlife.

How does Herbert achieve the typical dramatic start of the Metaphysical poem? Why would the poet-priest *ever sigh and pine*? Why are the similes of the fourth and fifth lines effective? How does the poet achieve the effect of the *lines* of poetry being *free*? Look at the rhythm, the layout, the rhyme scheme – are these patterned and regular or spontaneous and irregular?

To be *in suit* means to be following a lord, always in attendance and never independent. Why is the thorn a good metaphor for the life of the priest? It was medically the practice to *blood* patients, to bleed them and get rid of bad blood. How would Herbert wish to replace all the blood he has lost (meaning all the pain he has endured)? What style of life do the *wine* and *corn* of lines 10–11 represent? How have these vanished according to Herbert? How might the *year* be *lost* to the priest and why only to him? How does this line show envy?

A crown or garland of bay leaves was traditionally worn by the poet, or the hero, and came to be a metaphor for fame and success. What regrets is the poet voicing in lines 13–16?

Discuss the change of direction after line 15. What does the poet mean when he says to himself *thou hast hands*? What opportunities might he want to seize with these hands? In lines 18–26 Herbert characterises the life of the priest in very negative terms. Discuss each of the metaphors and adjectives he uses, bearing in mind that to *wink* meant to close both eyes. The *death's head* or memento mori was a real human skull which priests often kept on their desks to remind them of death – that life is short and the *sands* of time can quickly run out leaving little chance to live a good and holy life. The *rope* of lines 22–5 is reversed in line 29. How? Explain lines 30–32. Comment on the effectiveness of the closing lines.

Compare this poem in detail with any by the other poet-priests in this volume, Donne, Hopkins and Thomas.

ANDREW MARVELL

To His Coy Mistress

Had we but world enough, and time,
This coyness, Lady, were no crime.
We would sit down and think which way
To walk and pass our long love's day.
Thou by the Indian Ganges' side   5
Shouldst rubies find: I by the tide
Of Humber would complain. I would
Love you ten years before the Flood,
And you should, if you please, refuse
Till the conversion of the Jews.   10
My vegetable love should grow
Vaster than empires, and more slow;
An hundred years should go to praise
Thine eyes and on thy forehead gaze;
Two hundred to adore each breast;   15
But thirty thousand to the rest;
An age at least to every part,
And the last age should show your heart;
For, Lady, you deserve this state,
Nor would I love at lower rate.   20
    But at my back I always hear
Time's wingèd chariot hurrying near;
And yonder all before us lie
Deserts of vast eternity.
Thy beauty shall no more be found,   25
Nor, in thy marble vault, shall sound
My echoing song: then worms shall try
That long preserved virginity,
And your quaint honour turn to dust,
And into ashes all my lust: 30
The grave's a fine and private place,
But none, I think, do there embrace.

Now therefore, while the youthful hue
Sits on thy skin like morning dew,
And while thy willing soul transpires   35
At every pore with instant fires,
Now let us sport us while we may,
And now, like amorous birds of prey,
Rather at once our time devour
Than languish in his slow-chapt power.   40
Let us roll all our strength and all
Our sweetness up into one ball,
And tear our pleasures with rough strife
Thorough the iron gates of life:
Thus, though we cannot make our sun   45
Stand still, yet we will make him run.

What does *coyness* mean and why might the poet regard it
as a *crime* in his mistress? As in the poems of Donne and
the other Metaphysical poets, there is a very strong line of
argument running through the poem as the poet tries to
persuade his mistress to sleep with him. Briefly summarise
this argument in your own words, clearly preserving the
three stages of argument. Why is *carpe diem* the perfect
phrase to sum it up? How and why does the poet slow down
the rhythm in the phrase *long love's day*? What does the
phrase mean?

The exotic and the mundane (or ordinary) are summed up
in the poet's choice of rivers. He lived by the Humber (in
Hull) whilst the slow-flowing Ganges is thousands of miles
away. Of what might the poet *complain* in this ideal world?
Which *flood* is the poet referring to and when will the
conversion of the Jews be? What does the poet mean by
vegetable love? Contrast this with the *animal love* at the end
of the poem. Why would the *last age* describe the mistress'
heart? Why is *deserts of vast eternity* such an excellent
image for death? How does the poet seek to disgust and
frighten his mistress in the next lines? Which of the images
do you find most striking and why?

How does the poet achieve a change of tone after line 32? There is a pun on *willing*, the main meaning being alive, or able to will or control one's own destiny. What is the second meaning? To transpire is to breathe or to perspire. What physical effects is the poet hoping his poetry will have on his mistress in lines 35–6? *Slow-chapt* means slowly devouring. Why is this an effective image for *time*? How does the poet intend to turn the tables on time? What do the images of physical love in the remainder of the poem have in common? How are they very different from those in the first section? Do you find them appealing? How does the poet achieve the effects of energy and speed in these lines? Discuss the final couplet.

How persuasive do you find this poem?

'Strong lines' is one term used to describe the Metaphysical poets. How 'strong' do you find their poetry? Consider originality, opening lines, lines of argument, rhetorical devices and images designed to shock in your answer.

JOHN MILTON

Paradise Lost *(extract)*

Now came still ev'ning on, and twilight gray
Had in her sober livery all things clad;
Silence accompanied, for beast and bird,
They to their grassy couch, these to their nests
Were slunk, all but the wakeful nightingale;   5
She all night long her amorous descant sung;
Silence was pleased. Now glowed the firmament
With living sapphires; Hesperus that led
The starry host, rode brightest, till the moon
Rising in clouded majesty, at length   10
Apparent queen unveiled her peerless light,
And o'er the dark her silver mantle threw.

This passage is a description of 'evening in paradise.' What sounds and sights would you expect the scene to include?

From the fourth book of Milton's great epic poem 'Paradise Lost' (lines 598–609), the extract describes an evening when Adam and Eve, still innocent and living in the Garden of Eden, are about to retire to sleep. Milton uses personification five times in this brief passage, each time with a different effect. Why would he characterise *twilight* as one who dresses things in *sober livery*, the *nightingale* as a cathedral choirboy, *silence* as an appreciative audience awed by the nightingale's song, the evening star *Hesperus* as the leader of an army, and the *moon* as a *queen* dressed in silver? How does the final personification relate back to the first? What differences are there? Why might the nightingale's song be appropriately described as *amorous*? Explain the expressions *living sapphires* and *peerless light*.

The poet employs blank verse, enjambement, Miltonic inversion (where normal English word order is reversed like French or Latin) and references to classical gods and figures to give his great poem more epic weight and grandeur. Pick out the most striking instances of these within this passage and discuss their effectiveness. How does he achieve the effect of harmony in the passage?

ALEXANDER POPE

Essay on Criticism (extract)

Some to *Conceit* alone their taste confine,
And glitt'ring thoughts struck out at ev'ry line;
Pleas'd with a work where nothing's just or fit;
One glaring Chaos and wild heap of wit.
Poets like painters, thus, unskill'd to trace   5
The naked nature and the living grace,
With gold and jewels cover ev'ry part,
And hide with ornaments their want of art.
True Wit is Nature to advantage dress'd,
What oft was thought, but ne'er so well
   express'd;   10
Something, whose truth convinc'd at sight
   we find,
That gives us back the image of our mind.
As shades more sweetly recommend the light,
So modest plainness sets off sprightly wit.
For works may have more wit than does
   'em good,   15
As bodies perish thro' excess of blood.

Published in 1711 when Pope was only 22, the 'Essay on
Criticism' is the poet's attempt to lay down the rules of good
taste. Following the example of Dryden and the Augustan
poets of classical Rome, Pope defends a poised balance in
art as opposed to intense extremes. The poem fulfils its own
didactic principles of decorum, graceful expression and
balance. The heroic couplet – a pair of rhymed lines of
iambic pentameter – reached its apogee in the hands of
Pope, as he frequently balances one line against another
and even the first half of a line with the second, using the
caesura. Which of the couplets do you find the most elegant
and which the most thoughtful? Study the various ways
Pope uses balance in this extract.

Taking any of Pope's phrases from this extract, write an
essay in which you decide whether he is justified or
unjustified in his attack on the Metaphysical poets and their
love of *wit, conceit* and *excess*.

The Romantic Era

(1780–1830)

An age which opened explosively in two major political revolutions challenged many dearly held convictions of the old hierarchy both in literature and the wider world. For just as the young American nation and the French revolutionary forces overturned the might of an established colonial power and the monarch and aristocracy of the *ancien régime*, so the literary establishment was shaken with the arrival of such rebels as William Blake, William Wordsworth and Percy Shelley.

The poetic rebellion of these Romantic writers took two forms: their choice of subject matter, and the structure of their poetry. Unlike their predecessors the Augustans (of whom Alexander Pope was the greatest), they chose to write about a wild untamed nature and simple unrefined folk. To Pope, civilised sophistication was what humanity should be aiming for. To the Romantics, society, social rules and refinement were often to blame in corrupting the beauty of the human spirit. Whilst the Augustans liked their nature (including human nature) 'tamed', the Romantics preferred it in its elemental uncultivated state. Hence their celebration of children and simple country folk, who were more in touch with the natural instinctive state, less cluttered with rules of propriety. This can also partly explain their turning to less sophisticated times such as the Middle Ages or Ancient Greece.

Such a rebellion in taste accompanied a feeling that liberty and genuine emotion were important in people's lives. The passion for liberty often brought these poets into open conflict with the authorities. Blake was deeply associated with the revolutionary thinkers of the 1790s, a time of hope for Britain's lower classes that, following the example of the French Revolution, the British would make rapid advances in sharing power. Only landowners held the vote at this time and power and wealth were concentrated in the hands of the few. Such hopes for change were short-lived as William Pitt and his government quickly clamped down on any signs of rebellious thought, and free speech itself was severely diminished. This attack was accompanied by a growing sense of what was considered 'decent', and, of course 'indecent' too; the publishing of many of the poems of the Romantics were therefore acts of bravery. All of the poets here included were at one time or another attacked by critics for being dangerous radical thinkers whose poetry ought not to be encouraged. One of the main reasons for this, especially for the poems of Keats, Byron and Shelley, was that the poetry was considered too explicit in its sexual content. Britain, despite the excesses of the Prince Regent, was rapidly moving towards the Victorian values which dominated the country at least as far as the 1960s.

In form as well as content the Romantics rebelled against the work of their predecessors. The heroic couplet which had dominated poetry for so long was replaced by various alternatives. The ballad form associated with the simple and rustic was extensively used by Blake and Wordsworth. All of the poets turned to the blank verse favoured by Milton (but with fewer of his Latinate inversions); when they used the iambic rhyming couplet it was often with strong enjambement which, like blank verse, encourages flow and natural freedom. Their verses were more spontaneous and unrestricted, following the natural rhythms of speech and thought. When regular rhythms and end-stopping were used it was because the forms were folk songs which encouraged simplicity, though often with an underlying depth and profundity. Old forms such as the sonnet and the ode were invested with a new energy and intensity.

As well as championing liberal causes, the Romantics were fascinated with individual development and psychology, the processes of the imagination, and how we become ourselves. The greatest single expression of this curiosity is Wordsworth's 'Prelude' but it can be seen in Blake's and Keats' works also. Shelley, equally fascinated by the way the human brain works, is represented below by more explicitly political poetry. Unlike Keats, Shelley felt able to publish direct attacks on those in power. Keats believed that poetry should not be so explicitly political. He disliked poetry which seemed to have a purpose rather than being merely beautiful in its own right. However, if all of the Romantics share any common purpose, it was to celebrate the imaginative powers and freedom of the natural human being – and to oppose any forced restriction on the individual. And celebrate they did, in one of the most potent bursts of poetic creativity the nation has seen.

BIOGRAPHICAL NOTES

William Blake (1757–1827)

The only great poet of the English Romantic movement who was genuinely working class, Blake was the son of a hosier and himself trained as an engraver. This was an important trade in the eighteenth century as it was the only way of reproducing representations or prints of classic pictures, as well as new designs and illustrations for books and journals. Blake was a very accomplished engraver, both of others' work and his own original designs. His own books of poetry, beginning with *Poetical Sketches* (1783) were often lavishly illustrated, with only small amounts of the books published because of the time and care which was given over to their production. In order to appreciate the works just as Blake intended them, it might be useful to see an illustrated version. The small print runs of the works is one of the reasons for Blake's lack of fame in his lifetime. Other reasons included the obscurity of the works (some of the longer poems are notoriously difficult to understand) and the fact that he was such an outspoken rebel.

Blake claimed, through a character in 'Jerusalem', one of his longer poems, that he 'must Create a System, or be enslav'd by another Man's' and his verse certainly bears this statement out: the rebellion against the form of earlier poetry, as well as against the Enlightenment (see notes on

Pope) and puritanical repressive Christianity, is very evident throughout his longer more mystical texts and the shorter lyrics included here. *Songs of Innocence* was published in 1789 during the early stage of the French Revolution. Partly as an answer to the lack of change in Britain in the 1790s, Blake republished the book in 1794 alongside *Songs of Experience*. The two views of life, one full of hope and innocence, the other full of the bitter fruits of experience, go hand in hand.

William Wordsworth (1770–1850)

Born and brought up in the Lake District, Wordsworth's poetry is full of his passionate belief in the beauty and power of the English countryside, much of it expressed in almost mystical terms as a semi-religious experience. Nature was, to Wordsworth, not merely something beautiful but an expression both of the 'spirit' which sustained the universe and of the 'still, sad music of humanity' ('Lines Written Above Tintern Abbey'). His poetry was an effort to reconcile this 'sad music' with the spirit of nature. He quite often chose to write about ordinary country people rather than exalted 'important' folk, and chose the simple style of *Lyrical Ballads* as the expression of this choice. Written with his friend Coleridge, and published first in 1798, it was an extremely important Romantic text, one which puzzled and offended the critics of the time. Such early work reflects his radical liberal views at this time, views kindled by his visit to France of 1791 at the height of the Revolution. He came to regard the Revolution, especially after the 'terror' of the guillotine in the mid-1790s, as an extremely flawed example of the human endeavour to achieve the ideal and gradually became more conservative in his views until he was made Poet Laureate in 1843, having settled once more in his native Lake District.

Perhaps his greatest achievements were in the exploration of his own mind, in a combination of autobiography, psychology and philosophy which seeks to discover great universal truths based in his own experience. 'The Prelude',

the supreme expression of this strand of his work, was
begun in 1798 but was reworked and expanded throughout
the poet's life and only published after his death.

Percy Shelley (1792–1822)

The son of a baronet (a minor English lord), Shelley was
educated at Eton and Oxford. Ever the rebel, he was
expelled from university for publishing a pamphlet about
atheism, eloped twice with young and impressionable girls,
attempted to educate the working classes in obscure radical
theories and ended up living in Italy along with his great
friends Lord Byron and the liberal editor Leigh Hunt. His
poetry was always intelligent and full of ideas but sometimes
a little obscure. As the century progressed Shelley's
reputation gradually improved and some of his ideas about
equality and democracy began to seem a little less radical.

John Keats (1795–1821)

Unlike Wordsworth and Shelley, Keats was from the lower
middle classes, never went to Oxford or Cambridge and was
mocked by the journals for having the audacity to write and
publish poetry at all. The son of an ostler, he grew up in a
London coaching inn before the death of his father and the
departure of his mother left him a virtual orphan and the
eldest of four, responsible for his younger siblings. He
trained as a doctor but gave up this career after meeting his
hero Leigh Hunt, who encouraged him in the belief that, with
Shelley, he embodied the youthful hope of poetry in
England. He was strongly influenced by Wordsworth but in
the sudden and intense flowering of poetry between 1818
and 1819 he acquired his own poetic voice, one
characterised by intensity, rich ambiguous expression, and a
lush sensuousness. During 1818 he had seen one brother
emigrate to America, and then had to nurse his loved
younger brother Tom until his death by consumption (or
tuberculosis) in December of that year. The following winter
he was to recognise the symptoms of the disease in himself.

This effectively curtailed his brief and turbulent engagement to Frances Brawne, a neighbour who alternately enraptured and frustrated him. He journeyed to Italy to escape the English winter at the end of 1820, but died in Rome a few months after his twenty-fifth birthday. Attacked in his own day as a presumptuous upstart from the lower classes (and a friend of radicals like Hunt), his reputation grew quickly after his death, accompanied by the myth of the youthful genius supposedly killed by harsh insensitive criticism.

*H*oly Thursday

Twas on a Holy Thursday, their innocent faces clean,
The children walking two & two in red & blue &
    green;
Grey headed beadles walkd before with wands as
    white as snow,
Till into the high dome of Paul's they like Thames
    waters flow.

O what a multitude they seemed, these flowers of
    London town;   5
Seated in companies they sit with radiance all their
    own.
The hum of multitudes was there but multitudes of
    lambs,
Thousands of little boys & girls raising their innocent
    hands.

Now like a mighty wind they raise to heaven the voice
    of song
Or like harmonious thunderings the seats of heaven
    among.   10
Beneath them sit the aged men, wise guardians of
    the poor.
Then cherish pity, lest you drive an angel from your
    door.

*H*oly Thursday

Is this a holy thing to see,
In a rich and fruitful land,
Babes reduced to misery,
Fed with cold and usurous hand?

Is that trembling cry a song?   5
Can it be a song of joy?
And so many children poor?
It is a land of poverty!

And their sun does never shine.
And their fields are bleak & bare.   10
And their ways are fill'd with thorns.
It is eternal winter there.

For where-e'er the sun does shine,
And where-e'er the rain does fall:
Babe can never hunger there,   15
Nor poverty the mind appall.

The first of these two poems, from *Songs of Innocence*, describes the custom, begun in 1782, of marching destitute children from their charity schools all over London to attend services held in St Paul's Cathedral. This event took place on a Thursday over the Easter period but not Maundy Thursday (the Thursday before Easter, known to Roman Catholics as Holy Thursday, traditionally a time of giving to the poor), nor Ascension Day (commemorating Christ's ascent to heaven and known as Holy Thursday to the Anglicans). Blake seems to be suggesting, by naming the event Holy Thursday, that the singing of these children is as important as the two major Church occasions also known by that name. Beadles were local church officials one of whose functions was to ensure that the parish poor were properly cared for. Blake twice refers to them in terms which make them seem kindly and profound; how does he achieve this and what is the point of the simile he uses in line 3? How else might the *wands* be perceived by the small children? Pick out the images of innocence and of angelic purity in the poem, discussing how they work in context. What is different about the rhythm in lines 9–10? Why might Blake have wanted to change the rhythm here? The last line echoes some of St Paul's words in the Bible: 'Be not forgetful to entertain strangers: for thereby some have entertained angels unawares.' (Hebrews 13.2) What does Blake mean by *cherish pity* and what function does the line perform in the poem? What might the child's view be of this occasion?

What type of questions does the second 'Holy Thursday' begin with and what effect do these have? Britain was a *rich and fruitful land* in the 1790s but there was a huge gap between the rich and the poor. Blake was closely associated with groups of revolutionaries throughout this period and was later tried for sedition. In what two senses is this *green and pleasant land* a *land of poverty*? What would the *usurous hand* expect back in return? Why is it described as *cold*? Compare it with the picture of the beadles in the first poem. Compare the *trembling cry* with the *song* of the first poem – and perhaps also with Sylvia Plath's 'Morning Song'. Discuss the third stanza both in terms of its structure and its metaphors. What sort of society is Blake wishing for in the final stanza?

Having looked in detail at the second poem (and perhaps also at the two poems entitled 'Nurse's Song'), look back at the first and think whether Blake approved of the children being marched *two & two* to give thanks to the patrons of their schools. What type of worship would Blake find more fitting perhaps? What act raises them above the *aged men*? What might you now say about the pure waters of the Thames to which they are compared (see notes to 'London')?

Does the second poem make the first seem naïve or does the vision of the first still hold true? Compare R.S. Thomas' 'Window'.

A Poison Tree

I was angry with my friend:
I told my wrath, my wrath did end.
I was angry with my foe:
I told it not, my wrath did grow.

And I waterd it in fears,   5
Night and morning with my tears:
And I sunned it with smiles,
And with soft deceitful wiles.

And it grew both day and night.
Till it bore an apple bright.   10
And my foe beheld it shine,
And he knew that it was mine.

And into my garden stole.
When the night had veild the pole;
In the morning glad I see   15
My foe outstretchd beneath the tree.

Discuss to what extent openness is an essential quality in
friendship.

Originally entitled 'Christian Forbearance', this poem is a
fable of what happens when you suppress natural emotions.
This applies equally to so-called negative emotions as to
positive ones. What happens to nature because of this
suppression? Why was the speaker able to tell his friend of
his anger but not his foe? Discuss the metaphors in the
second stanza. Look also at the rhythm, especially in line 7
– why are the *smiles* long and drawn out? Why is an *apple
bright* such an appropriate metaphor for the fruit of this
suppressed emotion? Why do you suppose the foe wanted
the apple? Explain line 14. What makes the last couplet so
shocking?

Nurse's Song

When the voices of children are heard on the green
And laughing is heard on the hill,
My heart is at rest within my breast
And everything else is still.

'Then come home my children, the sun is gone down   5
And the dews of night arise;
Come còme leave off play, and let us away
Till the morning appears in the skies.'

'No no let us play, for it is yet day
And we cannot go to sleep;   10
Besides in the sky, the little birds fly
And the hills are all covered with sheep.'

'Well well go & play till the light fades away
And then go home to bed.'
The little ones leaped & shouted & laugh'd   15
And all the hills ecchoed.

NURSES Song

When the voices of children are heard on the green
And whisprings are in the dale:
The days of my youth rise fresh in my mind,
My face turns green and pale.

'Then come home children, the sun is gone down   5
And the dews of night arise
Your spring & your day, are wasted in play
And your winter and night in disguise.'

'Children's play should be carefully monitored.' 'Adults have short memories and have forgotten what it is to be a child.' 'Safety is the most important factor in bringing up children.' 'Play is less important than learning.' 'Spare the rod and spoil the child.' 'When I was young we wandered free for hours on end.' Discuss these concepts of bringing up children and decide whether children today have too much or too little freedom.

Who is the speaker in each song? Discuss in detail the subtle differences between the first two stanzas of each poem. Whose voice is missing from the second poem and what does this signify? Why are the titles different? Put into your own words the second stanza of the second poem. Are you convinced by the arguments? How are they different from those of the second stanza of the first poem? What is the implication of lines 11–12? How is this backed up by the clever rhyme of the last line? Describe the effect of the rhythm of the poem and why it is appropriate to the subject matter. One interpretation of the second poem is that the nurse is jealous of the children. Pick out details which reinforce this explanation. What might the *whisprings* be of in the dale and what might the *dews of night* represent? Green was traditionally the colour of the jealous spinster. Why does she want them to stop such play?

'The Romantics believed that children were much closer to nature and therefore we all ought to remember the child within us.' Discuss with reference to these two poems. You might also consider Wordsworth's 'My Heart Leaps Up'.

*O*n *Another's Sorrow*

Can I see another's woe,
And not be in sorrow too?
Can I see another's grief,
And not seek for kind relief?

Can I see a falling tear,   5
And not feel my sorrow's share?
Can a father see his child
Weep, nor be with sorrow fill'd?

Can a mother sit and hear
An infant groan, an infant fear?   10
No no never can it be.
Never never can it be.

And can he who smiles on all
Hear the wren with sorrows small,
Hear the small bird's grief and care   15
Hear the woes that infants bear –

And not sit beside the nest
Pouring pity in their breast,
And not sit the cradle near
Weeping tear on infant's tear?   20

And not sit both night & day,
Wiping all our tears away?
O! no never can it be.
Never never can it be.

He doth give his joy to all.   25
He becomes an infant small.
He becomes a man of woe.
He doth feel the sorrow too.

Think not, thou canst sigh a sigh,
And thy maker is not by.   30
Think not, thou canst weep a tear,
And thy maker is not near.

O! he gives to us his joy.
That our grief he may destroy;
Till our grief is fled & gone   35
He doth sit by us and moan.

One thing all the Romantics had in common is their belief in
the power of the imagination. Percy Shelley claimed that
'the great instrument of moral good is the imagination',
whilst Hazlitt the Romantic critic attempted to demonstrate
philosophically that without the sympathetic faculty of being
able to imagine yourself another, we would not be human.
Here Blake makes the philosophy more practical, more
rooted in the everyday. How does he achieve this?

How would you divide up the poem? What patterns do you
notice both within each section and in the poem as a whole?
Who is the *he* of stanza 4? Why do you think Blake does not
use a capital letter? What is the point of linking the *wren*
with the *infants* in the same stanza? How can you tell this is
one of the *Songs of Innocence*? What possible answer could
be given instead of lines 11–12? Why does Blake use
repetition, both here and throughout the poem? What links
does Blake suggest exist between the human and the divine?

This is the last of the *Songs of Innocence* and has no direct
counterpart in the *Songs of Experience*. Try to write your
own response to it, using the rhythms and phrases of the
original. Look carefully at the preceding pairs as models of
the way Blake perceived the different ways of looking at the
same experience.

The Sick Rose

O Rose thou art sick.
The invisible worm
That flies in the night,
In the howling storm:

Has found out thy bed   5
Of crimson joy:
And his dark secret love
Does thy life destroy.

 List all the terms you associate with roses.

A haunting but a difficult poem in which the rose,
symbolising passionate love, has been blighted because of
dark secret love instead of openness. Blake, in accordance
with many of the pro-revolutionaries of the 1790s, was
opposed to any suppression of our natural urges, including
sexual. Suppression, according to Blake – as according to
modern psychological studies – destroys inner life. How
does Blake make the opening of the poem so dramatic?
Why is the *worm* such an appropriate metaphor for
seemingly sinful passion? Why is it described as *invisible*
and associated with *night* and *storm* here? Why is *bed* such
a doubly appropriate term? Compare the poem with 'The
Garden of Love'.

The Garden of Love

I went to the Garden of Love,
And saw what I never had seen:
A Chapel was built in the midst,
Where I used to play on the green.

And the gates of this Chapel were shut,   5
And Thou shalt not writ over the door;
So I turn'd to the Garden of Love,
That so many sweet flowers bore,

And I saw it was filled with graves,
And tomb-stones where flowers should be: 10
And Priests in black gowns, were walking their rounds,
And binding with briars, my joys & desires.

Which poem in this selection is referred to in the phrase *to play on the green*? What kind of *love* might the poet be referring to? What do you suppose he means by *sweet flowers*? What is significant about the fact that the building is a chapel, that the chapel obstructs the play, that the words *Thou shalt not* are *writ over the door*, that the chapel is shut, that flowers are replaced by *tomb-stones* and that the priests wear *black*? Discuss the sounds of the words in the final line – focusing particularly on *briars*. Why does the poet choose this term? How would you describe the mood of the poem? How do you know it is a song of experience?

*T*he Tyger

Tyger, Tyger, burning bright,
In the forests of the night:
What immortal hand or eye,
Could frame thy fearful symmetry?

In what distant deeps or skies   5
Burnt the fire of thine eyes?
On what wings dare he aspire?
What the hand dare sieze the fire?

And what shoulder, & what art
Could twist the sinews of thy heart?   10
And when thy heart began to beat,
What dread hand? & what dread feet?

What the hammer? what the chain?
In what furnace was thy brain?
What the anvil? what dread grasp,   15
Dare its deadly terrors clasp?

When the stars threw down their spears
And water'd heaven with their tears:
Did he smile his work to see?
Did he who made the Lamb make thee?   20

Tyger, Tyger, burning bright,
In the forests of the night:
What immortal hand or eye,
Dare frame thy fearful symmetry?

Justly one of Blake's most famous poems, 'The Tyger'
portrays the *fearful* or sublime side of creation, that
embodied in *Songs of Experience*, after all the lambs in
Songs of Innocence. To deny that we have such a side is to
deny half of God's creation. Discuss the fourth line in detail.
How does the way the whole poem is phrased indicate
man's lack of knowledge? What else makes the tiger an
embodiment of all that is beyond man's control? List the
ways Blake makes the tiger beautiful and menacing. Why
does Blake use so much industrial imagery in stanza 4?
Link this with stanza 2. In what different ways is God's
strength emphasised throughout the poem? What two sides
of God are emphasised in stanza 5? What effect does seeing
the tiger have on the *stars* or angels? Why might this be?
How does stanza 5 change your view of the term *fearful
symmetry*? What changes has Blake made in the last stanza
from the first and why? Discuss the symmetries of the whole
poem, including the way Blake uses the sounds of the
words.

*L*ondon

I wander thro' each charter'd street,
Near where the charter'd Thames does flow.
And mark in every face I meet
Marks of weakness, marks of woe.

In every cry of every Man,   5
In every Infant's cry of fear,
In every voice, in every ban,
The mind-forg'd manacles I hear:

How the Chimney-sweeper's cry
Every blackning Church appalls,   10
And the hapless Soldier's sigh,
Runs in blood down Palace walls.

But most thro' midnight streets I hear
How the youthful Harlot's curse
Blasts the new-born Infant's tear   15
And blights with plagues the Marriage hearse.

The most explicit condemnation of life in London in the
1790s is contained in this verse. Some one hundred years
had passed since the Glorious Revolution had supposedly
established the rights and freedoms of the English people in
a process of liberation begun very tentatively as long ago as
Magna Carta in 1215 (a treaty signed on an island in the
Thames). However, the French Revolution, which had
seemed to promise universal privileges (such as the right to
vote), and far greater equality, had instead given the British
government the excuse to clamp down on dangerous
subversives such as those associated with Blake. Britain did
not have its own revolution at this time, although at times
the people seemed close to joining with their French
counterparts, and the conservative forces of Army and
Church did all in their power to constrain and repress the
citizens.

London holds ancient charters which guarantee certain liberties, but these were only granted to certain privileged inhabitants (mostly landowners). To 'charter' had also come to mean to 'limit' or to 'hire'. How do the words *wander* and *flow* work against these meanings in the first two lines? Instead of *charter'd* Blake originally chose the adjective 'dirty'. Why is his *charter'd* far more effective?

A *ban* was either an announcement made by the authorities or a new restriction placed on the citizens. It could also mean a curse. Find out what *manacles* are. Here they are both literal (many protestors and campaigners for free speech or extending the vote were imprisoned at this time) and metaphorical (representing the oppressive powers of Church and state). Originally Blake used 'german forged links', referring to King George III (who was of German descent) and the German soldiers he used to suppress the British. Why is *mind-forg'd* such a brilliant term for the habits of submissiveness in the face of oppression?

Why would a *chimney-sweeper* cry at this time? Discuss the attitude of a church which is appalled by such a cry. Why does *blackning* work on two levels? *Hapless* here means blameless. Why does the soldier *sigh*? Explain the following line. Why does Blake make the harlot *youthful*?

The *curse* of the harlot is both a verbal one and the curse of gonorrhea which can blind any offspring. Discuss the last line in the light of this remark. What does it reveal about the hypocrisy of those in power?

Is Wordsworth's 'Composed upon Westminster Bridge' the song of innocence to Blake's song of experience in terms of their responses to London?

'Deceptively profound.' To which of Blake's poems does this seem the most appropriate description?

Originally all of these poems were printed in lovingly crafted editions with accompanying illustrations by the author. Find a copy of some of the pictures and write about what they add to your interpretation of the poems.

WILLIAM WORDSWORTH

*E*xpostulation and Reply

'Why William, on that old grey stone,
'Thus for the length of half a day,
'Why William, sit you thus alone,
'And dream your time away?

'Where are your books? that light bequeath'd   5
'To beings else forlorn and blind!
'Up! Up! and drink the spirit breath'd
'From dead men to their kind.

'You look round on your mother earth,
'As if she for no purpose bore you;   10
'As if you were her first-born birth,
'And none had lived before you!'

One morning thus, by Esthwaite lake,
When life was sweet I knew not why,
To me my good friend Matthew spake,   15
And thus I made reply.

'The eye it cannot chuse but see,
'We cannot bid the ear be still;
'Our bodies feel, where'er they be,
'Against, or with our will.   20

'Nor less I deem that there are powers,
'Which of themselves our minds impress,
'That we can feed this mind of ours,
'In a wise passiveness.

'Think you, mid all this mighty sum   25
'Of things for ever speaking,
'That nothing of itself will come,
'But we must still be seeking?

' – Then ask not wherefore, here, alone,
'Conversing as I may,   30
'I sit upon this old grey stone,
'And dream my time away.'

Is daydreaming a waste of time?

The argument is based loosely on a disagreement between
Wordsworth and William Hazlitt who was writing a
philosophical book at the time. What is the main thrust of
the 'expostulation' or criticism given by 'Matthew'? What
should Wordsworth be doing instead? How are lines 8 and
12 connected?

Summarise Wordsworth's reply. Whose argument do you
find more convincing? Should inspiration and ideas come
from hard study or from 'nature'? What does *a wise
passiveness* mean? Why is the *old grey stone* an appropriate
place for Wordsworth to be sitting? How had Wordsworth
been *conversing* before Matthew came along?

Compare and contrast the ways Wordsworth, Keats and
Yeats present daydreaming in 'Expostulation and Reply', 'O
thou whose face hath felt the Winter's wind' and 'The Lake
Isle of Innisfree' respectively.

The Tables Turned; An Evening Scene, on the Same Subject

Up! up! my friend, and clear your looks,
Why all this toil and trouble?
Up! up! my friend, and quit your books,
Or surely you'll grow double.

The sun above the mountain's head,   5
A freshening lustre mellow,
Through all the long green fields has spread,
His first sweet evening yellow.

Books! 'tis a dull and endless strife,
Come, hear the woodland linnet,   10
How sweet his music; on my life
There's more of wisdom in it.

And hark! how blithe the throstle sings!
And he is no mean preacher;
Come forth into the light of things,   15
Let Nature be your teacher.

She has a world of ready wealth,
Our minds and hearts to bless –
Spontaneous wisdom breathed by health,
Truth breathed by chearfulness.   20

One impulse from a vernal wood
May teach you more of man;
Of moral evil and of good,
Than all the sages can.

Sweet is the lore which nature brings;   25
Our meddling intellect
Misshapes the beauteous forms of things;
– We murder to dissect.

Enough of science and of art;
Close up these barren leaves;   30
Come forth, and bring with you a heart
That watches and receives.

What activities do you consider a 'waste of time'? Might
others find value in these acts?

Wordsworth is perhaps overstating the case in this
companion piece to the previous poem. Clearly he did read
extensively himself. However, there is genuine feeling in his
warning against society's general habit of assuming that
walking in the countryside was a waste of time considered in
terms of both the improvement of your own mind and the
prosperity of your country. What are the benefits according
to the poem? Wordsworth spent a great deal of time in such
walks – what evidence is there in the poem that such walks
had a profound effect on him?

What does the brilliant phrase *we murder to dissect* mean?
The *barren leaves* here mean pages; why is it such an
appropriate phrase for the products of analytical minds?

What do you notice about the general vocabulary, the length
of line, the rhythm and the rhyme scheme of these poems?
Why is it so appropriate to choose a ballad form?

The Prelude (extract)

(i)

One evening (surely I was led by her)
I went alone into a shepherd's boat,
A skiff that to a willow tree was tied
Within a rocky cave, its usual home.
'Twas by the shores of Patterdale, a vale   5
Wherein I was a stranger, thither come
A schoolboy traveller, at the holidays.
Forth rambled from the village inn alone,
No sooner had I sight of this small skiff,
Discovered thus by unexpected chance,   10
Than I unloosed her tether and embarked.
The moon was up, the lake was shining clear
Among the hoary mountains; from the shore
I pushed, and struck the oars and struck again
In cadence, and my little boat moved on,   15
Even like a man who walks with stately step
Though bent on speed. It was an act of stealth
And troubled pleasure, nor without the voice
Of mountain-echoes did my boat move on;
Leaving behind her still, on either side,   20
Small circles glittering idly in the moon,
Until they melted all into one track
Of sparkling light. A rocky steep uprose
Above the cavern of the willow tree,
And now, as suited one who proudly rowed   25
With his best skill, I fixed a steady view
Upon the top of that same craggy ridge,
The bound of the horizon, for behind
Was nothing but the stars and grey sky.
She was an elfin pinnace; lustily   30
I dipped my oars into the silent lake,
And, as I rose upon the stroke, my boat
Went heaving through the water like a swan;
When, from behind that craggy steep till then
The bound of the horizon, a huge cliff,   35
As if with voluntary power instinct,

Upreared its head. I struck and struck again,
And growing still in stature the huge cliff
Rose up between me and the stars, and still,
With measured motion, like a living thing,   40
Strode after me. With trembling hands I turned,
And through the silent water stole my way
Back to the cavern of the willow tree;
There in her mooring-place I left my bark, –
And through the meadows homeward went, with grave   45
And serious thoughts; and after I had seen
That spectacle, for many days, my brain
Worked with a dim and undetermined sense
Of unknown modes of being; in my thoughts
There was a darkness, call it solitude   50
Or blank desertion. No familiar shapes
Of hourly objects, images of trees,
Of sea or sky, no colours of green fields;
But huge and mighty forms, that do not live
Like living men, moved slowly through my mind   55
By day, and were the trouble of my dreams.

        (ii)
And in the frosty season, when the sun
Was set, and visible for many a mile
The cottage windows through the twilight blazed,
I heeded not the summons: happy time
It was indeed for all of us – to me   5
It was a time of rapture! Clear and loud
The village clock tolled six, – I wheeled about,
Proud and exulting like an untired horse
That cares not for its home. All shod with steel,
We hissed along the polished ice in games   10
Confederate, imitative of the chase
And woodland pleasures, – the resounding horn,
The pack loud bellowing, and the hunted hare.
So through the darkness and the cold we flew,

And not a voice was idle; with the din,   15
Meanwhile, the precipices rang aloud;
The leafless trees and every icy crag
Tinkled like iron; while the distant hills
Into the tumult sent an alien sound
Of melancholy not unnoticed, while the stars   20
Eastward were sparkling clear, and in the west
The orange sky of evening died away.
Not seldom from the uproar I retired
Into a silent bay, or sportively
Glanced sideway, leaving the tumultuous throng,   25
To cut across the image of a star
That gleamed upon the ice; and oftentimes,
When we had given our bodies to the wind,
And all the shadowy banks on either side
Came sweeping through the darkness, spinning still   30
The rapid line of motion, then at once
Have I, reclining back upon my heels,
Stopped short; yet still the solitary cliffs
Wheeled by me – even as if the earth had rolled
With visible motion her diurnal round!   35
Behind me did they stretch in solemn train,
Feebler and feebler, and I stood and watched
Till all was tranquil as a dreamless sleep.

As these extracts, especially the second, share many of the
themes of Blake's poems entitled 'Nurse's Song', look at the
notes marked ☼ to those poems before reading these.

Both these extracts come from the first book of
Wordsworth's great twelve or thirteen-book poem which has
since come to be known as 'The Prelude'. He knew it simply
as the poem he wrote to Coleridge, explaining the growth of
his own mind. He revised and changed the poem all his life,
but this edition is that of 1805–6, and thus closer to his
youthful intentions than the later edition of 1850. Book One
concerns childhood and schooltime. In both extracts,
Wordsworth is discussing the effect on the young poet of
Nature, here personified as the *she* of line 1. Whilst the first
is a rather sombre, terrifying experience, the second is much

more exhilarating. Both share a strong sense of movement, of the living power of the natural world and the spirit behind that world as well as of the perspective of the onlooking boy.

(i) What impulses lead the child to the boat? Whose is the boat? What tells us that his boating is unplanned, spontaneous? Why do you think he includes the lines which describe why he is staying in this region, lines which merely seem to delay his story? Describe the progress of the boy on the lake in your own words. What is his state of mind? Why has he *fixed a steady view* on a hill opposite? A *pinnace* is a large rowing boat: why does he give his own *skiff* so grand a title? Why is his own *pinnace* merely *elfin*? Explain *lustily*. Explain carefully, with due reference to perspective, what happens in the next lines. Analyse the sentence and line structure (especially the placing of the word *upreared*) to explain how Wordsworth recaptures the suspense and surprise of the child. Comment on the reactions of the boy, both immediately and over more time. What does he believe is happening? What long-term effects does it have on him?

(ii) What tells us that the young Wordsworth was disobedient? Why is this not looked on in an unkindly way by the older poet looking back? How does he recreate the sense of excitement of his youth, the importance of make-believe? How does he evoke the sense of movement and of noise in the extract? Pick out the details and what they contribute. Why in particular would the hills send *an alien sound/Of melancholy*? What does the fact that he *retired* from the *tumultuous throng* tell us of this child who 'is father of the man' (see 'My Heart Leaps Up')? How does he view himself in relation to the other children? Which motion on the part of the skater resulted in the cliffs seeming to move, even after he stopped? Compare the use of the word *wheeled* with that of *upreared* in the first extract. How does Wordsworth make this fairly ordinary event sound extremely majestic and important in the final lines? What impact must the event have had on him and how do we know?

*N*utting

It seems a day
(I speak of one from many singled out)
One of those heavenly days that cannot die;
When, in the eagerness of boyish hope,
I left our cottage-threshold, sallying forth   5
With a huge wallet o'er my shoulder slung,
A nutting-crook in hand; and turned my steps
Tow'rd some far-distant wood, a Figure quaint,
Tricked out in proud disguise of cast-off weeds
Which for that service had been husbanded,   10
By exhortation of my frugal Dame –
Motley accoutrement, of power to smile
At thorns, and brakes, and brambles, – and in truth
More ragged than need was! O'er pathless rocks,
Through beds of matted fern, and tangled thickets,   15
Forcing my way, I came to one dear nook
Unvisited, where not a broken bough
Drooped with its withered leaves, ungracious sign
Of devastation; but the hazels rose
Tall and erect, with tempting clusters hung,   20
A virgin scene! – A little while I stood,
Breathing with such suppression of the heart
As joy delights in; and with wise restraint
Voluptuous, fearless of a rival, eyed
The banquet; or beneath the trees I sat   25
Among the flowers, and with the flowers I played;
A temper known to those who, after long
And weary expectation, have been blest
With sudden happiness beyond all hope.
Perhaps it was a bower beneath whose leaves   30
The violets of five seasons re-appear
And fade, unseen by any human eye;
Where fairy water-breaks do murmur on
For ever; and I saw the sparkling foam,
And – with my cheek on one of those green stones,   35
That, fleeced with moss, under the shady trees,
Lay round me, scattered like a flock of sheep –

I heard the murmur and the murmuring sound,
In that sweet mood when pleasure loves to pay
Tribute to ease; and, of its joy secure,   40
The heart luxuriates with indifferent things,
Wasting its kindliness on stocks and stones,
And on the vacant air. Then up I rose,
And dragged to earth both branch and bough,
     with crash
And merciless ravage: and the shady nook   45
Of hazels, and the green and mossy bower,
Deformed and sullied, patiently gave up
Their quiet being: and unless I now
Confound my present feelings with the past,
Ere from the mutilated bower I turned   50
Exulting, rich beyond the wealth of kings,
I felt a sense of pain when I beheld
The silent trees, and saw the intruding sky –
Then, dearest Maiden, move along these shades
In gentleness of heart; with gentle hand   55
Touch – for there is a spirit in the woods.

Why do vandals destroy things?

What begins as a simple pastoral ends as a brutal and
unexplained scene of destruction followed by guilt. The poet
is remembering a scene from his youth when he went in his
rough clothes and equipment (cast-off weeds, motley
accoutrement, the nutting-crook to pull down the branches
and the wallet or bag to put in the nuts) to collect hazelnuts.
The spirit of boyish adventure is both recaptured and
slightly mocked by the older wiser poet, looking back at his
youthful self. However when he discovers the virgin scene of
a bower of trees unfound by any others, the tone changes to
one of idyllic beauty, just as the temper or mood of the boy
changes to one of stillness and wonder. What makes the

figure of the boy amusing? Why is he dressed as he is? List the expressions from lines 14–25 which tell us that the boy is in territory where none have gone before? What makes it so *tempting*? Why do you think the poet includes the detail of the *wise restraint* of the boy? Explain lines 27–9. How does the poet emphasise the idyllic, peaceful nature of the *bower* in lines 30–42? What makes the change of mood so sudden? (Refer to the enjambement on line 42 and the sounds of the words in the next two lines; contrast line 38.) How, according to the poet, do the trees respond? What makes the boy *rich beyond the wealth of kings* in his imagination?

Do you think he really felt a *sense of pain* or does he *confound* or confuse his feelings as a man with those of the boy? What is there in the poem to suggest that this boy might feel guilt for such a savage rape of nature? At the end of the poem Wordsworth addresses his younger sister and best friend Dorothy. Explain what he means by the last line.

Are we justified in using nature to increase our *wealth*? What *spirit* should this be done in? Find a copy of 'The Ancient Mariner' by Coleridge and compare the two poems. What would have made these poems about exploration and discovery extremely relevant to Wordsworth's time?

Choose one of the extracts from 'The Prelude' and compare and contrast it with 'Nutting'. Look at the presentation of emotion and experience, the structure of the narrative and the lessons to be learned from each passage.

My Heart Leaps Up

My heart leaps up when I behold
    A rainbow in the sky:
So was it when my life began;
So is it now I am a man;
So be it when I shall grow old,   5
    Or let me die!
The Child is father of the Man;
And I could wish my days to be
Bound each to each by natural piety.

How would you describe the mood of the poem and the tone
of line 6? What do you notice about lines 3–5? What figure
of speech is used in line 7, what does it mean and do you
agree?

The Child is father of the man – both are full of *natural
piety*. How does Wordsworth show this to be true in 'Nutting'
and the two extracts from 'The Prelude'?

Composed upon Westminster Bridge

Earth has not anything to show more fair:
Dull would he be of soul who could pass by
A sight so touching in its majesty:
This City now doth, like a garment, wear
The beauty of the morning; silent, bare,   5
Ships, towers, domes, theatres, and temples lie
Open unto the fields, and to the sky;
All bright and glittering in the smokeless air.
Never did sun more beautifully steep
In his first splendour, valley, rock, or hill;   10
Ne'er saw I, never felt, a calm so deep!
The river glideth at his own sweet will:
Dear God! the very houses seem asleep;
And all that mighty heart is lying still!

This remarkable sonnet finds, in the midst of inudstrial London, the *mighty heart* of the most industrialised (some would say advanced) country on earth at the time, the most beautiful sight imaginable. It accuses, by implication, the city dwellers of being *dull* not to appreciate what was there in front of them. Discuss the extended metaphor in lines 4–5. What time is the poem set and how does this make a tremendous difference to the scene? What verb is repeated in the sixth and final lines and why is this significant? How does enjambement *open* up lines 6–7? What does Wordsworth instinctively compare the beauty of the scene to in lines 9–11, and what is surprising about the comparison?

Compare Blake's perspective of the same city in 'London'.

The World is Too Much With Us

The world is too much with us; late and soon
Getting and spending, we lay waste our powers:
Little we see in Nature that is ours;
We have given our hearts away, a sordid boon!
This Sea that bares her bosom to the moon;   5
The winds that will be howling at all hours,
And are up-gathered now like sleeping flowers;
For this, for everything, we are out of tune;
It moves us not. – Great God! I'd rather be
A Pagan suckled in a creed outworn   10
So might I, standing on this pleasant lea,
Have glimpses that would make me less forlorn;
Have sight of Proteus rising from the sea;
Or hear old Triton blow his wreathèd horn.

This poem is a passionate plea to re-establish the link
between what Hazlitt termed the 'natural' and the 'spirit of
humanity' as opposed to the 'artificial ... spirit of fashion
and the world'. How does Wordsworth shock his Christian
readership in this sonnet? How does *getting and spending*
destroy *our powers* and what powers are these? Ironically, in
such a trade-oriented world, Wordsworth believes we have
made a *boon* or gift of the most important thing in our lives.
Discuss what you think he means by this. How does the
tone change in line 4? What does he mean by *out of tune*?

Proteus and Triton were sea gods in the *outworn* beliefs of
Greek mythology. What does the fact that the Greeks had
gods of nature prove about their priorities and why does
Wordsworth find this appealing? Work out the rhyme
scheme to find out where the natural divisions should fall in
the poem. Wordsworth delays his change of direction from
exposition in the octet to conclusion in the sestet by half a
line. What effect does this have?

*T*he *Solitary Reaper*

Behold her, single in the field,
Yon solitary Highland lass!
Reaping and singing by herself;
Stop here, or gently pass!
Alone she cuts and binds the grain,   5
And sings a melancholy strain;
O listen! for the Vale profound
Is overflowing with the sound.

No Nightingale did ever chaunt
More welcome notes to weary bands   10
Of travellers in some shady haunt,
Among Arabian sands:
A voice so thrilling ne'er was heard
In spring-time from the Cuckoo-bird,
Breaking the silence of the seas   15
Among the farthest Hebrides.

Will no one tell me what she sings? –
Perhaps the plaintive numbers flow
For old, unhappy, far-off things,
And battles long ago: 20
Or is it some more humble lay,
Familiar matter of to-day?
Some natural sorrow, loss, or pain,
That has been, and may be again?

Whate'er the theme, the Maiden sang   25
As if her song could have no ending;
I saw her singing at her work,
And o'er the sickle bending;–
I listened, motionless and still;
And, as I mounted up the hill,   30
The music in my heart I bore,
Long after it was heard no more.

The critic William Hazlitt, who knew Wordsworth personally, remarked that Wordsworth's 'Muse', the guiding spirit of his poetry, was 'a levelling one'. By this he meant that, instead of dealing with the great and mighty, with kings and princes and heroes and heroines, Wordsworth's poetry, 'along with the revolutionary movement of our age', is more concerned with the ordinary public, the poor and needy and gives to those people a voice. This is certainly the case in this poem which is much more concerned with *familiar matter of to-day* than any more conventionally glorious *battles long ago.* Wordsworth here finds the glamour in the ordinary situation of a girl singing, implying that her griefs and joys are as important as those of the great.

Who do you think the poet is addressing throughout the poem? What might the alternatives to *stop here, or gently pass* be? The valley is *profound* or deep. What secondary meaning might the adjective have? How does Wordsworth emphasise the exotic glamour of the song in the second stanza? Contrast this with phrases from the first. Why are the comparisons natural and homely as well as exotic? Perhaps the girl was singing in Scots or Gaelic which explains all the questions in stanza 3 – but it also allows Wordsworth to speculate before enjoying the music for its own sake. How do we know the last two lines are true?

 To what extent do you find Hazlitt's remarks quoted above useful in describing Wordsworth's work?

Is Wordsworth more than just a nature poet? How effectively does he explore other themes in this selection?

*O*zymandias

I met a traveller from an antique land,
Who said – 'Two vast and trunkless legs of stone
Stand in the desert ... . Near them, on the sand,
Half sunk a shattered visage lies, whose frown,
And wrinkled lip, and sneer of cold command,   5
Tell that its sculptor well those passions read
Which yet survive, stamped on these lifeless things,
The hand that mocked them, and the heart that fed;
And on the pedestal, these words appear:
My name is Ozymandias, King of Kings,   10
Look on my Works, ye Mighty, and despair!
Nothing beside remains. Round the decay
Of that colossal Wreck, boundless and bare
The lone and level sands stretch far away.'

How much that has been built in this century will survive as
long as the pyramids have done? Can you name any pieces
of architecture which deserve to survive? Who are the most
powerful people on our planet? Can you think of a world
leader of our time who will be remembered in ten or even
two centuries?

Written late in 1817 whilst Shelley was living at Marlow in
Berkshire, this sonnet was one of a series of 'poetry
competitions' that the young poets of the day often indulged
in. The circle included John Keats, Horace Smith, John
Hamilton Reynolds and Leigh Hunt, the radical editor of the
liberal magazine *The Examiner*. It was he who discovered
first Keats and then Shelley, and began bringing them to the
attention of the public. This sonnet, written in competition
(perhaps not timed, though often Hunt would set time limits
of fifteen minutes!) was first published in *The Examiner* in
January 1818. Ozymandias (the Greek name for Rameses

II, 1304–1237 BC) was the pharaoh of Egypt during Moses'
exodus from that land.

What does Shelley mean by the phrases *antique land*,
trunkless legs and *shattered visage*? Why do you think the
traveller pauses halfway through line 3? What do we find out
about the sculptor, and what is revealed about the pharaoh?
How can the *passions* survive the death of the pharaoh, the
man with the *heart that fed* such feelings? Whose was the
hand which *mocked* or imitated and criticised these
passions? What is Shelley suggesting to us about the proper
role of the artist in society? What do you think Ozymandias
meant when he had lines 10–11 carved on the pedestal of
his statue? Why are the words now ironic? Comment on the
stark simplicty of the next half line. Who are the *mighty* of
Shelley's day and what is he trying to tell them? How does
Shelley use the sounds of the words in the last two lines to
emphasise the futility of human empires?

Compare the ways Shelley and Keats use history and myth
to comment on the mighty of their times in 'Ozymandias'
and 'Hyperion'. Is it true, as Keats claimed, that Shelley's
'purpose' is too obvious or do you agree with Shelley that
one of the functions of the artist is to 'mock' the mighty, to
be 'an unacknowledged legislator of the world'?

The Mask of Anarchy
Written on the Occasion of the Massacre at Manchester

As I lay asleep in Italy
There came a voice from over the Sea,
And with great power it forth led me
To walk in the visions of Poesy.

I met Murder on the way –   5
He had a mask like Castlereagh –
Very smooth he looked, yet grim;
Seven bloodhounds followed him:

All were fat; and well they might
Be in admirable plight,   10
For one by one, and two by two,
He tossed them human hearts to chew
Which from his wide cloak he drew.

Next came Fraud, and he had on,
Like Eldon, an ermined gown;   15
His big tears, for he wept well,
Turned to mill-stones as they fell.

And the little children, who
Round his feet played to and fro,
Thinking every tear a gem,   20
Had their brains knocked out by them.

Clothed with the Bible, as with light,
And the shadows of the night,
Like Sidmouth, next, Hypocrisy
On a crocodile rode by.   25

And many more Destructions played
In this ghastly masquerade,
All disguised, even to the eyes,
Like Bishops, lawyers, peers, or spies.

Last came Anarchy: he rode   30
On a white horse, splashed with blood;
He was pale even to the lips,
Like Death in the Apocalypse.

And he wore a kingly crown;
And in his grasp a sceptre shone;   35
On his brow this mark I saw –
'I AM GOD, AND KING, AND LAW!'

    ****

'And these words shall then become
Like Oppression's thundered doom
Ringing through each heart and brain,   40
Heard again – again – again –

'Rise like Lions after slumber
In unvanquishable number –
Shake your chains to earth like dew
Which in sleep had fallen on you –   45
Ye are many – they are few.'

This incredibly forceful poem, not widely known or
published until long after Shelley's death, was the poet's
response (written from Shelley's new home in Italy) to what
had become known as the Peterloo Massacre. In August
1819 a huge march of protestors had gathered in St Peter's
Field, Manchester to campaign for an extension to the vote.
Before the 1832 Parliamentary Reform Act only wealthy
landowners had the right to vote; it was not until 1884 that
there was a universal vote for males and 1928 before
women were allowed to vote at all. There was a huge
atmosphere of defiance in the country at the price of food
and the oppressive regime which disallowed many protests.

Militiamen (a kind of cross between army and police) misunderstood orders, charged the crowd and killed at least six, injuring perhaps five hundred including women and children.

Included are the first nine stanzas and the last two, where Shelley calls directly on the people of England. In the beginning of the poem, Shelley follows the artist in 'Ozymandias' by mocking the mighty of his time – in terms which are perhaps better remembered than any of the accomplishments of these political figures. So offend a poet at your peril! Castlereagh, the Foreign Secretary, had ordered similar charges on civilians in Ireland and supported Britain's alliance with seven other *bloodhounds* – European countries who, after Napoleon's defeat at Waterloo (after which Peterloo was named), joined forces to prevent such liberal changes as the abolition of slavery. Eldon was the Lord Chancellor (hence the *gown*); Sidmouth was the Home Secretary who had new churches built to pacify the people. To gain an idea of the poem's power, try substituting names of present-day leaders, tyrants and bullies instead of these nineteenth-century politicians. Why is the figure of Hypocrisy shown on a *crocodile* after references to the Bible? The whole *mask* is a *masquerade*, a dance of death, in which the characters are personifications who look very like the members of the government. Account for the power of each picture. Why is it a mask of *anarchy*? How does Shelley use emotive language to gain his power? Why does stanza 3 have five lines? What is meant by the phrase *thundered doom*? Account for the repetition in line 41. Why are the people referred to as in *chains* and *in sleep*? What is the implication of the last line?

The poem has been called Shelley's 'rallying hymn to non-violent resistance'. Can you find any hints in the extract that it calls for even more than what Blake called 'mental fight'? Why do you think Leigh Hunt chose not to publish it until 1832?

JOHN KEATS

On First Looking into Chapman's Homer

Much have I travell'd in the realms of gold,
 And many goodly states and kingdoms seen;
 Round many western islands have I been
Which bards in fealty to Apollo hold;
Oft of one wide expanse had I been told   5
 That deep-brow'd Homer ruled as his demesne;
 Yet never did I breathe its pure serene
Till I heard Chapman speak out loud and bold:
Then felt I like some watcher in the skies
 When a new planet swims into his ken;   10
Or like stout Cortez when with eagle eyes
 He star'd at the Pacific – and all his men
Look'd at each other with a wild surmise –
 Silent, upon a peak in Darien.

This, the greatest of the poems of Keats' youth, was composed after spending an exhilarating night reading the Elizabethan poet, George Chapman. Chapman's translation of the epic Greek poetry of Homer (first published in 1614) was virtually unknown in the early nineteenth century. The more widely known version, by Alexander Pope, attempted to 'tidy up' the rough 'bold' qualities of the Greek poet, whereas Chapman had been prone to more exaggeration. Keats, who did not know Greek, was immediately impressed by the sense that Chapman's version had opened up for him some more of *the realms of gold* of classic poetry. The sense of privilege and discovery led Keats to make extended similes (the favourite device of the epic poet), comparing himself to discoverers and explorers. The astronomer Herschel had discovered the planet Uranus in 1781. It is typical of the haste with which the poem was written that Keats confused the Spanish conqueror of such literal *realms of gold* as Mexico with the discoverer Balboa who really first set European eyes on the Pacific west of the Americas.

To remind himself of the rhyme scheme of the Petrarchan sonnet, Keats wrote it down the side of the page. When you do the same, work out where the octet ends and the sestet begins. Is there a change of subject matter? Why do you think Keats had only *travell'd* in the *western islands* of European literature? Apollo was the Greek god of poetry; what do you think Keats means by *in fealty*? Why are *wide expanse* and *pure serene* such appropriate terms for Homer's poetry? What do they tell us about the range of emotions and moods (as well as the settings) in his work? Why is the Pacific such a suitable comparison for Keats' sense of youthful discovery? Why is the last line of the sonnet so successful?

Compare Wordsworth's 'Nutting'. What different strategies do they use to capture the excitement of youthful discovery and wonder?

O thou whose face hath felt the Winter's wind

'O thou whose face hath felt the Winter's wind;
Whose eye has seen the Snow-clouds hung in Mist
And the black-elm tops 'mong the freezing Stars
To thee the Spring will be a harvest-time –
O thou whose only book has been the light   5
Of supreme darkness which thou feddest on
Night after night, when Phœbus was away
To thee the Spring shall be a tripple morn –
O fret not after Knowledge – I have none
And yet my song comes native with the warmth   10
O fret not after Knowledge – I have none
And yet the Evening listens – He who saddens
At thought of Idleness cannot be idle,
And he's awake who thinks himself asleep.'

Never published in his life-time, this sonnet was included in
a letter to Keats' friend, John Hamilton Reynolds, a letter in
which Keats defended his current lazy mood. He concluded
that it is better to be like the passive flower than the
hurrying bee and introduced the sonnet with these words:
'I was led into these thoughts, my dear Reynolds, by the
beauty of the morning operating on a sense of Idleness –
I have not read any Books – the Morning said I was right –
I had no Idea but of the Morning and the Thrush said I was
right – seeming to say – ...' The whole poem then is the
'speech' of the personified thrush, a bird which seems to
repeat its gentle song like a refrain.

The poem was written on February 19th, 1818, only three
months after Keats had finished his first long poem,
'Endymion'. His ambition was urging him to learn more, to
read and gain wisdom so that he might become one of the
great poets of England. The self-discipline to do this, to give
up his medical career and hope to earn his living as a writer,
is one of the many incredible sides to this young poet. Here

however he shows a different side. The whole sonnet was a response to Wordsworth's defence of 'a wise passiveness' in 'Expostulation and Reply'.

Why had Keats' face *felt the Winter's wind* both literally and metaphorically? Refer in your answer to the biographical notes. Explain the transferred epithet *freezing Stars* and the reference to the *black-elm tops* visible against them. What mood dominates the opening three lines of the poem? There are two paradoxes in lines 4–6, the second of which suggests that Keats has found more knowledge in *darkness* than in the conventional *light* of book learning. What might he mean by feeding on *supreme darkness* here? Compare Wordsworth's 'Expostulation and Reply' lines 5–6 in your answer.

Phœbus was a title of Apollo, the Greek god of the sun and of poetry; in what two senses has this god been away in the last few months of Keats' life? Which lines or phrases in the poem try to echo the melodic repetitions of the thrush? Which suggest that more great poetry will come if Keats waits rather than struggling? Which tell us that the thrush's song is spontaneous? Why do you suppose Keats does not rhyme his sonnet? Explain the last three lines.

Compare the poem with Wordsworth's 'Expostulation and Reply'. Explore the differences as well as similarities in the approaches, styles and forms of the poems. Which do you find the most successful? You might also look at Larkin's 'Toads' or 'After Apple-Picking' by Robert Frost.

Hyperion (extract)

Deep in the shady sadness of a vale
Far sunken from the healthy breath of morn,
Far from the fiery noon, and eve's one star,
Sat gray-hair'd Saturn, quiet as a stone,
Still as the silence round about his lair;   5
Forest on forest hung above his head
Like cloud on cloud. No stir of air was there,
Not so much life as on a summer's day
Robs not one light seed from the feather'd grass,
But where the dead leaf fell, there did it rest.   10
A stream went voiceless by, still deadened more
By reason of his fallen divinity
Spreading a shade: the Naiad 'mid her reeds
Press'd her cold finger closer to her lips.

Along the margin-sand large foot-marks went,   15
No further than to where his feet had stray'd,
And slept there since. Upon the sodden ground
His old right hand lay nerveless, listless, dead,
Unsceptred; and his realmless eyes were closed;
While his bow'd head seem'd list'ning to the Earth,   20
His ancient mother, for some comfort yet.

Imagine the court of a successful king in ancient times, the
movement and business all about him, rarely alone, always
in demand. Describe the scene briefly in adjectives; who
might be present and how might the king react? What
leisure pursuits might the king indulge in?

The 'fragment' of 'Hyperion' was abandoned by Keats late in
1818, although he later attempted to rework the poem in a
different form. Of this epic poem only two books were
completed, each over 300 lines long, and a third begun.
This is the opening of the first book where Keats describes
the *realmless* Saturn. Based on Greek myth, the tale
concerned the passing of power from one generation (the
Titans) to another (the Olympians) and the pain that

caused. Saturn, who had himself taken power from his
father Uranus, was defeated by Jupiter (or Zeus) his son.
Hyperion was the only Titan to maintain power and that was
only until Apollo grew strong enough to take over
Hyperion's role as god of the sun. The poem begins just
after the defeat of the Titans and describes the despairing
former king.

Describe the atmosphere Keats creates in the first five lines.
How does he evoke the feeling of depth here? How does he
emphasise the stillness in the following lines? Why are the
seed and the *dead leaf* perfect images for this conflict
between the generations? What effect does Saturn have on
the stream and why? Explain the actions of the *Naiad*, or
water nymph, the spirit of the stream. What do the following
terms tell us about the progress and present situation of
Saturn: *gray-hair'd*, *quiet as a stone*, *fallen divinity*, *stray'd*,
sodden ground, *nerveless*, *listless*, *dead*, *bow'd head*?
Consider their contexts carefully. What does Keats mean by
an *unsceptred* right hand and *realmless eyes*? Why were the
latter closed? Earth's *ancient mother* was called Tellus; it
was she who had predicted that Saturn's sons would take
power away from him. Will there be any *comfort* from such a
source? The poem has been admired for the way it stations
its characters and creates imposing almost statuesque
attitudes for them. Sketch Saturn as he is pictured in this
scene, perhaps including the phrases from the poem. Keats
was most concerned with the sounds of the words in this
passage. Trace the alliteration and assonance patterns.

 How does Keats emphasise the enormity of the tragedy of
Saturn in this opening? You might compare Shelley's
'Ozymandias' for its theme, or Tennyson's 'The Kraken' for
the sense of scale and power.

*L*a Belle Dame sans Merci

O what can ail thee knight at arms
    Alone and palely loitering?
The sedge has withered from the Lake
    And no birds sing!

O what can ail thee knight at arms   5
    So haggard and so woe-begone?
The squirrel's granary is full
    And the harvest's done.

I see a lily on thy brow
    With anguish moist and fever dew,   10
And on thy cheeks a fading rose
    Fast withereth too –

I met a Lady in the Meads
    Full beautiful, a faery's child
Her hair was long, her foot was light   15
    And her eyes were wild –

I made a Garland for her head,
    And bracelets too, and fragrant Zone:
She look'd at me as she did love
    And made sweet moan –   20

I set her on my pacing steed
    And nothing else saw all day long
For sidelong would she bend and sing
    A faery's song –

She found me roots of relish sweet   25
    And honey wild and manna dew
And sure in language strange she said
    'I love thee true' –

She took me to her elfin grot
    And there she wept and sigh'd full sore   30
And there I shut her wild wild eyes
    With kisses four.

And there she lulled me asleep
    And there I dream'd – Ah Woe betide!
The latest dream I ever dreamt   35
    On the cold hill side.

I saw pale kings and Princes too
    Pale warriors, death pale were they all;
They cried 'La belle dame sans merci
    Thee hath in thrall.'   40

I saw their starv'd lips in the gloam
    With horrid warning gaped wide
And I awoke and found me here
    On the cold hill's side

And this is why I sojourn here   45
    Alone and palely loitering;
Though the sedge is wither'd from the Lake
    And no birds sing --

Make a brief list of the things you would expect a knight in shining armour (a figure from medieval times, either real or legendary) to be doing. What qualities would he need in the fulfilment of his duties? Would you expect his relationship with women to help or hinder him in his assignments?

Written during the first months of Keats' relationship with Frances Brawne, this poem seems to deal with the distractions which a man with a sense of destiny might yield to as well as the dangers of trusting to beautiful women. The title, translated as 'the beautiful woman without mercy', was taken from a medieval French poem by Alain Chartier. It was a common convention in such poems to speak of the bewitching power of the beloved woman and to try to persuade her to love by calling her merciless. Here Keats seems to take these qualities more literally. The speaker of the first three stanzas meets a knight and asks what is wrong with him. What is to loiter? The third and fourth lines of the first two stanzas seem to be indirect answers to the questions. What do they tell us and what mood do they provide? What clues in the third stanza tell us that the knight is unwell, possibly dying? Discuss the metaphors used. In stanza 4 the knight begins his reply concerning what happened to him in the meads or meadows. Pick out the suggestions that the woman may prove to be unreliable. How is this confirmed in his dream? How do we know that the knight fell in love? Look carefully at the rhythm of the poem. What do you notice about the last line of each stanza and what effect does this have? Why do you think Keats chooses the ballad form? Pick out old-fashioned expressions in the poem saying why they are appropriate.

One critic has remarked: 'This short romance calls our attention to the extreme anxiety Keats felt toward his feminine subject matter, even as he could not turn away from it.' Discuss the way the poet successfully conveys a combination of anxiety and attraction in this poem.

This Living Hand, now Warm and Capable

This living hand, now warm and capable
Of earnest grasping, would, if it were cold
And in the icy silence of the tomb,
So haunt thy days and chill thy dreaming nights
That thou would wish thine own heart dry of blood   5
So in my veins red life might stream again,
And thou be conscience-calm'd – see here it is
I hold it towards you –

Keats dearly wanted to follow his great idol Shakespeare
and produce great poetic drama. His one finished play, *Otho
the Great*, was less than successful despite some passages
of beautiful verse. In this fragment, one of the last things
Keats wrote, we see perhaps signs of real promise in terms
of dramatic poetry. There is an obvious physical element
and an arresting ending. It was possibly written for inclusion
in a play Keats was planning about Queen Elizabeth I and
her favourite the Earl of Leicester, who was eventually
executed. How does Keats achieve the immediacy of the
piece? Pick out the most effective phrases and describe how
they achieve their power.

Compare Donne's 'The Apparition'. How successfully does
Keats recreate the world of the Renaissance in his poem?
Which do you find the most dramatic and chilling?

Ode to a Nightingale

My heart aches, and a drowsy numbness pains
    My sense, as though of hemlock I had drunk,
Or emptied some dull opiate to the drains
    One minute past, and Lethe-wards had sunk:
'Tis not through envy of thy happy lot,   5
    But being too happy in thine happiness, –
        That thou, light-winged Dryad of the trees,
          In some melodious plot
Of beechen green, and shadows numberless,
    Singest of summer in full-throated ease.   10

O, for a draught of vintage! that hath been
    Cool'd a long age in the deep-delved earth,
Tasting of Flora and the country green,
    Dance, and Provençal song, and sunburnt mirth!
O for a beaker full of the warm South,   15
    Full of the true, the blushful Hippocrene,
        With beaded bubbles winking at the brim,
          And purple-stained mouth;
That I might drink, and leave the world unseen,
    And with thee fade away into the forest dim: 20

Fade far away and quite forget
    What thou among the leaves hast never known,
The weariness, the fever, and the fret
    Here, where men sit and hear each other groan;
Where palsy shakes a few, sad, last grey hairs,   25
Where youth grows pale, and spectre-thin, and dies;
    Where but to think is to be full of sorrow
        And leaden-eyed despairs,
Where Beauty cannot keep her lustrous eyes,
    Or new Love pine at them beyond tomorrow.   30

Away! away! for I will fly to thee,
   Not charioted by Bacchus and his pards,
But on the viewless wings of Poesy,
   Though the dull brain perplexes and retards:
Already with thee! tender is the night,   35
   And haply the Queen-Moon is on her throne,
      Cluster'd around by all her starry Fays;
         But here there is no light,
Save what from heaven is with the breezes blown
   Through verdurous glooms and winding
       mossy ways.   40

I cannot see what flowers are at my feet,
   Nor what soft incense hangs upon the boughs,
But, in embalmed darkness, guess each sweet
   Wherewith the seasonable month endows
The grass, the thicket, and the fruit-tree wild;   45
   White hawthorn, and the pastoral eglantine;
      Fast fading violets cover'd up in leaves;
         And mid-May's eldest child,
The coming musk-rose, full of dewy wine,
      The murmurous haunt of flies on summer eves.   50

Darkling I listen; and, for many a time
   I have been half in love with easeful Death,
Call'd him soft names in many a mused rhyme,
   To take into the air my quiet breath;
      Now more than ever seems it rich to die,   55
To cease upon the midnight with no pain,
   While thou art pouring forth thy soul abroad
         In such an ecstasy!
Still wouldst thou sing, and I have ears in vain –
   To thy high requiem become a sod.   60

Thou wast not born for death, immortal Bird!
　　No hungry generations tread thee down;
The voice I hear this passing night was heard
　　In ancient days by emperor and clown:
Perhaps the self-same song that found a path　　65
　　Through the sad heart of Ruth, when, sick
　　　　for home,
　　　　She stood in tears amid the alien corn;
　　　　The same that oft-times hath
Charm'd magic casements, opening on the foam
　　Of perilous seas, in faery lands forlorn.　　70

Forlorn! the very word is like a bell
　　To toll me back from thee to my sole self!
Adieu! the fancy cannot cheat so well
　　As she is fam'd to do, deceiving elf.
Adieu! adieu! thy plaintive anthem fades　　75
　　Past the near meadows, over the still stream,
　　Up the hill-side; and now 'tis buried deep
　　　　In the next valley-glades:
Was it a vision, or a waking dream?
　　Fled is that music: – Do I wake or sleep?　　80

List as many ways of escaping our daily anxieties as you
can. Which do you find the most effective? To what extent
do you believe we should use these rather than 'facing up'
to the reality around us?

One of Keats's undisputed masterpieces, this ode was
written in May 1819. Its refusal to find easy answers in the
poet's response to death and despair makes this poem both
challenging and richly rewarding. Keats here displays the
quality he described as 'negative capability', or being
capable of contradictory attitudes instead of desperately
trying to prove one given position. In its use of a symbol (in
this case the song of the nightingale) for the ideal and
eternal, as opposed to the changeable and mortal world of
mankind, the poem resembles the 'Ode on a Grecian Urn'.

Keats' younger brother Tom had died of consumption (or
tuberculosis) the previous December and in this ode the

poet attempts to come to terms with a world so cruel that *youth grows pale, and spectre-thin, and dies*, a world full of sorrows which the nightingale cannot feel. Keats wishes to be as numb as the bird. In the first stanza Keats describes a pleasure so powerful that it pains him, bringing with it a *numbness* to the pain of the real world. Already we are in the world of paradox, for it is in his seeming escape from death that Keats will come to learn more of it. In stanza 2, he considers wine in his efforts to forget; however, he accomplishes his momentary escape not through alcohol but *on the viewless wings of Poesy* – through the power of the imagination so necessary for poetry. However, instead of a heavenly escape, Keats remains resolutely earth-bound surrounded by flowers (stanza 5) and wishes for a painless death. The nightingale is immortal, he claims (stanza 6), because its song is unchanging through the generations, offering consolation and perhaps sadness for mankind throughout the centuries. Suddenly the poet is brought back to his sense of his *sole self* because his imagination or *fancy* has failed him. But the questions of the last two lines suggest that the poet remains unsure which is the reality, the visionary world or the world of suffering to which he has returned.

Pick out the images of, or subtle allusions to, death in the poem. You will notice that even in the seemingly most escapist passages, death is present, until death is the ultimate escape in stanza 6. Why does the poem change tense suddenly in stanza 4? What do you notice about the rhyme in line 60? (A sod is a section of turf and thus insensitive.)

 Do you find the poem ultimately more life-affirming or escapist?

*O*de on Melancholy

No, no, go not to Lethe, neither twist
   Wolf's bane, tight-rooted, for its poisonous wine;
Nor suffer thy pale forehead to be kiss'd
   By nightshade, ruby grape of Proserpine;
Make not your rosary of yew-berries,   5
   Nor let the beetle, nor the death-moth be
      Your mournful Psyche, nor the downy owl,
A partner in your sorrow's mysteries;
   For shade to shade will come too drowsily,
      And drown the wakeful anguish of the soul.   10

But when the melancholy fit shall fall
   Sudden from heaven like a weeping cloud,
That fosters the droop-headed flowers all,
   And hides the green hill in an April shroud;
Then glut thy sorrow on a morning rose,   15
   Or on the rainbow of the salt sand-wave,
      Or on the wealth of globed peonies;
Or if thy mistress some rich anger shows,
   Emprison her soft hand, and let her rave,
      And feed deep, deep upon her peerless eyes.   20

She dwells with Beauty – Beauty that must die;
   And Joy, whose hand is ever at his lips
Bidding adieu; and aching Pleasure nigh,
   Turning to poison while the bee-mouth sips:
Ay, in the very temple of Delight   25
   Veil'd Melancholy has her sovran shrine,
      Though seen of none save him whose strenuous
        tongue
Can burst Joy's grape against his palate fine;
   His soul shall taste the sadness of her might,
      And be among her cloudy trophies hung.   30

A whole tradition of wallowing in self-pity, fascination with
death and the dark side of life had grown up at the same time
as the Romantic era. Known as the Gothic, this tradition is

what Keats has in mind when he writes his own version of
what the melancholy mood should be like in order to be
artistically creative. In the first stanza he rejects any worship
of death because it would *drown the wakeful anguish of the
soul.* In the second stanza he substitutes a more creative
melancholy mood which should be *fed* not with gloomy
images, but those of beauty, because as he concludes in the
final stanza, joy and melancholy are inseparable, both parts
of life. There is no such thing as one without the other and
thus to worship one of the two separately is to shut oneself off
from the full beauty of life. As with the 'Ode to a Nightingale',
it is in the rich phraseology, the condensed and unexpected
expressions, that the glory of this poem lies.

What do the first two words of the poem imply? *Lethe* was
the river in the mythical Greek underworld which caused
forgetfulness. *Wolfsbane* and *nightshade* are poisonous
plants. What else is associated with death and darkness in
stanza 1? *Psyche* was the Greek goddess of the soul,
represented by a butterfly; the *rosary* is the necklace of
beads used for Catholic prayers. Why, in the melancholic,
would these be replaced by a *death-moth* and *yew-berries*
respectively? Why is *downy owl* such an effective phrase?
How is the sound of this phrase picked up in the next three
lines? Explain carefully how the *weeping cloud* of stanza 2
is both productive and depressing. A series of rich images
follow, experiences which complement the melancholy
mood, ranging from the ordinary (the rose) to the unusual
(rainbow effects on beaches), from the life-giving (the round
peony flower is named after Paion, the physician of the
Greek gods) to the violent. All of these experiences can be
added to the melancholy to give beauty.

Why would a mistress live *with Beauty ... that must die*?
Discuss the personifications in stanza 3. What kind of
characters are described and why is their action appropriate
to their title? What is the only type of person who can fully
see Melancholy's shrine? What two qualities must he have?
The last line suggests a goddess who 'collects' poets as
trophies. In what ways is she similar to the lady in 'La Belle
Dame sans Merci'?

To Autumn

Season of mists and mellow fruitfulness,
    Close bosom-friend of the maturing sun;
Conspiring with him how to load and bless
    With fruit the vines that round the thatch-eves run;
To bend with apples the moss'd cottage-trees,   5
    And fill all fruit with ripeness to the core;
        To swell the gourd, and plump the hazel shells
With a sweet kernel; to set budding more,
    And still more, later flowers for the bees,
    Until they think warm days will never cease,   10
        For Summer has o'er-brimm'd their clammy cells.

Who hath not seen thee oft amid thy store?
    Sometimes whoever seeks abroad may find
Thee sitting careless on a granary floor,
    Thy hair soft-lifted by the winnowing wind;   15
Or on a half-reap'd furrow sound asleep,
    Drows'd with the fume of poppies while thy hook
        Spares the next swath and all its twined flowers:
And sometimes like a gleaner thou dost keep
    Steady thy laden head across a brook;   20
    Or by a cyder-press, with patient look,
        Thou watchest the last oozings hours by hours.

Where are the songs of Spring? Ay, where are they?
    Think not of them, thou hast thy music too, –
While barred clouds bloom the soft-dying day,   25
    And touch the stubble-plains with rosy hue;
Then in a wailful choir the small gnats mourn
    Among the river sallows, borne aloft
        Or sinking as the light wind lives or dies;
And full-grown lambs loud bleat from hilly bourn;   30
    Hedge-crickets sing; and now with treble soft
    The red-breast whistles from a garden-croft;
        And gathering swallows twitter in the skies.

As with the odes 'To a Nightingale' and 'On Melancholy', Keats uses extensive personification in this the last of his great odes, written in September of 1819. The whole poem is addressed almost like a hymn to the season. Often described as the most perfect of Keats's poems, there is an amazing poise about it, a mood of calm acceptance as opposed to some of the urgent questioning of earlier work. The sense of richness extends beyond the amazing abundance of the harvest to the wealth of sensory perceptions recorded and the sheer profusion of meanings which the poem is able to hold. When Keats wrote to Shelley a year later, advising him to 'load every rift of your subject with ore' it was perhaps such poems as 'To Autumn' which he had in mind. In the same letter Keats criticised his fellow poet for showing too much 'purpose' in his poetry as he attempted to prove things instead of letting the poetry speak for itself. It is perhaps worth bearing in mind that Keats wrote this poem only a week after the horrific murder of demonstrating people by government soldiers at the Peterloo massacre in Manchester. Among other things the people had been demonstrating against was the lack of power – and the price of bread. Never can there have been a better illustration of the difference between the two poets than that Shelley's purposeful response was 'The Mask of Anarchy' whilst Keats calmly composed an ode to the plenty of the harvest. On a more personal note, the 'harvest' of poetry which the thrush had predicted in 'O thou whose face' was nearly at an end. A feeling of this seems to pervade the poem, especially the end. Within eighteen months, Keats would die, like his brother, of tuberculosis. By the end of 1819, he knew he had the disease and composed very little more poetry.

Make a list of the five senses and catalogue Keats' use of images from these senses within the poem. Does a pattern emerge? Which sense would you expect to dominate a poem and which to be least used? Does Keats use all five? How does Keats create a sense of plenty in the first stanza?

What consonants are predominantly used? Are these soft or hard sounds? How do they fit in with the picture of the season in the first line? Keats creates an archetypal, or typical, old-fashioned English autumn scene. How? Where is there a hint that there is about to be a change?

The second stanza shows the personified Autumn in a series of roles as labourer, resting after the harvest (both inside and out), or as a *gleaner* (a poor person who was allowed to collect the leftover grains from the fields) or watching the squeezing of the apples for cider. Account for the beauty of line 15. Gleaning had been made illegal in 1818. What do you think Keats is (gently) hinting by including such a figure? How does he achieve the effect of crossing a boundary from line 19 to line 20? Why is *oozings* such a successful word?

What might the *songs of Spring* be? Keats gently hints at death and the end of the day and the season in the final stanza. List the examples. How might the cricket and the *full-grown lambs* add to this feeling? The robin and the swallows give a sense of continuity and hope but also of completion and finality respectively. Why?

 Is the poem ultimately hopeful, sombre or merely objective in its picture of the close of the growing year?

 Which of the odes did you find most successful?

 Keats claimed that *intensity* is what is essential in poetry. To what extent has he achieved this in his own work? You might consider the presentation of sensual experience, emotion, pain and dream worlds in your answer.

The Victorian Age

(1830–1900)

It is scarcely surprising that an age of such rapid reform in terms of politics, industry, science and economy should cling so desperately to the notion of conformity in manners and morality. The poetry of the period aptly reflects this duality, making few technical innovations (if we except the virtually unpublished Hopkins) whilst recording the underlying changes in thought which marked the age as a turning point.

The great age of reform began in earnest in 1832, when the industrial middle classes were given the right to vote for a member of parliament, a right which previously had only been granted to landowners. This right was extended in 1867 to many of the new urban workers until finally in 1884 agricultural labourers could vote. (Women had to wait until the twentieth century.) Industrialisation, a process begun in the previous century, now leapt forward encouraged by a new individualism and made possible by the huge population explosion of the century; numbers living in England and Wales had multiplied from nine to twenty-six million between 1801 and 1881. Cheap labour was never so ruthlessly exploited particularly in the manufacturing urban workforce. Disease was rife and mortality high, and efforts to improve these conditions (including such great Victorian engineering feats as the sewer systems, many of which survive to this day) were notable features of the age. Perhaps these conditions may explain the standard Victorian prejudices against dirt and against sex. 'Cleanliness is next to Godliness', a phrase much ridiculed in our own day, might have held more relevance for a society where the benefits of hygiene were only just being fully discovered. Similarly the typical Victorian prudery was perhaps an unconscious attempt to check such a massive population growth as well as a reaction to the increased incidence of sexually transmitted diseases.

Literacy increased enormously during the age, meaning that the reading public and therefore the market for literature was expanded, ensuring the real earning power of such favourite authors as Dickens, Thackeray and Tennyson. Not since the theatre of Shakespeare's day had great literature been so accessible to so many ranks in society. It was all a part of the great democratising process of the age, the belief in the greatest good for the greatest number. It is also testament to the enormous ambition for self-improvement in a society which, whatever else it was, was never apathetic or lacking a sense of determination and duty. This duty was reinforced by the Protestant work ethic – that, since 'the Devil makes work for idle hands', it is better to be continually employed on something useful, or you are likely to turn to sin. A reaction to this ethic is seen in the escapist imaginary worlds explored by Brontë or Tennyson, though even here the investment of time and energy towards creating them is typically Victorian, typically thorough!

If this was an age of progress and pride (shown most clearly in the Great Exhibition of 1851), of expanding Empire, increasing moralising and earnest self-confidence, then for others (especially the intellectuals) it was also an age of Darwin and doubt. Darwin's *Origin of Species* of 1859 was only one key text in the questioning of age-old faiths about God's creation. For many of the age's great thinkers and artists there was to be no way back to faith, as exhibited clearly in Arnold's 'Dover Beach'. If Hopkins made the great answer to Arnold's doubt, Tennyson and Browning remained ambivalent. Meanwhile Emily Brontë, a clergyman's daughter, was working out her own answers to the problems of faith. Like many of the Victorian poets she was strongly influenced by the Romantics' belief in the power of Nature – and if her faith in spirituality was strong, it was also remarkably independent. At their greatest, all of the poets here represented – from the seemingly conventional Poet Laureate Tennyson to the fiercely isolated Brontë – formed their own system.

BIOGRAPHICAL NOTES

Alfred Lord Tennyson (1809–92)

The third surviving son of a Lincolnshire rector, Tennyson
went to Trinity College, Cambridge, and published his first
great volume of verse in 1830. His friend Arthur Hallam died
in 1833 – an event which made a huge impression on
Tennyson. He became engaged to Emily Sellwood but was
not married until 1850. In the same year, after the death of
Wordsworth, Tennyson was made Poet Laureate. Living on
the Isle of Wight he discharged his official duties (odes on
Royal birthdays etc.) received his civil list pension and
became the most popular poet of the age. One of the
greatest lyricists in the language, Tennyson considered
himself the heir to the younger generation of Romantics and
shared their love of the past, if not their radical politics. His
greatest works (such as 'In Memoriam') perfectly captured
the concerns of the age (faith and progress) as well as
dealing with the eternal human concerns of love and death.

Robert Browning (1812–89)

The son of a clerk in the Bank of England, Browning was
educated largely at home, reading in his father's large
library. Browning's early literary ambitions lay chiefly in the
field of drama where he had some success in 1835 with
Paracelcus. However it was in poetry where he was to
achieve lasting fame after a period of some obscurity. He
courted another famous poet of the day, Elizabeth Barrett,
and they finally married and eloped to Italy in 1846. He did
not return to live in England until after her death in 1866 by
which time he had achieved critical acclaim if not the
commercial success enjoyed by Tennyson.

Emily Brontë (1818–48)

The fourth daughter of the Reverend Patrick Brontë, curate of Haworth on the Yorkshire moors, Emily grew up with a great deal of freedom, supported by her siblings but extremely shy of any other society. Her mother had died in 1821 and in 1824 her father sent the eldest of the girls to boarding school, where in harsh conditions both Mary and Elizabeth contracted consumption and died. Charlotte, the next oldest, largely assumed the role of mother and protector despite being only two years older than Emily. She it was who survived her siblings and oversaw the publication of their posthumous work. Only for short periods did Emily leave a home to which she was fiercely attached – to boarding school, where she was taught by Charlotte, to teach in a large school near Halifax, and finally to Belgium with Charlotte, where she attempted to improve her language skills in the hope of founding a school herself. During all of these times she was intensely homesick not merely for the moors, but for the extremely close bond she had built with Anne her younger sister – a bond which resulted in the creation of an imaginary realm, Gondal, to rival Angria, the realm created by Charlotte and her brother Branwell. Many of her poems are based on this realm, which was also to become the basis for her lasting belief in the amorality of art: that good and evil intensely imagined can not only coexist but must be presented equally, without judgement. This belief reached its height in her one novel *Wuthering Heights*, published in 1847 under the pseudonym Ellis Bell – since none of the sisters wanted to be patronised as 'mere' women writers. The three had already published poetry in 1846 under the names Acton, Currer and Ellis Bell. In 1848, after nursing her brother until his death, Emily contracted consumption and died, followed just over twelve months later by her sister Anne.

Matthew Arnold (1822–88)

The eldest son of the famous headmaster of Rugby School, on leaving Balliol College, Oxford, Arnold became an

Inspector of Schools. His first volume of poems was published in 1849 and in 1851 he married. He became less prolific in poetry, finding the age 'wanting in moral grandeur' and turned his attention instead to essays and criticism. He became Professor of Poetry at Oxford and was one of the foremost cultural thinkers of his day. His belief in education and literature as a replacement for the civilising powers of religion was extremely influential.

Gerard Manley Hopkins (1844–89)

Born in Stratford, Essex, the eldest son of middle-class High Anglican parents, Hopkins attended Balliol College, Oxford from 1863, where he wrote much poetry. Most of this he destroyed in 1868, having decided to become not merely a Catholic, but a Jesuit – a member of a very strict sect of Roman Catholics. He trained as a priest, and with the permission of the Jesuit authorities felt able to write poetry once more in 1876. The pieces he wrote were considered too difficult for the reading public and so were never published in his lifetime. Hopkins worked in various parishes in Chesterfield, London, Oxford and for difficult periods in Liverpool and Glasgow. He returned to academic life in Roehampton, where he had trained, and eventually in 1884 became Professor of Classics in Dublin. However, he felt overwhelmed by the administrative work, fell ill and died in March 1889 of typhoid. His work remained largely unpublished until 1918 (after the Modernist innovations of Eliot and others) when his friend Robert Bridges felt that the reading public was ready for such original work. Hopkins had developed several theories in poetry which made him a great innovator: he believed that the poet must seek to capture the 'inscape' or essential quality of what he described, and that the sounds and rhythms of the language ought to be captured in what he called 'sprung rhythm'. Basically this involves counting only stressed syllables rather than total numbers of syllables in each line. Despite these innovations his concerns with faith and the way God and Nature interrelated mark him as a poet very much of his time.

ALFRED LORD TENNYSON

Mariana

With blackest moss the flower-pots
Were thickly crusted, one and all:
The rusted nails fell from the knots
That held the pear to the gable-wall.
The broken sheds looked sad and strange: 5
Unlifted was the clinking latch;
Weeded and worn the ancient thatch
Upon the lonely moated grange.
She only said, 'My life is dreary,
He cometh not,' she said;   10
She said, 'I am aweary, aweary,
I would that I were dead!'

Her tears fell with dews at even;
Her tears fell ere the dews were dried;
She could not look on the sweet heaven,   15
Either at morn or eventide.
After the flitting of the bats,
When thickest dark did trance the sky,
She drew her casement-curtain by,
And glanced athwart the glooming flats.   20
She only said, 'The night is dreary,
He cometh not,' she said;
She said, 'I am aweary, aweary,
I would that I were dead!'

Upon the middle of the night,   25
Waking she heard the night-fowl crow:
The cock sung out an hour ere light:
From the dark fen the oxen's low
Came to her: without hope of change,
In sleep she seemed to walk forlorn,   30
Till cold winds woke the gray-eyed morn
About the lonely moated grange.

She only said, 'The day is dreary,
He cometh not,' she said;
She said, 'I am aweary, aweary,   35
I would that I were dead!'

About a stone-cast from the wall
A sluice with blackened waters slept,
And o'er it many, round and small,
The clustered marish-mosses crept.   40
Hard by a poplar shook alway,
All silver-green with gnarlèd bark:
For leagues no other tree did mark
The level waste, the rounding gray.
She only said, 'My life is dreary,   45
He cometh not,' she said;
She said, 'I am aweary, aweary,
I would that I were dead!'

And ever when the moon was low,
And the shrill winds were up and away,   50
In the white curtain, to and fro,
She saw the gusty shadow sway.
But when the moon was very low,
And wild winds bound within their cell,
The shadow of the poplar fell   55
Upon her bed, across her brow.
She only said, 'The night is dreary,
He cometh not,' she said;
She said, 'I am aweary, aweary,
I would that I were dead!'   60

All day within the dreamy house,
The doors upon their hinges creaked;
The blue fly sung in the pane; the mouse

Behind the mouldering wainscot shrieked,
Or from the crevice peered about.   65
Old faces glimmered through the doors,
Old footsteps trod the upper floors,
Old voices called her from without.
She only said, 'My life is dreary,
He cometh not,' she said;   70
She said, 'I am aweary, aweary,
I would that I were dead!'

The sparrow's chirrup on the roof,
The slow clock ticking, and the sound
Which to the wooing wind aloof   75
The poplar made, did all confound
Her sense; but most she loathed the hour
When the thick-moted sunbeam lay
Athwart the chambers, and the day
Was sloping toward his western bower.   80
Then, said she, 'I am very dreary,
He will not come,' she said;
She wept, 'I am aweary, aweary,
O God, that I were dead!'

What sort of things make you depressed? Try to describe
your mood and attitude to things around you (the weather,
your surroundings, other people) when affected by this
despair.

Together with the next two pieces this was published in
1832, when Tennyson was twenty-three years old. Like
much of his early work it concerns the subjective projection
of feelings onto the surroundings, and the kind of detached
solitude and dwelling on one's own (often melancholy)
mood which characterised his own youth. The 'heroine'
seems incapable of breaking out of the cycle of misery, a
cycle echoed in the rhythmical repetitions of the stanzas.

What are the signs that the place has been neglected in the first stanza? Why do you think Tennyson begins with these? The phrase *moated grange*, taken from Shakespeare's play *Measure for Measure*, refers to the type of medieval country-house which was surrounded by a moat for protection. What is the effect of the moat here? What might be the reasons that Mariana's lover *cometh not*?

In what sense is Mariana in tune with nature in the second stanza? The *glooming flats* refers to the land about Lincolnshire where the poem is set. Why is this an appropriate background for Mariana? What is the effect of the chorus at the end of each stanza? Trace carefully the differences between these refrains (especially in the final stanza) saying why they are appropriate to each stanza. One critic, Paul Turner, has commented on the 'circular rhyme scheme' being one factor in creating 'a living picture of utter dejection'. What do you think he means by this? Before the third stanza there is very little enjambement. Why do you suppose Tennyson includes this suggestion of change in the third stanza? Is the hope of change fulfilled?

Tennyson, who grew up in the fenlands of Lincolnshire, noted that *marish-mosses* are 'little marsh-moss lumps that float on the surface of water'. What is the effect of the two rhyming verbs in lines 38 and 40? What effect does the poplar tree have in the fourth and fifth stanzas? Who are the *old faces*? Look carefully at the sounds of the words and the repetitions in the seventh and eighth stanzas – how does Tennyson perfectly capture the feeling of entrapped inactivity here? We can see why these tedious details would *confound* or annoy her – but why do you suppose that sunset is the hour she most *loathed*?

Compare with Browning's 'Porphyria's Lover'.

Song – The Owl

When cats run home and light is come,
And dew is cold upon the ground,
And the far-off stream is dumb,
And the whirring sail goes round,
And the whirring sail goes round;   5
Alone and warming his five wits,
The white owl in the belfry sits.

When merry milkmaids click the latch,
And rarely smells the new-mown hay,
And the cock hath sung beneath the thatch   10
Twice or thrice his roundelay,
Twice or thrice his roundelay;
Alone and warming his five wits,
The white owl in the belfry sits.

A peculiarly haunting poem, this 'song', like many of
Tennyson's works, employs the device of a type of medieval
ballad, the 'roundelay', with a repeated chorus or refrain.
What provides the central sounds around which the two
stanzas are constructed? What time is the poem set and
what are the clues? Why would the barn owl be safely in the
belfry or church-loft at this stage? Explore the differences –
especially those of mood – between the first three lines of
the first and second stanzas. The poem echoes two plays of
Shakespeare. In *Love's Labours Lost* Shakespeare had
described how 'nightly sings the staring owl,/Tu-whoo …/
Tu-whit to-who'; whilst in *King Lear* the madman Tom
a'Bedlam had repeatedly exclaimed 'Bless thy five wits!
Tom's a-cold.' The wits are here the five senses but there
seems to be a pun based on the first Shakespeare quotation.
There is also a feeling of loneliness and isolation in the
poem. How does Tennyson achieve this?

The Kraken

Below the thunders of the upper deep;
Far, far beneath in the abysmal sea,
His ancient, dreamless, uninvaded sleep
The Kraken sleepeth: faintest sunlights flee
About his shadowy sides: above him swell   5
Huge sponges of millennial growth and height;
And far away into the sickly light,
From many a wondrous grot and secret cell
Unnumbered and enormous polypi
Winnow with giant arms the slumbering green.   10
There hath he lain for ages and will lie
Battening upon huge seaworms in his sleep,
Until the latter fire shall heat the deep;
Then once by man and angels to be seen,
In roaring he shall rise and on the surface die.   15

The scale and elemental nature of this work give it an epic feel despite being only fifteen lines long. The Kraken is a mythical sea creature, only presented to our view momentarily – and here associated with beasts which will rise out of the sea on judgement day according to the biblical Book of Revelations (Books 8 and 13). How does Tennyson achieve the sense of scale here, and the sense of being far removed from the human world? *Polypi* here are octopuses or cuttlefish. How can they *winnow* the seas, separating the food from the non-food? To *batten* is to thrive at another's expense. How can the Kraken achieve this even *in his sleep*? What is meant by the *latter fire*? Explain the legend which Tennyson invents in the last line.

Compare with Keats' 'Hyperion' or Shelley's 'Ozymandias'.

*T*he Eagle

(fragment)

He clasps the crag with crooked hands;
Close to the sun in lonely lands,
Ringed with the azure world, he stands.

The wrinkled sea beneath him crawls;
He watches from his mountain walls,   5
And like a thunderbolt he falls.

 Find examples of hyperbole, personification, simile,
alliteration, assonance and metaphor in this brief poem.
Explain their effectiveness in context, and how they add to
the impact of the poem and the majesty of the eagle,
traditionally king of the birds. How do the rhyme and rhythm
contribute to the inevitability of the eagle's power?

Ulysses

It little profits that an idle king,
By this still hearth, among these barren crags,
Matched with an agèd wife, I mete and dole
Unequal laws unto a savage race,
That hoard, and sleep, and feed, and know not me.   5

I cannot rest from travel: I will drink
Life to the lees: all times I have enjoyed
Greatly, have suffered greatly, both with those
That loved me, and alone; on shore, and when
Through scudding drifts the rainy Hyades   10
Vexed the dim sea: I am become a name;
For always roaming with a hungry heart
Much have I seen and known; cities of men
And manners, climates, councils, governments,
Myself not least, but honoured of them all;   15
And drunk delight of battle with my peers,
Far on the ringing plains of windy Troy.

I am a part of all that I have met;
Yet all experience is an arch wherethrough
Gleams that untravelled world, whose margin fades   20
For ever and for ever when I move.
How dull it is to pause, to make an end,
To rust unburnished, not to shine in use!
As though to breathe were life. Life piled on life
Were all too little, and of one to me   25
Little remains: but every hour is saved
From that eternal silence, something more,
A bringer of new things; and vile it were
For some three suns to store and hoard myself,
And this grey spirit yearning in desire   30
To follow knowledge like a sinking star,
Beyond the utmost bound of human thought.

This is my son, mine own Telemachus,
To whom I leave the sceptre and the isle –
Well-loved of me, discerning to fulfil   35
This labour, by slow prudence to make mild

A rugged people, and through soft degrees
Subdue them to the useful and the good.
Most blameless is he, centred in the sphere
Of common duties, decent not to fail   40
In offices of tenderness, and pay
Meet adoration to my household gods,
When I am gone. He works his work, I mine.

   There lies the port; the vessel puffs her sail:
There gloom the dark broad seas. My mariners,   45
Souls that have toiled, and wrought, and thought
   with me –
That ever with a frolic welcome took
The thunder and the sunshine, and opposed
Free hearts, free foreheads – you and I are old;
Old age hath yet his honour and his toil;   50
Death closes all: but something ere the end,
Some work of noble note, may yet be done,
Not unbecoming men that strove with Gods.
The lights begin to twinkle from the rocks:
The long day wanes: the slow moon climbs: the deep   55
Moans round with many voices. Come, my friends,
'Tis not too late to seek a newer world.
Push off, and sitting well in order smite
The sounding furrows; for my purpose holds
To sail beyond the sunset, and the baths   60
Of all the western stars, until I die.
It may be that the gulfs will wash us down:
It may be we shall touch the Happy Isles,
And see the great Achilles, whom we knew.
Though much is taken, much abides; and though   65
We are not now that strength which in old days
Moved earth and heaven; that which we are, we are;
One equal temper of heroic hearts,
Made weak by time and fate, but strong in will
To strive, to seek, to find, and not to yield.   70

Like Tennyson's most famous poem, the long philosophical work 'In Memoriam' (published in 1850), 'Ulysses' is a response to the early death of his friend, Arthur Hallam. Hallam, only 22 when he died, was a scholar of enormous promise.

Tennyson described 'Ulysses' as giving his 'feeling about the need of going forward and braving the struggle of life'. Ulysses was a figure from Classical epic poetry, a hero of the Trojan War – and, unlike Achilles his fellow Greek, a survivor; in Homer's 'Odyssey', he is described as a wandering adventurer, who near the end of his life had settled in Ithaca in the Mediterranean. In Tennyson's version the king decides to go on one final journey, leaving his son in charge of the *savage race* of Ithaca. He obviously dislikes the staleness of his life as well as the frustration of not being able to achieve fairness in law-giving (line 4) amongst a selfish people.

The *Hyades* are stars which were said to bring about storms, whilst the *Happy Isles* were a legendary group of islands said to lie beyond the Pillars of Hercules at Gibraltar, which to the Greeks was the boundary of the known world. Ulysses' journey beyond such a boundary seems to represent the Victorian thirst for progress as much as Tennyson's own ambition. It has been claimed (by Matthew Arnold among others) that the slow pace of the poem works against Ulysses' stated desire for movement (see especially lines 19–21 and 53–5). How valid do you find this criticism? The heroic eagerness for action is certainly a contrast to the introspective Tennyson's early central figures such as the passive Mariana.

 Compare this poem either with 'Mariana' or with Keats' 'Hyperion' in their depictions of strength and weakness. How do the poets affect our sympathies in these works?

To what extent do you find Ulysses admirable in this poem? He has been referred to as intolerant and impulsive. Are these accusations justified? Do you think Tennyson is ambivalent about his character?

*B*reak, break, break

Break, break, break,
On thy cold gray stones, O Sea!
And I would that my tongue could utter
The thoughts that arise in me.

O well for the fisherman's boy,   5
That he shouts with his sister at play!
O well for the sailor lad,
That he sings in his boat on the bay!

And the stately ships go on
To their haven under the hill;   10
But O for the touch of a vanished hand,
And the sound of a voice that is still!

Break, break, break,
At the foot of thy crags, O Sea!
But the tender grace of a day that is dead   15
Will never come back to me.

Written in spring 1834, whilst Tennyson was living in
Somersby, Lincolnshire, this is another beautiful and
evocative response to Hallam's death. If, like the ships
described in the third stanza, life (and natural forces) must
go on after such an event, this does not prevent the illogical
and very human heartfelt response of this yearning emotion
to reverse time.

How does the sea *break* on the shore and why is this word
repeated? What else is breaking apart from the sea? Why
are the *stones* described with such harsh adjectives?
Describe the contrast between the first two stanzas in detail.
Why is it appropriate that Tennyson is here describing the
young? What effect does seeing them have on him? *Haven*
is linguistically close to 'heaven'. What would you expect
lines 11–12 to describe considering that Tennyson was a
devout Christian writing for a devoutly Christian readership?
Why is his response more honest than conventional?

The Charge of the Light Brigade

Half a league, half a league,
Half a league onward,
All in the valley of Death
Rode the six hundred.
'Forward, the Light Brigade!   5
Charge for the guns!' he said:
Into the valley of Death
Rode the six hundred.

'Forward, the Light Brigade!'
Was there a man dismayed?   10
Not though the soldier knew
Some one had blundered:
Their's not to make reply,
Their's not to reason why,
Their's but to do and die: 15
Into the valley of Death
Rode the six hundred.

Cannon to the right of them,
Cannon to the left of them,
Cannon in front of them   20
Volleyed and thundered;
Stormed at with shot and shell,
Boldly they rode and well,
Into the jaws of Death,
Into the mouth of Hell   25
Rode the six hundred.

Flashed all their sabres bare,
Flashed as they turned in air
Sabring the gunners there,
Charging an army, while   30
All the world wondered:
Plunged in the battery-smoke
Right through the line they broke;
Cossack and Russian

Reeled from the sabre-stroke   35
Shattered and sundered.
Then they rode back, but not
Not the six hundred.

Cannon to the right of them,
Cannon to the left of them,   40
Cannon behind them
Volleyed and thundered;
Stormed at with shot and shell,
While horse and hero fell,
They that had fought so well   45
Came through the jaws of Death,
Back from the mouth of Hell,
All that was left of them,
Left of six hundred.

When can their glory fade?   50
O the wild charge they made!
All the world wondered.
Honour the charge they made!
Honour the Light Brigade!
Noble six hundred!   55

First published in the weekly magazine *The Examiner* on
9 December, 1854, the poem commemorated the ill-fated
charge of six hundred soldiers into a virtual death trap, a
valley heavily defended. The charge had occurred in
October during the Crimean War which Britain was fighting
against Russia. *The Times* referred to 'some hideous
blunder' on the part of the British commanders and it was
after reading the report that Tennyson responded.

How does Tennyson use rhythm and repetition to capture
the sound of the cavalry in the first stanza? How are these
same devices used differently in the second and third
stanzas? Examine the various ways the bravery of the men
is emphasised during the poem. Compare the third and fifth
stanzas, noting especially the differences. How does the poet
use punctuation effectively in the final stanza? In a later
version of the poem, Tennyson omitted lines 5–12, but then
regretted the decision and reinserted them. With reference to
his role as Poet Laureate, explain why he left them out. Do
you think the poem is better with or without these lines?
Does the poem, in your view, celebrate blind heroism or
criticise blind leadership? What makes these men heroic?
Look at 'Ulysses' to establish what Tennyson was likely to
admire in men.

Compare the poem with any based on the First World War –
Sassoon's 'The General' or Owen's 'Dulce et Decorum est'
might be particularly appropriate. Consider what the poems
are trying to achieve before analysing how effective they are
in fulfilling these aims.

Crossing the Bar

Sunset and evening star,
And one clear call for me!
And may there be no moaning of the bar,
When I put out to sea,

But such a tide as moving seems asleep,   5
Too full for sound and foam,
When that which drew from out the boundless deep
Turns again home.

Twilight and evening bell,
And after that the dark!   10
And may there be no sadness of farewell,
When I embark;

For though from out our bourne of Time and Place
The flood may bear me far,
I hope to see my Pilot face to face   15
When I have crost the bar.

Written in October 1889 whilst crossing the Solent, the poem is in part a response to Tennyson's serious illness earlier that year. The *bar* is the sandbank across the harbour mouth, the boundary or *bourne* to travel across – here representing our final boundary, death. It was Tennyson's wish that this poem should be at the end of all editions of his poems. Explain the sound which the sea might make on this sandbank – what does this *moaning* represent? Compare the image of the tide to that used by Arnold in 'Dover Beach'. How would a full tide help practically? What is the deeper meaning of lines 7–8?

The *call* is a marine term, a summons to duty. Who might be calling Tennyson here? Who do you think the *pilot* or navigator of Tennyson's ship of life is?

'In this selection, Tennyson explores the contrasting characteristics of the passive and vulnerable and the active and decisive, without fully committing himself to which he favours.' Discuss.

'Twice or thrice his roundelay.' Explore Tennyson's use of repetition, rhyme and rhythm for various effects in different poems.

ROBERT BROWNING

Porphyria's Lover

The rain set early in tonight,
    The sullen wind was soon awake,
It tore the elm-tops down for spite,
    And did its worst to vex the lake:
    I listened with heart fit to break.   5
When glided in Porphyria; straight
    She shut the cold out and the storm,
And kneeled and made the cheerless grate
    Blaze up, and all the cottage warm;
    Which done, she rose, and from her form   10
Withdrew the dripping cloak and shawl,
    And laid her soiled gloves by, untied
Her hat and let the damp hair fall,
    And, last, she sat down by my side
    And called me. When no voice replied,   15
She put my arm about her waist,
    And made her smooth white shoulder bare,
And all her yellow hair displaced,
    And stooping, made my cheek lie there,
    And spread, o'er all, her yellow hair,   20
Murmuring how she loved me – she
    Too weak, for all her heart's endeavour,
To set its struggling passion free
    From pride, and vainer ties dissever,
    And give herself to me for ever.   25
But passion sometimes would prevail,
    Nor could tonight's gay feast restrain
A sudden thought of one so pale
    For love of her, and all in vain:
    So, she was come through wind and rain.   30
Be sure I looked up at her eyes
    Happy and proud; at last I knew
Porphyria worshipped me; surprise
    Made my heart swell, and still it grew

While I debated what to do.   35
That moment she was mine, mine, fair,
    Perfectly pure and good: I found
A thing to do, and all her hair
    In one long yellow string I wound
Three times her little throat around,   40
And strangled her. No pain felt she;
    I am quite sure she felt no pain.
As a shut bud that holds a bee,
    I warily oped her lids: again
    Laughed the blue eyes without a stain.   45
And I untightened next the tress
    About her neck; her cheek once more
Blushed bright beneath my burning kiss:
    I propped her head up as before,
    Only, this time my shoulder bore   50
Her head, which droops upon it still:
    The smiling rosy little head,
So glad it has its utmost will,
    That all it scorned at once is fled,
    And I, its love, am gained instead!   55
Porphyria's love: she guessed not how
    Her darling one wish would be heard.
And thus we sit together now,
    And all night long we have not stirred,
    And yet God has not said a word!   60

What are your expectations of the poem based on the title? Read the poem in excerpts of five lines, briefly recording your impressions of character and situation before proceeding.

This macabre gothic tale was first published in 1842 in Browning's fourth volume of verse, *Dramatic Lyrics*. The title of the publication aptly describes what was to become Browning's most characteristic formal development, the dramatic monologue. In the advertisement to this edition, the poet described these works as 'though for the most part Lyric in expression, always Dramatic in principle, and so many utterances of so many imaginary persons, not mine.' What kind of atmosphere does the poet create in the opening lines – especially with the device of personification? What clues does this give you as regards personality? What effect does Porphyria's entrance have on this atmosphere? Describe her efforts to bring comfort to the man. What reasons does he give for not responding? Which lines tell us that he is utterly wrapped up in himself? How does he propose to prolong the moment of triumph forever? Why is the image so shocking in the context of the poem? Look particularly at the enjambement in lines 37–41. How does Browning gain the impact of immediacy in lines 50–51? What is the point of the last line? Look back to earlier parts of the poem which suggest that the man is mad. Describe the cyclical rhyme scheme – what does it imply about the man's state of mind? Originally titled 'Madhouse Cell', the poem is perhaps a reflection of changing attitudes towards lunatics, leading to some efforts at empathy. Why is it important that we do not know the man is mad at the beginning?

Compare Tennyson's 'Mariana'.

My Last Duchess

That's my last Duchess painted on the wall,
Looking as if she were alive; I call
That piece a wonder, now: Frà Pandolf's hands
Worked busily a day, and there she stands.
Will't please you sit and look at her? I said   5
'Frà Pandolf' by design, for never read
Strangers like you that pictured countenance,
The depth and passion of its earnest glance,
But to myself they turned (since none puts by
The curtain I have drawn for you, but I)   10
And seemed as they would ask me, if they durst,
How such a glance came there; so, not the first
Are you to turn and ask thus. Sir, 't was not
Her husband's presence only, called that spot
Of joy into the Duchess' cheek: perhaps   15
Frà Pandolf chanced to say 'Her mantle laps
Over my lady's wrist too much,' or 'Paint
Must never hope to reproduce the faint
Half-flush that dies along her throat;' such stuff
Was courtesy, she thought, and cause enough   20
For calling up that spot of joy. She had
A heart – how shall I say? – too soon made glad,
Too easily impressed; she liked whate'er
She looked on, and her looks went everywhere.
Sir, 't was all one! My favour at her breast,   25
The dropping of the daylight in the West,
The bough of cherries some officious fool
Broke in the orchard for her, the white mule
She rode with round the terrace – all and each
Would draw from her alike the approving speech,   30
Or blush, at least. She thanked men, – good!
      but thanked
Somehow – I know not how – as if she ranked
My gift of a nine-hundred-years-old name
With anybody's gift. Who'd stoop to blame
This sort of trifling? Even had you skill   35
In speech – (which I have not) – to make your will

Quite clear to such an one, and say, 'Just this
Or that in you disgusts me; here you miss,
Or there exceed the mark' – and if she let
Herself be lessoned so, nor plainly set   40
Her wits to yours, forsooth, and made excuse,
– E'en then would be some stooping; and I choose
Never to stoop. Oh sir, she smiled, no doubt,
Whene'er I passed her; but who passed without
Much the same smile? This grew; I gave commands;   45
Then all smiles stopped together. There she stands
As if alive. Will't please you rise? We'll meet
The company below, then. I repeat,
The Count your master's known munificence
Is ample warrant that no just pretence   50
Of mine for dowry will be disallowed;
Though his fair daughter's self, as I avowed
At starting, is my object. Nay we'll go
Together down, sir. Notice Neptune, though,
Taming a sea-horse, thought a rarity,   55
Which Claus of Innsbruck cast in bronze for me!

One of the greatest of Browning's dramatic monologues, this poem is probably based on Alfonso II (1533–98) the fifth Duke of Ferrara who married the fourteen-year-old Lucrezia de'Medici in 1558. She died in 1561 and there were some suspicions of poisoning. This chilling tale of arrogance and male power concerns a man for whom a woman is to be another work of art (Alfonso was known to be egotistical and possessive as well as being a great patron of the arts). The Duke is to be imagined talking to an envoy, or representative, of a wealthy Count whose daughter is to become engaged to the Duke but we do not find this out immediately (see lines 49–53). It seems at first as though he is showing around a tourist. How does Browning achieve the effect of speech in the poem? What actually happens during the course of the poem? *Frà Pandolf* is a painter invented by Browning. Why did the Duke disapprove of his *last Duchess*? Which phrases mark him as an arrogant man? What do you suppose happens to the Duchess when all smiles stopped together? What happens to the Duke's flowing style at this point? Explain how Browning uses enjambement so effectively in the sentence *There she stands / As if alive.* What causes you to doubt the Duke's smooth words in lines 48–53? What is the point of the last three lines?

Which of these dramatic monologues do you find the most effective?

Compare with either Shelley's 'Ozymandias' or Auden's 'Epitaph on a Tyrant'. Which do you find the most effective portrayal of arrogance?

EMILY BRONTË

High waving heather, 'neath stormy blasts bending

High waving heather, 'neath stormy blasts bending,
Midnight and moonlight and bright shining stars;
Darkness and glory rejoicingly blending,
Earth rising to heaven and heaven descending,
Man's spirit away from its drear dungeon sending,   5
Bursting the fetters and breaking the bars.

All down the mountain sides, wild forests lending
One mighty voice to the life-giving wind;
Rivers their banks in the jubilee rending,
Fast through the valleys a reckless course wending,   10
Wider and deeper their waters extending,
Leaving a desolate desert behind.

Shining and lowering and swelling and dying,
Changing for ever from midnight to noon;
Roaring like thunder, like soft music sighing,   15
Shadows on shadows advancing and flying,
Lightning-bright flashes the deep gloom defying,
Coming as swiftly and fading as soon.

Briefly describe two types of contrasting winter weather, one calm and the other violent.

Written in December 1836, this poem is a celebration, not only of the moors where Brontë spent so much time but of the feeling of freedom which they brought to her. Analysed grammatically each stanza is an incomplete sentence with no finite verb, merely a catalogue of present participles (verbs ending in -ing, which cannot make a sentence complete). However, this merely adds to the sense of movement, power and never-ending natural processes which she describes. The poem needs to be read aloud to appreciate its full power.

Pick out the powerful verbs used throughout the poem and explain their impact in context. Look at the sounds of the words as well as the meaning. How would you describe the rhythm of the poem? What effect is Brontë trying to achieve? Bearing in mind that a *glory* can mean a halo, pick out the examples of antithesis, or contrast, which the poet uses – especially in the first stanza and the last. What two types of weather are being described? Lines 4–6 describe man's response to the freedom of the winds on the moors. What do you think Brontë means by the spirit's *drear dungeon?* In what sense is the heather of the first line a symbol of man's spirit? How can forests *lend* a voice to the wind and how can the wind be *life-giving* (7–8)? Which term in the second stanza implies that the weather inspires wild celebration? Describe the pace of the stanza and how it is achieved. What might the shadows be which move so swiftly over the landscape in the final stanza?

Compare Hopkins' 'Inversnaid' with this poem.

A *little while, a little while*

A little while, a little while,
The noisy crowd are barred away;
And I can sing and I can smile
A little while I've holyday!

Where wilt thou go, my harrassed heart?   5
Full many a land invites thee now;
And places near and far apart
Have rest for thee, my weary brow.

There is a spot 'mid barren hills
Where winter howls and driving rain,   10
But if the dreary tempest chills
There is a light that warms again.

The house is old, the trees are bare
And moonless bends the misty dome
But what on earth is half so dear,   15
So longed for as the hearth of home?

The mute bird sitting on the stone,
The dank moss dripping from the wall,
The garden-walk with weeds o'ergrown,
I love them – how I love them all!   20

Shall I go there? or shall I seek
Another clime, another sky,
Where tongues familiar music speak
In accents dear to memory?

Yes, as I mused, the naked room,   25
The flickering firelight died away
And from the midst of cheerless gloom
I passed to bright, unclouded day –

A little and a lone green lane
That opened on a common wide;   30
A distant, dreamy, dim blue chain
Of mountains circling every side;

A heaven so clear, an earth so calm,
So sweet, so soft, so hushed an air
And, deepening still the dream-like charm,   35
Wild moor-sheep feeding everywhere –

That was the scene; I knew it well,
I knew the path-ways far and near
That winding o'er each billowy swell
Marked out the tracks of wandering deer.   40

Could I have lingered but an hour
It well had paid a week of toil,
But truth has banished fancy's power;
I hear my dungeon bars recoil –

Even as I stood with raptured eye   45
Absorbed in bliss so deep and dear
My hour of rest had fleeted by
And given me back to weary care.

In what ways, and when, is work like a prison? What else
would you rather be doing?

Composed in December 1838, when Brontë was teaching in
Law Hill School, near Halifax, this poem is a cry for greater
freedom, for more time to indulge her imagination rather
than the *weary care* of the prison-like schoolwork. The air of
artless simplicity, like Blake's, is largely achieved in the
eight syllable, flowing rhythm, iambic and childish. In what
two senses is the *little while* of freedom a *holyday*? Which
lines describe her home? In which lines does she long for
home, even with all its imperfections? What role do the
questions play in the poem? The sixth stanza speaks of
other options. How would she (in her brief hour of freedom)
travel to other climates than home? The last lines of this
stanza probably refer to the characters of Gondal, her
imaginary world. How does Brontë use alliteration to
emphasise the magic of her transformation in the next two

stanzas? Why is *chain* an odd but appropriate choice of word? Describe the visionary world she creates in your own words. Why is *charm* so appropriate?

 Compare the poem with Keats' 'Ode to a Nightingale', D.H. Lawrence's 'Last Lesson of the Afternoon', Yeats' 'Lake Isle of Innisfree', or Larkin's 'Toads'. In what different ways do they explore the differences between the harsh prison of truth and ideal worlds of freedom?

Riches I hold in light esteem

Riches I hold in light esteem
And Love I laugh to scorn
And lust of Fame was but a dream
That vanished with the morn –

And if I pray, the only prayer   5
That moves my lips for me
Is – 'Leave the heart that now I bear
And give me liberty.'

Yes, as my swift days near their goal
'Tis all that I implore –   10
Through life and death, a chainless soul
With courage to endure!

Written in May 1841 whilst Emily was living back at
Haworth, this is the first in this selection which Emily herself
chose for inclusion in the publication of 1846. Which of the
three qualities of *Riches*, *Love* or *Fame* has the poet found
the most tempting and how do you know? Why might the
second stanza have seemed shocking in 1846? Why do you
think the poem was given the title 'The Old Stoic' when it
was first published? What rejections are needed in order to
earn *a chainless soul*? Relate this concept to other
references to chains and prisons in her work.

*T*o *Imagination*

When weary with the long day's care,
And earthly change from pain to pain,
And lost, and ready to despair,
Thy kind voice calls me back again –
O my true friend, I am not lone   5
While thou canst speak with such a tone!

So hopeless is the world without,
The world within I doubly prize;
Thy world where guile and hate and doubt
And cold suspicion never rise;   10
Where thou and I and Liberty
Have undisputed sovereignty.

What matters it that all around
Danger and grief and darkness lie,
If but within our bosom's bound   15
We hold a bright unsullied sky,
Warm with ten thousand mingled rays
Of suns that know no winter days?

Reason indeed may oft complain
For Nature's sad reality,   20
And tell the suffering heart how vain
Its cherished dreams must always be;
And Truth may rudely trample down
The flowers of Fancy newly blown.

But thou art ever there to bring   25
The hovering visions back and breathe
New glories o'er the blighted spring
And call a lovelier life from death,
And whisper with a voice divine
Of real worlds as bright as thine.   30

I trust not to thy phantom bliss,
Yet still in evening's quiet hour
With never-failing thankfulness
I welcome thee, benignant power,
Sure solacer of human cares   35
And brighter hope when hope despairs.

Written in September 1844, a time when the sisters were in
despair over plans to start a school, the poem once more
celebrates the powers of the imagination to bring solace.
However the poem also looks briefly at the negative aspect
of the imagination. It was published in 1846.

Compare Keats' 'Ode to a Nightingale'. What, according to
both poems, are the drawbacks of the imagination or
Fancy? What are the benefits?

Cold in the earth, and the deep snow piled above thee!

Cold in the earth, and the deep snow piled above thee!
Far, far removed, cold in the dreary grave!
Have I forgot, my Only Love, to love thee,
Severed at last by Time's all-wearing wave?

Now, when alone, do my thoughts no longer hover   5
Over the mountains on Angora's shore;
Resting their wings where heath and fern-leaves cover
That noble heart for ever, ever more?

Cold in the earth, and fifteen wild Decembers
From those brown hills have melted into spring –   10
Faithful indeed is the spirit that remembers
After such years of change and suffering!

Sweet Love of youth, forgive if I forget thee
While the World's tide is bearing me along:
Sterner desires and darker hopes beset me,   15
Hopes which obscure but cannot do thee wrong.

No other Sun has lightened up my heaven;
No other Star has ever shone for me:
All my life's bliss from thy dear life was given –
All my life's bliss is in the grave with thee.   20

But when the days of golden dreams had perished
And even Despair was powerless to destroy,
Then did I learn how existence could be cherished,
Strengthened and fed without the aid of joy;

Then did I check the tears of useless passion,   25
Weaned my young soul from yearning after thine;
Sternly denied its burning wish to hasten
Down to that tomb already more than mine!

And even yet, I dare not let it languish,
Dare not indulge in Memory's rapturous pain;   30
Once drinking deep of that divinest anguish,
How could I seek the empty world again?

A starkly honest portrayal of grief for a long-dead lover, this poem is based not on real-life experience (though surely the crushing blow of the loss of mother and sisters feeds into the authenticity of the vision) but on two characters in the Gondal saga and was originally titled 'R[osina] Alcona to J[ulius] Brenzaida'. When the poem was published in 1846, certain alterations were made including changing the name of Angora (an imaginary kingdom adjacent to Gondal and ruled by Brenzaida) and giving the poem a new title, 'Remembrance'. These changes were designed to make the poem more general in its application. The speaker fluctuates in the poem between wishing to end a life without her loved one and forcing herself to fight on. How does the speaker emphasise the distance between the living and the dead in the first stanza? The critic F.R. Leavis comments that the *brown hill* represents the hardness of the speaker's spirit which withstands all the vicissitudes, or changing fortunes, of life since Brenzaida's death. What has Rosina learnt to do in response to this shattering death?

Compare this poem with Tennyson's responses to death in 'Ulysses' and 'Break, break, break'.

Emily Brontë

*S*tar

Ah! why, because the dazzling sun
Restored my earth to joy
Have you departed, every one,
And left a desert sky?

All through the night, your glorious eyes   5
Were gazing down in mine,
And with a full heart's thankful sighs
I blessed that watch divine!

I was at peace, and drank your beams
As they were life to me   10
And revelled in my changeful dreams
Like petrel on the sea.

Thought followed thought – star followed star
Through boundless regions on,
While one sweet influence, near and far,   15
Thrilled through and proved us one.

Why did the morning rise to break
So great, so pure a spell,
And scorch with fire the tranquil cheek
Where your cool radiance fell?   20

Blood-red he rose, and arrow-straight
His fierce beams struck my brow:
The soul of Nature sprang elate,
But mine sank sad and low!

My lids closed down – yet through their veil   25
I saw him blazing still;
And bathe in gold the misty dale,
And flash upon the hill.

I turned me to the pillow then
To call back Night, and see   30
Your worlds of solemn light, again
Throb with my heart and me!

It would not do – the pillow glowed
And glowed both roof and floor,
And birds sang loudly in the wood,   35
And fresh winds shook the door.

The curtains waved, the wakened flies
Were murmuring round my room,
Imprisoned there, till I should rise
And give them leave to roam.   40

O Stars and Dreams and Gentle Night;
O Night and Stars return!
And hide me from the hostile light
That does not warm, but burn –

That drains the blood of suffering men;   45
Drinks tears, instead of dew:
Let me sleep through his blinding reign,
And only wake with you!

Written in April 1865, this is one of Brontë's most successful poems. Once again she explores the relationship between imaginary (dream) worlds and the *hostile* truth of everyday reality. However, here she acknowledges the necessity of involving herself with that sunshine-filled world (it is no coincidence that she chooses such a positive image), because otherwise what would happen to the flies? Responsibility for other lives raises its head here – however reluctantly. Who is the poet speaking to? Discuss in detail the *sweet influence* of these beings. Why is the poet compared to a *petrel*, a seabird which flies miles from land? How does this image follow naturally on from others in stanza 3? How is the sun made to appear destructive in the poem? Look carefully at each image used to describe the character Brontë addresses. Are there any instances where the image of the sun is more positive? Why can the speaker not recall the images of night? What sort of sunshine (real life) does the speaker long for and what does she dread?

*S*tanzas

Often rebuked, yet always back returning
To those first feelings that were born with me,
And leaving busy chase of wealth and learning
For idle dreams of things which cannot be:

Today, I will seek not the shadowy region;   5
Its unsustaining vastness waxes drear;
And visions rising, legion after legion,
Bring the unreal world too strangely near.

I'll walk, but not in old heroic traces,
And not in paths of high morality,   10
And not among the half-distinguished faces,
The clouded forms of long-past history.

I'll walk where my own nature would be leading:
It vexes me to choose another guide:
Where the gray flocks in ferny glens are feeding;   15
Where the wild wind blows on the mountain side.

What have those lonely mountains worth revealing?
More glory and more grief than I can tell:
The earth that wakes *one* human heart to feeling
Can centre both the worlds of Heaven and Hell.   20

The authorship of this poem has been disputed since no manuscript in Emily's hand has been found. However it seems unlikely that the more conventionally Christian Charlotte (who published this and the following poem in 1850) could have written the final stanzas. The poem seems to extend the partial recognition of the necessity of the 'real' world from the previous poem. In fact it rejects the *shadowy region* of the *unreal world* – at least for one day. The third and fourth stanzas turn on the literal and metaphorical meanings of 'walk'. How can one *walk* through history, or philosophy, or biography? How does she choose to walk instead? Why is her *own nature* such an appropriate *guide* – much more than any other? Which figure in the Bible promised to be our 'guide' and shepherd? What point is Emily revealing here? Why might the last stanza be seen as shocking for a Christian minister's daughter in Victorian England? What does she mean when she claims that earth can *centre ... Heaven and Hell*? What contradictory qualities must earth contain? Why is it more significant than religious morality, according to this view?

Blake commented that he must 'create a system or be the slave of another man's'. To what extent is the remark appropriate when considering Emily Brontë's poetry?

No coward soul is mine

No coward soul is mine
No trembler in the world's storm-troubled sphere
I see Heaven's glories shine
And Faith shines equal arming me from Fear

O God within my breast   5
Almighty ever-present Deity
Life, that in me hast rest
As I Undying Life, have power in Thee

Vain are the thousand creeds
That move men's hearts, unutterably vain,   10
Worthless as withered weeds
Or idlest froth amid the boundless main

To waken doubt in one
Holding so fast by thy infinity
So surely anchored on   15
The steadfast rock of Immortality

With wide-embracing love
Thy spirit animates eternal years
Pervades and broods above,
Changes, sustains, dissolves, creates and rears   20

Though Earth and moon were gone
And suns and universes ceased to be
And thou wert left alone
Every Existence would exist in thee.

There is not room for Death   25
Nor atom that his might could render void
Since thou art Being and Breath
And what thou art may never be destroyed.

Referred to by Charlotte as the last words written by Emily, the poem expresses her undying faith in an eternal being – whether the conventional God of Christianity, the kind of deity Wordsworth often seemed to have in mind, or a more personal divinity in line with earlier poems in this collection is not made clear. Her faith remains unshaken by mere worldly influences such as sickness, other beliefs, and even death itself. What gives the opening statement its power and clarity? One critic refers to the 'impassioned invocation of the second stanza' and the 'formulation of the workings of the deity in the fifth stanza'. How does Brontë achieve these very different qualities – the first showing deep emotion, the second intellectual clarity? Why are the *thousand creeds* of other men *vain* to shake her own belief?

Charlotte's comment that 'Liberty was the breath of Emily's nostrils; without it, she perished' is particularly appropriate to her poetry. Discuss.

'Emily Brontë's poetry is as much about carving out a world of "sovereignty", of discovering a voice for the passive voiceless heroines of much Victorian literature, as it is about imagination.' 'Emily's espousal of a life of proud, isolated autonomy is celebrated in [her] poems.' Discuss. You might like to look at the work of Tennyson and Browning's 'Porphyria's Lover' in your answer.

Does Brontë's poetry rise above escapism?

MATTHEW ARNOLD

Dover Beach

The sea is calm tonight.
The tide is full, the moon lies fair
Upon the straits; – on the French coast the light
Gleams and is gone; the cliffs of England stand,
Glimmering and vast, out in the tranquil bay.   5
Come to the window, sweet is the night-air!

Only, from the long line of spray
Where the sea meets the moon-blanched land.
Listen! you hear the grating roar
Of pebbles, which the waves draw back, and fling,   10
At their return, up the high strand,
Begin, and cease, and then again begin,
With tremulous cadence slow, and bring
The eternal note of sadness in.

Sophocles long ago   15
Heard it on the Aegean, and it brought
Into his mind the turbid ebb and flow
Of human misery; we
Find also in the sound a thought,
Hearing it by this distant northern sea.   20

The Sea of Faith
Was once, too, at the full and round earth's shore
Lay like the folds of a bright girdle furl'd.
But now I only hear
Its melancholy, long, withdrawing roar,   25
Retreating, to the breath
Of the night-wind, down the vast edges drear
And naked shingles of the world.

Ah, love, let us be true
To one another! for the world, which seems   30
To lie before us like a land of dreams,
So various, so beautiful, so new,

Hath really neither joy, nor love, nor light,
Nor certitude, nor peace, nor help for pain;
And we are here as on a darkling plain   35
Swept with confused alarms of struggle and flight,
Where ignorant armies clash by night.

Written in 1851, whilst Arnold was on honeymoon in Dover, this the most famous of his poems concerns faith and fidelity. As the couple start out on married life, Arnold looks not only at their own faith in each other, but at the whole of the decline in religious faith which was so alarming to a nation (and a world) so used to taking religious belief for granted. How does the poet create an air of idyllic simplicity in the first stanza? Who is he talking to? Explain the epithet *moon-blanch'd* to describe the land. How does it add to the air of purity? Why is reference to the moon appropriate in this poem so concerned with tides? How does Arnold capture the rhythm of the waves in the second stanza? Look at the rhyme scheme and the lengths of the lines throughout the poem. With reference to the introduction to this section, explain why *the Sea of Faith* is no longer *at the full*. A *girdle* is a medieval word for a belt, here *bright* because it represents the line of sea spray seen from high above all around the island. Why do you suppose this belt is *furl'd*? Why is a medieval word so appropriate when describing the *Sea of Faith* at high tide? How does Arnold perfectly capture the *withdrawing roar* of both tide at the turn, and religion in decline? Why are the beaches described as *naked*? What does Arnold turn to as a brief comfort in the final stanza? Relate the images here to those in the first stanza. What is the main difference? In the last three lines, Arnold implies that suddenly in a faithless world the enemies and evil are not known easily: all the old certitudes are gone.

GERARD MANLEY HOPKINS

God's Grandeur

The world is charged with the grandeur of God.
It will flame out, like shining from shook foil;
It gathers to a greatness, like the ooze of oil
Crushed. Why do men then now not reck his rod?
Generations have trod, have trod, have trod;   5
And all is seared with trade; bleared, smeared, with toil;
And wears man's smudge and shares man's smell: the soil
Is bare now, nor can foot feel, being shod.

And, for all this, nature is never spent;
There lives the dearest freshness deep down things;   10
And though the last lights of the black West went
Oh, morning, at the brown brink eastward, springs –
Because the Holy Ghost over the bent
World broods with warm breast and with ah! bright wings.

Think of three images, either man-made or natural, which might best describe for you the grandeur and power of the divine.

The confidence of this sonnet contrasts massively with Arnold's ponderings and (later) Eliot's self-doubt. There is a sureness in this piece even more strong than that of the Metaphysicals which in some ways it resembles. Explore the sounds of the words and the alliteration and assonance throughout the poem. Why are the metaphysical conceits in the first four lines both surprising and effective in emphasising the power of God (both quickly in lightning, and slowly in geological changes)? What are the normal associations of oil? In what ways does Hopkins reclaim the power of this natural product, finding beauty in unexpected places? Which line tells us that faith is declining so that the rule of God is no longer to be taken for granted? Comment on line 5 and compare it to a similar line in Keats' 'Ode to a Nightingale'. How does Hopkins improve on his original? Compare line 8 with a work of another poet-priest, R.S. Thomas' 'Cynddylan on a Tractor'. How does Hopkins make use of the volta, the change of direction governed by the change in rhyme scheme? The *freshness deep down things* is perhaps what Hopkins meant by 'inscape' (see Biographical Notes). How does he make this quality sound not stale but alive? Where is the dawn described as a reassuring sign of God's care for the world?

*H*eaven-Haven
A nun takes the veil

I have desired to go
Where springs not fail,
To fields where flies no sharp and sided hail
And a few lilies blow.

And I have asked to be   5
Where no storms come,
Where the green swell is in the havens dumb,
And out of the swing of the sea.

Belonging to his first burst of creative activity, there are
fewer of the complications of Hopkins' later style in this
poem. However already the poet's concerns with a Catholic
retreat combine with his love of the sounds and rhythms of
the language. What does 'taking the veil' signify? In what
ways are the images the nun chooses in the first stanza
different from those of the second stanza? Decide whether
the nun is speaking literally, metaphorically or both in the
first stanza. What does she mean by *sided hail*? Why does
she choose *lilies* as the flowers which will *blow* or grow in
her haven? Why would the *green swell* of the sea be *dumb*
in the *havens*? What does the sea represent here?

Compare the poem with Yeats' 'Lake Isle of Innisfree'.

Compare the different ways Tennyson, Arnold and Hopkins
use the image of the sea in their poems about faith,
'Crossing the Bar', 'Dover Beach' and 'Heaven-Haven'.

*P*ied *Beauty*

Glory be to God for dappled things –
For skies of couple-colour as a brinded cow;
For rose-moles all in stipple upon trout that swim;
Fresh-firecoal chestnut-falls; finches' wings;
Landscape plotted and pieced – fold, fallow, and plough;   5
And all trades, their gear and tackle and trim.

All things counter, original, spare, strange;
Whatever is fickle, freckled (who knows how?)
With swift, slow; sweet, sour; adazzle, dim;
He fathers-forth whose beauty is past change: 10
        Praise him.

'The pursuit of perfection may lead to intolerance or even vicious destruction.' Discuss with reference to the history of the nineteenth and twentieth centuries. Are imperfections tolerated in your own environment (family or friends)?

As an unconventional innovator, Hopkins must have felt by 1878 that his poetry did not fit with what was happening in literature around him. The Victorian age was very critical of all that ran counter to convention. Here he celebrates the 'inscape' of all that seems *original* and *spare* or not strictly necessary. List those things which he finds *dappled*.

How does he make each seeming imperfection sound beautiful? Look especially at the harmonies he creates with alliteration and assonance, as though they belong in the world; also note the words ending in *-le* which ripple through the poem. Also look for the compound words and epithets that imply a connection between different aspects of God's creation. For instance, fresh glowing red-brown chestnuts (or the autumnal leaves) are compared to *firecoal* probably by association with roasting chestnuts. Why are these things *dappled*? How is God different from the paradoxical and changeable natures of his creations?

*I*nversnaid *Sept. 28 1881*

The darksome burn, horseback brown,
His rollrock highroad roaring down,
In coop and in comb the fleece of his foam
Flutes and low to the lake falls home.

A windpuff-bonnet of fawn-froth 5
Turns and twindles over the broth
Of a pool so pitchblack, fell-frowning,
It rounds and rounds Despair to drowning.

Degged with dew, dappled with dew
Are the groins of the braes that the brook
   treads through, 10
Wiry heathpacks, flitches of fern,
And the beadbonny ash that sits over the burn.

What would the world be, once bereft
Of wet and of wildness? Let them be left,
O let them be left, wildness and wet; 15
Long live the weeds and the wilderness yet.

After seven weeks working in the parish of St Joseph's,
Glasgow, Hopkins was given two days' leave and spent it at
Loch Lomond, where he found the tiny hamlet of Inversnaid,
with its waterfall. The poem describes the steepest part of
the *burn* or stream, Arklet Water, before depicting its calmer
upper reaches. The poet revels not only in the energy of the
wild water but in the sounds of local and north-country
dialect words. *Coop* describes the narrows where the water
is confined and therefore more powerful; a *comb* is a ridge,
dividing the water; *twindles* means splits in two; a *fell* is a
hill; *degged* means sprinkled; *braes* are steep banks;
heathpacks are heathers; *flitches* are flakes; the *beadbonny*
is the rowan or mountain ash. Justify *horseback brown*,
rollrock highroad and *fleece of his foam*. *Flutes* here means
spreads. With a little thought that which seems so
condensed and strange makes perfect sense. How can these
pools turn *Despair to drowning*? Refer to Hopkins' own
feelings about his vocation in your answer. Compare the last
line with the previous poem.

Compare the depiction of landscape in Brontë's 'High
waving heather'.

*T*hou art indeed just, Lord

Thou art indeed just, Lord, if I contend
With thee; but, sir, so what I plead is just.
Why do sinners' ways prosper? and why must
Disappointment all I endeavour end?
Wert thou my enemy, O thou my friend,   5
How wouldst thou worse, I wonder, than thou dost
Defeat, thwart me? Oh, the sots and thralls of lust
Do in spare hours more thrive than I that spend,
Sir, life upon thy cause. See, banks and brakes
Now, leavèd how thick! lacèd they are again   10
With fretty chervil, look, and fresh wind shakes
Them; birds build – but not I build; no, but strain,
Time's eunuch, and not breed one work that wakes.
Mine, O thou lord of life, send my roots rain.

Written in March 1889, only months before his death, this sonnet records Hopkins' despair in his new post in University College, Dublin. Nothing that he does seems to produce any fruit. His poems are ignored, his parish work and preaching are a disappointment and now even academia results in frustration. Even *sots* or drunks and other sinners seem to *thrive* more than he. How does Hopkins, like Herbert and Donne before him, achieve the feeling of a conversation with God? Consider rhythms as well as vocabulary. *Chervil* or cow-parsley is known as Queen Anne's lace; here Hopkins, seeming to digress, describes its *fretty* or fine-toothed leaves. Why is this digression appropriate to what he was saying before? Consider the season he writes about. Which word tells us which season this is? What might the *fresh wind* represent in his own life? In what dual metaphorical sense is he *time's eunuch*? Explain the last line.

Even Hopkins is beset with doubt at times. Contrast this with any other poem which seems to you most sure in its faith and most effective in conveying that faith.

'All things counter, original, spare, strange.' Discuss with reference to either Hopkins or Emily Brontë.

The First World War and Beyond (1900-1939)

The turn of the century, so neatly described by Hardy, brought with it fresh hope but tremendous fears. The pace of change in lifestyles has never been faster than in the twentieth century and advancing technology brought us new and more devastating ways to destroy each other as well as innovations which were designed to make our lives easier and longer. This paradox lies at the heart of some of the greatest poetry of the century. The sense of nostalgia for more simple, less mechanised ways of life was strongly expressed by such poets as Hardy, Frost, Edward Thomas and D.H. Lawrence, as it was later by R.S. Thomas and Seamus Heaney. The 'tribal' territorial and destructive side of human nature, fed rather than tamed by our new machines, are here explored, not merely in the great poetry which came out of the First World War, but less directly in poets such as Frost and Hughes and in the troubled later work of Seamus Heaney.

As the old orders of class and religion have declined, so there has been great technical innovation in poetry. The old forms (the sonnet, the heroic couplet, rhyme itself) are less often used reflecting the lack of harmony and order in our lives. Free verse, the lack of end-rhyme, and an avoidance of regular pattern in rhythm, is best exemplified in the work of Lawrence. For him it is the natural expression of his desire to escape the accepted truths and become more like the natural world, spontaneous and free – not merely free of the old hierarchies based on class, but of the new masters, the machines themselves – which according to Lawrence and R.S. Thomas increasingly rule our lives.

Events which directly affect the poetry include the First World War, which formed a watershed in English life. The vote for women soon followed, the old respect for class was never the same again, the new machinery (especially the car and the tractor) began to dominate, old country ways changed. At the same time, as Eliot's verse records, life in the new urban areas seemed alienated from the old certainties of religion, the sense of common accepted values. All seemed shallow and petty. The British Empire had reached its zenith and, exhausted by this war and the depression a little later, would never be quite the force it had been. Heroes were not the same and the taste for old heroic verse in the style of Tennyson faded to be replaced by the everyman figure, the 'hero' as victim, the ordinary man manipulated by circumstances (society, war, the machinery of modern life) and powerless to change things. The tone of the poetry (wry, ironic, almost world-weary) often reflected this change.

As one empire faded a new one emerged to replace it – albeit one with the same language. The American empire, based on trade and culture backed up by military force rather than outright territorial conquest, replaced the British as the dominant world power and, for the first half of the century at least, brought the fresh optimism of the triumphant successor – not merely in economic and political terms but also in literature. Fuelled by the myth of the American Dream – that by hard work the virgin land could be conquered, ensuring independence and freedom for oneself and one's family – the culture in the United States survived the Depression and the Wall Street Crash to emerge dominant and essentially proud. Whilst some (like T.S. Eliot) found the lack of heritage there worrying enough to prefer England, other poets (like Auden) felt exhilarated by the opportunities this young nation seemed to offer.

BIOGRAPHICAL NOTES

Thomas Hardy (1840–1928)

A great novelist as well as a major poet, Hardy was born into a working class family in rural Dorset. He achieved considerable fame in his lifetime as a novelist, but some hostile criticism contributed to his decision to give up prose and focus on what he thought of as the greatest art, poetry. Like Wordsworth and Browning, Hardy tried to write poetry in a language close to that of speech. His poetry was admired only by a few critics during his lifetime but has since been recognised as some of the greatest lyric verse of modern times.

Rupert Brooke (1887–1915)

Rupert Brooke, the son of a housemaster at Rugby school, was educated there and went on to study at Cambridge. Intelligent, athletic and 'the most handsome man in England', according to Yeats, he acquired a reputation as a golden youth. He enlisted at the outbreak of war and died of blood poisoning on board ship in the Aegean at the age of 27, having seen little action. Despite this he wrote several famous sonnets which seemed to capture a national sentiment of glorious sacrifice, typifying the national mood in the first months of the war.

Siegfried Sassoon (1886–1967)

A tremendously courageous fighter during the First World War, Sassoon earned the M.C. only to throw it away later when he became so frustrated by the way the war was being conducted. He organised public protests against the methods and tactics employed by the generals but suffered shell-shock and was regarded as mad. After the war he published religious and rural poetry.

Wilfred Owen (1893–1918)

Perhaps the greatest of the poets who wrote about the experiences of trench warfare, Owen came from a more humble background than Sassoon, his father being a railway worker. Fellow officers in the war, they met in hospital and Sassoon encouraged Owen's work. He returned to France in 1918 and won the M.C., but was killed a week before the Armistice. Most of his great poems, technically sophisticated and full of indignation and compassion, were written in the last year of his life. Like Keats, whose work strongly influenced him, Owen died at the age of 25 and his reputation grew after his own lifetime.

William Butler Yeats (1865–1939)

Born and educated in Dublin, Yeats was a convinced Irish Nationalist, believing that the Ireland which had been ruled by the English for several centuries should now be free to govern its own affairs. His early works were heavily influenced by Celtic or early Irish literature and tried to create a new vibrant tradition. Gradually his poetry became more political, less backward looking, but he also wrote some of the most powerful love poems in the language, many of them for a beautiful and extreme Nationalist, Maude Gonne. With the granting of independence for some of Ireland in 1921, Yeats served as a Senator in the government, thus returning to the Renaissance tradition of mingled roles in poetry and politics.

Edward Thomas (1878–1917)

Initially a prose writer, focusing on biography, criticism and descriptions of the British countryside, Thomas was encouraged by his friend Robert Frost to try writing poetry. It seems to have been the First World War which spurred him on to record some of the ways of the countryside, which were changing fast, and he did so memorably and beautifully before volunteering for the trenches and losing his life at the battle of Arras.

T.S. Eliot (1888–1965)

One of the most influential figures in English literature, Eliot was an American who came to England during the First World War and eventually became a British citizen. His poetry, in common with other Modernist works, attempted to break up the old narrative continuities of traditional Victorian poetry in favour of a seeming chaos of impressions. In his criticism he looked back to the Metaphysicals as an ideal, admiring the way they combined thought and feeling in their work.

Robert Frost (1874–1963)

Brought up in the New England farmland of the North East coast of America which was to inspire much of his work, Frost lived in England for a spell just before the First World War and published his first volume of poetry. Edward Thomas reviewed the volume favourably and was influential in Frost's early popularity. The two became very close friends for a short but extremely influential and fruitful period, before Frost returned to America in 1915. He taught in several colleges but continued to write poetry, celebrating the ordinary, everyday occurrences of the countryside, but finding in them something profound, something which illuminates our lives as human beings – much as Wordsworth had done before him. Both poets attempted to write in a less grand, more colloquial fashion, in keeping with their rural subject matter. Both, however, have moments of almost visionary lucidity, when eternal themes and extremely dark subject matter surface in their seemingly plain, ordinary tales. Like Edward Thomas, Frost looks with a very modern eye at the fast-changing traditions of country life amidst the increasing mechanisation of the industrialised societies of Britain and the United States.

D.H. Lawrence (1885–1930)

Primarily known as a novelist, Lawrence was one of the first working-class figures to emerge as a major prose writer in English. Heavily influenced by his more middle-class mother (whose death in 1910 deeply affected him) as well as his mining father, Lawrence was encouraged to develop a 'white collar' career as a clerk and later a teacher, rather than in the coal mines. However, he always retained his father's sensual characteristics along with his mother's more cerebral ones. It is this combination, and the opening up of new veins of interest (working-class life, sex and the new psychology so influenced by Freud), which makes his writing so fascinating. At the time, Lawrence's work was regarded as obscene and often banned. An instinctive rebel, he flouted decorum and convention to elope with Frieda Weekley, the wife of his old professor at Nottingham. She was six years older than Lawrence, and had three children, but was deeply unsatisfied with her married life. After her divorce the two married and enjoyed a passionate but extremely stormy life together, rarely living in one country for more than a couple of years. Unfit for service himself, Lawrence was a leading opponent of the First World War, which he regarded as an enormous waste of human life for petty, territorial motives. His wife was German and the two were persecuted as possible spies during the war. He later moved to Italy, Australia, America and Mexico. His poetry often explores many of the same themes as his novels, but unlike his prose style, which was rarely very experimental, Lawrence quickly developed away from traditional metres and structures in favour of free verse.

W. H. Auden (1907–73)

The greatest poet of his generation, Auden was the son of a doctor and was brought up in Birmingham before going to Christ Church, Oxford. He was heavily committed to anti-Fascist campaigning during the 1930s and his socially conscious poetry reflects this strongly. He was famous for using up-to-date language as well as contemporary images, which led to his type of verse being branded 'pylon poetry'. He left Britain in 1939 for the United States and became an American citizen in 1946. His work became much more personal and complex after this time and increasingly religious in tone.

THOMAS HARDY

The Darkling Thrush

I leant upon a coppice gate
    When Frost was spectre-gray,
And Winter's dregs made desolate
    The weakening eye of day.
The tangled bine-stems scored the sky   5
    Like strings of broken lyres,
And all mankind that haunted nigh
    Had sought their household fires.

The land's sharp features seemed to be
    The Century's corpse outleant,   10
His crypt the cloudy canopy,
    The wind his death-lament.
The ancient pulse of germ and birth
    Was shrunken hard and dry,
And every spirit upon earth   15
    Seemed fervourless as I.

At once a voice arose among
    The bleak twigs overhead
In a full-hearted evensong
    Of joy illimited;   20
An aged thrush, frail, gaunt, and small,
    In blast beruffled plume,
Had chosen thus to fling his soul
    Upon the growing gloom.

So little cause for carolings   25
    Of such ecstatic sound
Was written on terrestrial things
    Afar or nigh around,
That I could think there trembled through
    His happy good-night air   30
Some blessed Hope, whereof he knew
    And I was unaware.

The end of a year, a decade or most especially a century is often a time for reflection on the past and of looking forward to the future. As the new millennium gets under way, list the factors which make you optimistic and those which make you pessimistic about what may happen. Now do the same thing imagining that you were on the brink of the twentieth century. What great social, engineering and military changes were about to happen? Would an intelligent observer have been able to predict what would occur? Are people better off now than they were when the twentieth century began?

The poem is set in 1900. How is it possible to tell not only this, but the time of year and time of day? Look at the first four lines and explain each expression. Why does the poet use capital letters for *frost* and *winter*? The *bine-stems* are the thin creeping stems of plants such as the hop (a climbing plant used to flavour beer); discuss the simile comparing them to *strings of broken lyres*, bearing in mind what the lyre had been used for in olden times.

Discuss the extended metaphor in the first four lines of the second stanza. A *germ* in this context is a seed; what has happened to the seed's potential for new life? What is the poet's own outlook on the birth of this new century?

How does the poem change after its midpoint? Almost immediately there is an echo of Keats' 'full-throated' nightingale – as if the *strings of broken lyres*, the spirit of poetry from which the thrush sings, have been mended. Comment on the phrases *blast beruffled* and *fling his soul*.

Hardy has often been accused of pessimism. In what ways (and to what extent) is this true in the poem (even the final stanza) and in what ways is it not?

In Time of 'The Breaking of Nations' *(1915)*

Only a man harrowing clods
    In a slow silent walk
With an old horse that stumbles and nods
    Half asleep as they stalk.

Only thin smoke without flame   5
    From the heaps of couch-grass:
Yet this will go onward the same
    Though Dynasties pass.

Yonder a maid and her wight
    Come whispering by: 10
War's annals will cloud into night
    Ere their story die.

What would you say are the most significant inventions in the history of the human race? Which are the things which ensure our continued survival on the planet?

The title refers to a verse in the Bible when the prophet Jeremiah is calling upon God to bring vengeance upon Israel's enemy, Babylon: 'Thou art my battle axe and weapons of war: for with thee will I break in pieces the nations, and with thee will I destroy kingdoms' (Jeremiah 51, verse 20). The first 'world' war, then called simply 'the Great War', was a time when both sides called upon their God (the same God!) to bring them victory as they attempted to break the opposition. The war, as Hardy noted, may decide the fate of *dynasties*, but in the grand scheme of things it perhaps mattered less than the politicians (and priests) thought.

How is the man made to appear insignificant in the first stanza (especially after such a title)? What is to *harrow* and why is it so necessary for the human race (even in the days when horses are no longer used)? How would you describe the pace of the second line? How and why is this achieved? *Couch-grass*, a persistent weed, had to be uprooted and then burned to prevent regrowth. Why will this outlast the war? Why do you think Hardy uses the old-fashioned expression *wight* (meaning person, here a man) in the last stanza? What have this couple in common with the man and the fire of the previous stanzas? Why is *whispering* such an effective term to describe them? What does the poet mean by the last two lines? How is the whole poem a denial of its first word?

Compare Edward Thomas' 'As the Team's Head-brass' and Heaney's 'Follower'. What do these poems tell us about continuity in the human race?

RUPERT BROOKE

The Soldier

If I should die, think only this of me:
   That there's some corner of a foreign field
That is for ever England. There shall be
   In that rich earth a richer dust concealed;
A dust whom England bore, shaped, made aware,   5
   Gave, once, her flowers to love, her ways to roam,
A body of England's, breathing English air,
   Washed by the rivers, blest by suns of home.

And think, this heart, all evil shed away,
   A pulse in the eternal mind, no less   10
      Gives somewhere back the thoughts by England given;
Her sights and sounds; dreams happy as her day;
   And laughter, learnt of friends; and gentleness,
      In hearts at peace, under an English heaven.

This, the most famous of Brooke's five 'War Sonnets', first appeared early in 1915 (before the battle of the Somme) to an ecstatic public reception. Brooke quickly became the nation's poet of war, effortlessly expressing the nation's effortless feelings of superiority. Where does this sense of superiority show in the poem? How do the form and rhythm of the poem add to its effortless tone? What does the poet mean by *a dust whom England bore* ...? What kind of life is described in the lines which follow?

What do you think Brooke means by *a pulse in the eternal mind* (linked with the previous line)? How do you think the soul of Brooke would repay what England had given him? The last line refers to the idyllic English skies – but what does it suggest about English ideas of heaven? What might this suggest about English ideas about God during this war? Why do you think Brooke was so popular a poet at this time? Brooke died of blood poisoning on his way to the Dardanelles in Turkey shortly after the publication of this poem and was buried on the island of Scyros. Does this fact affect your attitude to the poem?

Compare this poem with any by Wilfred Owen – perhaps the 'Anthem for Doomed Youth' might be most appropriate. Consider not merely their attitudes to the war (and relevant backgrounds), but also the way they used their forms, their vocabularies and figures of speech, the public they had in mind, the beginnings and endings of their poems, and any other relevant factors.

SIEGFRIED SASSOON

The General

'Good-morning; good-morning!' the General said
When we met him last week on our way to the line.
Now the soldiers he smiled at are most of 'em dead,
And we're cursing his staff for incompetent swine.
'He's a cheery old card', grunted Harry to Jack   5
As they slogged up to Arras with rifle and pack.

But he did for them both by his plan of attack.

Read the poem aloud quickly and try to describe the rhythm of it. What type of poetry does it remind you of? Look at the line structures to see how Sassoon achieves this. What effect do you think he is aiming at? What is it easy to miss in the third line? Why is there a gap before the final line? How would you describe the tone of the poem?

The imaginary general's *plan of attack* was perhaps based on the British habit of bombarding the opposition trenches ceaselessly for several days before unleashing the soldiers to walk across no-man's land in an orderly manner to take ground. Not surprisingly, the Germans merely dug themselves deeper and deeper, and waited for the bombardment to finish. They then set about machine-gunning down the brave but ill-advised soldiers who were slowly advancing hampered by barbed wire, shell holes created by their own bombing and the inevitable sea of mud. Any 'success' was measured in yards rather than miles. Meanwhile Douglas Haig, Commander-in-Chief, persisted blindly, relying on the fact that with Britain's empire, we could afford to lose two men to every German. His 'plan of attack' was based on attrition, completely ignoring the human cost.

WILFRED OWEN

The Send-Off

Down the close, darkening lanes they sang their way
To the siding-shed,
And lined the train with faces grimly gay.

Their breasts were stuck all white with wreath and spray
As men's are, dead.   5

Dull porters watched them, and a casual tramp
Stood staring hard,
Sorry to miss them from the upland camp.
Then, unmoved, signals nodded, and a lamp
Winked to the guard.   10

So, secretly, like wrongs hushed-up, they went.
They were not ours:
We never heard to which front these were sent.

Nor there if they yet mock what women meant
Who gave them flowers.   15

Shall they return to beatings of great bells
In wild train-loads?
A few, a few, too few for drums and yells,
May creep back, silent to village wells
Up half-known roads.   20

Despite never looking directly at the battlefront, this poem is a bitter condemnation of the callous slaughter of war as soldiers are secretly, not publicly, sent off. It is as if the public is ashamed and not proud of what it is doing to these men.

Siding-sheds, or sheds at the side of railway tracks, are normally associated with the loading of goods or livestock. Why is it significant that the soldiers are loaded here, in the middle of the countryside lanes rather than in a station? Three of the first four words of the poem are oppressive, depressing terms. What does the soldier's singing show about them? Link the oxymoronic *grimly gay*. How can the soldiers be said to *line* the train?

To explain the *wreath and spray* read the fifth stanza. To the observing poet, these white flowers are a portent, or forewarning, of what will happen to the men. What do you suppose the women meant by giving them the flowers? Why is what actually will happen a mockery of the women's gestures? Why do you suppose the porters are *dull* and, like the signals, *unmoved*? Who is moved and why? The personification of signals and lamp gives an atmosphere of conspiracy and unfeeling inhumanity. How?

The line *They were not ours* is ambiguous. At first you assume that the poet is being as unfeeling as the porter, but the colon at the end of the line demands you read on to discover that he actually means they were not of his army division and therefore he lost touch. The line, following on from the previous one, is a condemnation of the callousness of the *wrongs hushed-up* of the slaughter on the battlefront.

Would the roads of the last line be *half-known* because they had changed or because the soldiers had changed?

Dulce et Decorum Est

Bent double, like old beggars under sacks,
Knock-kneed, coughing like hags, we cursed through
   sludge,
Till on the haunting flares we turned our backs,
And onwards our distant rest began to trudge.
Men marched asleep. Many had lost their boots,   5
But limped on, blood-shod. All went lame, all blind;
Drunk with fatigue; deaf even to the hoots
Of gas-shells dropping softly behind.

Gas! Gas! Quick, boys! – An ecstasy of fumbling,
Fitting the clumsy helmets just in time,   10
But someone still was yelling out and stumbling
And floundering like a man in fire or lime.
Dim through the misty panes and thick green light,
As under a green sea, I saw him drowning.

In all my dreams before my helpless sight   15
He plunges at me, guttering, choking, drowning.

If in some smothering dreams, you too could pace
Behind the wagon that we flung him in,
And watch the white eyes writhing in his face,
His hanging face, like a devil's sick of sin;   20
If you could hear, at every jolt, the blood
Come gargling from the froth-corrupted lungs,
Bitter as the cud
Of vile, incurable sores on innocent tongues, –
My friend, you would not tell with such high zest   25
To children ardent for some desperate glory,
The old Lie: *Dulce et decorum est*
Pro patria mori.

List the qualities you would regard as essential or typical in a hero – how they should look, behave and so on.

Would you be prepared to die for your country? Under what circumstances?

A certain amount of background information is necessary when reading this poem. As Britain went about building an empire, the largest the world has ever seen, it often turned for inspiration to another famous empire, that of Rome. Both dominions were conquered using superior fighting techniques to those of the 'savages' or 'barbarians'; both relied on the superior discipline and organisation of their troops and administrators, and both developed a huge feeling of national superiority as a result of their success. In order to maintain such success certain myths were developed and fostered. One of these was summed up in the famous phrase of the Roman poet Horace: 'Dulce et decorum est pro patria mori' – it is sweet and proper to die for your country. The Latin phrase became widely referred to in the education of young gentlemen in England, obviously to encourage obsessive national pride. The whole notion of a patriotism prepared to risk death was certainly encouraged amongst all classes and the phrase became perhaps a shorthand way of referring to the kind of blind patriotic fervour which swept Britain at the outbreak of war in 1914 – a fervour both epitomised and encouraged by the famous poster of Lord Kitchener pointing and saying 'Your country needs YOU'. When Owen entitled his poem 'Dulce et Decorum Est' he would be confident that many of his readers would have understood the Latin tag and known the remainder of the phrase. This would have made the opening of the poem and the gory details which followed all the more shocking.

The poem begins with an account of the troops returning to an area behind the front lines after a period at the battlefront, before telling of a surprise gas attack and the psychological effects of that attack and finally turning on the civilian reader. In what ways are the characteristics of the conventional hero overturned in the opening stanza? How much pride and discipline is in evidence here? How and why does Owen throw huge emphasis onto the first word of the poem? Note the use of alliteration throughout the stanza for harsh emphasis.

The *flares* would have been used to light up the opposition so as to make easier targets for bombs or, as in this case, gas shells. Why are they described as *haunting*? Why would the gas shells *hoot* (or taunt) in the imaginations of the soldiers? How does the pace change in the second stanza? Why does the poet use so many present participles (verbs ending in *–ing*)? Are the helmets really *clumsy*? (Look up 'transferred epithet' in the Glossary.) The effect of the green nerve gas was to give a burning, choking sensation if you were not quick enough to put on your helmet, eventually causing unconsciousness. How does Owen get these effects across to the reader?

How and why does the tense change in the third stanza?

When, in the final stanza, the poet addresses the civilians at home, he had in mind specifically Jessie Popes, author of much jingoistic patriotic poetry and children's books. What is the tone of his expression *my friend*? Who else might the poet have in mind? How has the poet proved to such people that the *old Lie* is false?

 Compare Tennyson's 'Charge of the Light Brigade'. Focus especially on the depiction of the glory and heroism of war.

Strange Meeting

It seemed that out of battle I escaped
Down some profound dull tunnel, long since scooped
Through granites which titanic wars had groined.
Yet also there encumbered sleepers groaned,
Too fast in thought or death to be bestirred.   5
Then, as I probed them, one sprang up, and stared
With piteous recognition in fixed eyes,
Lifting distressful hands as if to bless.
And by his smile, I knew that sullen hall,
By his dead smile I knew we stood in Hell.   10
With a thousand pains that vision's face was grained;
Yet no blood reached there from the upper ground,
And no guns thumped, or down the flues made moan.
'Strange friend,' I said, 'here is no cause to mourn.'
'None,' said the other, 'save the undone years,   15
The hopelessness. Whatever hope is yours,
Was my life also; I went hunting wild
After the wildest beauty in the world,
Which lies not calm in eyes, or braided hair,
But mocks the steady running of the hour,   20
And if it grieves, grieves richlier than here.
For by my glee might many men have laughed,
And of my weeping something had been left,
Which must die now. I mean the truth untold,
The pity of war, the pity war distilled.   25
Now men will go content with what we spoiled.
Or, discontent, boil bloody, and be spilled.
They will be swift with swiftness of the tigress,
None will break ranks, though nations trek from progress.
Courage was mine, and I had mystery,   30
Wisdom was mine, and I had mastery;
To miss the march of this retreating world
Into vain citadels that are not walled.
Then when much blood had clogged their chariot-wheels
I would go up and wash them from sweet wells,   35
Even with truths that lie too deep for taint.
I would have poured my spirit without stint

But not through wounds; not on the cess of war.
Foreheads of men have bled where no wounds were.
I am the enemy you killed, my friend.   40
I knew you in this dark; for so you frowned
Yesterday through me as you jabbed and killed.
I parried; but my hands were loath and cold.
Let us sleep now ...'

The most challenging of Owen's poems in this selection, both
in terms of difficulty and with regard to the wide-ranging
thrust of this harsh evaluation of twentieth-century society, it
needs to be read and re-read to appreciate all its subtleties.
The narrator of the poem descends into a realm, further and
further from the battlefield, a realm he identifies as Hell. Yet,
unlike the hell of the trenches themselves, this is a silent
world where there seems *no cause to mourn*. There he meets
one who recognises him, a *strange friend* who rises from the
dead to speak to him. The remainder of the poem is the
speech of this 'friend' who eventually reveals that he is *the
enemy you killed*. The surreal situation is quite different from
the harsh realism of much of the war poetry and gives the
poem much larger scope for a visionary view of the larger
significance of the war within the progress of civilisation.
There is also a suggestion that the *strange friend* is actually a
doppelganger, or double, of the poet himself – perhaps his
own suppressed self. This parallels much of the psychological
work of the day: as the poet puts it, *foreheads of men have
bled where no wounds are* – some of the most telling wounds
of the war have been psychological rather than physical.

Ultimately the figure of this other seems to be not merely an
enemy whom the narrator had killed as he *frowned ...
through* him, but a representative of the ideal poet, a figure
Shelley had described as one of the 'unacknowledged
legislator of the world', one who provided the morality of
modern society where religion failed – and a figure who, like
Owen himself, was to be tragically killed before he could
deliver that message. Fittingly, the manuscript suggests that
the poem, like Owen's life, was curtailed before it reached
completion.

The couplets of half rhyme allow for much greater freedom
of vocabulary than a normal rhyme scheme. What
emotional effect does this have here?

What kind of place does the poet descend to? What kind of
person was the *strange friend* before he died? What would
he have accomplished had he lived? What does he predict
will happen now in society? What does he mean by *none
will break ranks*? With regard to what happened in
Germany after the war, how was he proved right?

'In its refusal to draw a clear line between friend and foe,
between self and others, this poem is considerably in
advance of its time.' Discuss. Read the introductory notes to
the next section (The Modern Age) before answering.

The Dead-Beat

He dropped, – more sullenly than wearily,
Lay stupid like a cod, heavy like meat,
And none of us could kick him to his feet;
Just blinked at my revolver, blearily;
– Didn't appear to know a war was on,   5
Or see the blasted trench at which he stared.
'I'll do 'em in,' he whined, 'If this hand's spared,
I'll murder them, I will.'

              A low voice said,
'It's Blighty, p'raps, he sees; his pluck's all gone,   10
Dreaming of the valiant, that aren't dead:
Bold uncles, smiling ministerially;
Maybe his brave young wife, getting her fun
In some new home, improved materially.
It's not these stiffs have crazed him; nor the Hun.'   15

We sent him down at last, out of the way.
Unwounded; – stout lad, too, before that strafe.
Malingering? Stretcher-bearers winked, 'Not half!'
Next day I heard the Doc.'s well whiskied laugh:
'That scum you sent last night soon died. Hooray!'   20

Define bravery and describe brave things you have seen or done. What then is cowardice?

This brief narrative gives a picture of the official attitude towards cowardice in the shape of *malingering* (pretending to be ill to avoid combat). Even in 1998, the government refused to pardon the hundreds of men court-martialled and then shot for various 'acts of cowardice' in these most extreme conditions. However, the bravery of the men was acknowledged as well as the extreme psychological pressures they must have endured to react as they did.

How is the soldier characterised in the first stanza of the poem? What injury has he received in the latest bombardment or *strafe*? What do you suppose has made him lose his *pluck* or bravery? The man speaking in the second stanza guesses that it is neither the dead bodies nor the Germans but, oddly, the people at home back in *Blighty* (slang term for Britain) who have had this effect. Who do you at first think he means when he threatens to *murder them*? What attitude does the poet have towards the doctor and how do we know?

Mental Cases

Who are these? Why sit they here in twilight?
Wherefore rock they, purgatorial shadows,
Drooping tongues from jaws that slob their relish,
Baring teeth that leer like skulls' teeth wicked?
Stroke on stroke of pain, – but what slow panic   5
Gouged these chasms round their fretted sockets?
Ever from their hair and through their hands' palms
Misery swelters. Surely we have perished
Sleeping, and walk hell; but who these hellish?

– These are men whose minds the Dead have ravished.   10
Memory fingers in their hair of murders,
Multitudinous murders they once witnessed.
Wading sloughs of flesh these helpless wander,
Treading blood from lungs that had loved laughter.
Always they must see these things and hear them,   15
Batter of guns and shatter of flying muscles,
Carnage incomparable, and human squander,
Rucked too thick for these men's extrication.

Therefore still their eyeballs shrink tormented
Back into their brains, because on their sense   20
Sunlight seems a blood-smear; night comes blood-black;
Dawn breaks open like a wound that bleeds afresh.
– Thus their heads wear this hilarious, hideous,
Awful falseness of set-smiling corpses.
– Thus their hands are plucking at each other;   25
Picking at the rope-knouts of their scourging;
Snatching after us who smote them, brother,
Pawing us who dealt them war and madness.

In this harrowing poem, Owen tries to explain to us why some of the victims of shell shock, who must have seemed clinically insane, behaved as they did. He spent several months suffering from the condition in the summer of 1917 and it was in the specialist psychological hospital of Craiglockhart that he met Siegfried Sassoon, a fellow sufferer.

Purgatory is the place where souls go to await the judgement of God – and to purge away the sins they have committed, hopefully in preparation for heaven. Here there seems very little hope and merely a hellish punishment – but for sins not committed.

Having asked in the first stanza *Who are these …?*, the poet explains in the second what *multitudinous murders* they have witnessed, too many *for these men's extrication* – that is, too many for them to separate themselves from, so that they feel guilty as well as overwhelmed. By calling them murders, rather than casualties, what is Owen suggesting? Everything they see is now tinged with this blood so that they seem already dead. What do you notice about the way the last three lines begin? With what are these actions normally associated? Are they meant to be read literally, metaphorically or both? Think about each action. The *rope-knouts* refer back to the *stroke on stroke* of purgatorial punishment in the first stanza. What do the last two lines imply?

*A*nthem for Doomed Youth

What passing-bells for these who die as cattle?
   – Only the monstrous anger of the guns.
   Only the stuttering rifles' rapid rattle
Can patter out their hasty orisons.
No mockeries now for them; no prayers nor bells,   5
   Nor any voice of mourning save the choirs, –
The shrill, demented choirs of wailing shells;
   And bugles calling for them from sad shires.

What candles may be held to speed them all?
   Not in the hands of boys but in their eyes   10
Shall shine the holy glimmers of goodbyes.
   The pallor of girls' brows shall be their pall;
Their flowers the tenderness of patient minds,
And each slow dusk a drawing-down of blinds.

List those things you associate with English church services, especially funerals. What would you expect to hear, see or smell?

This sonnet is an extended metaphor in which the sounds of battle are the sad replacement for a proper funeral. The word *mockeries*, which Owen used also in 'The Send Off', implies a savage condemnation of the hypocrisy of a Church which failed to oppose the slaughter of these innocents (in the name, perhaps, of the very English 'Field Marshal God' of the next poem), but was happy enough to *mourn* them as heroes, fighting for the greater glory of the British Empire. Despite the distasteful thought of a funeral being made up of such sounds and sights as guns and shells, Owen suggests that it is more appropriate perhaps for such a death than the traditional memorial service.

A *passing-bell* was the traditional sign, a mournful tolling bell, that a soul had passed away in death; *orisons* are prayers; choirs and candle-bearers in processions would traditionally be boys. *Shires* are the traditional counties where the soldiers might have come from; a *pall* is the sheet draped over a coffin; at a traditional funeral the blinds would have been drawn over windows as a sign of mourning and respect. Explain carefully what replaces each of these traditional features, both using quotation and then in your own words.

Why do you think the poem is separated into two stanzas? Work out the rhyme scheme. What do you notice about the last two lines? Is this reflected in a change of tone?

Compare and contrast 'The Soldier' by Rupert Brooke.

*I*nspection

'You! What d'you mean by this?' I rapped.
'You dare come on parade like this?'
'Please, sir, it's –' ' 'Old yer mouth,' the sergeant snapped.
'I take is name, sir?' – 'Please, and then dismiss.'

Some days 'confined to camp' he got   5
For being 'dirty on parade'.
He told me, afterwards, the damned spot
Was blood, his own. 'Well, blood is dirt,' I said.

'Blood's dirt,' he laughed, looking away,
Far off to where his wound had bled   10
And almost merged for ever into clay.
'The world is washing out its stains,' he said.
'It doesn't like our cheeks so red:
Young blood's its great objection.
But when we're duly white-washed, being dead,   15
The race will bear Field Marshal God's inspection.'

Everyone has been told off for something trivial or stupid at one time, but have you ever had to tell anyone else off and realised afterwards that you were in the wrong? What is it like to be on both sides of the divide?

The grimly comic reversal, whereby the private soldier rebuked at the beginning of the poem becomes the instructor to the supposedly superior officer at the end, is heavy with bitter sarcasm. Written in Craiglockhart, it is heavily influenced by Siegfried Sassoon in its regular rhythm and harsh sarcasm.

The *damned spot* is a reference to the spot of blood in *Macbeth* which Lady Macbeth cannot wash off because it is a symbol of irremovable, unchanging guilt. Unlike Lady Macbeth's guilt this is of course not the soldier's own but everyone else's. The *world* refers to society rather than the planet. It seems, quite naturally to the put-upon soldier, victim of a war over which he has no control, that society is deliberately squeezing the life-blood out of its own young people. Comment on the bitter tone of the last line. To be whitewashed was to be cleaned in a superficial, surface-only manner – for, as Lady Macbeth found out, blood will eventually 'have blood'. There will be revenge for this awful punishment of the young – even if it is only divine justice. Of course the problem is that even God will be a *Field Marshal* – does this mean He is an uncaring distant snob, like Haig whose 'plan of attack' Sassoon had so viciously attacked in 'The General'?

Compare Sassoon's 'The General'.

W.B. YEATS

The Lake Isle of Innisfree

I will arise and go now, and go to Innisfree,
And a small cabin build there, of clay and wattles made:
Nine bean-rows will I have there, a hive for the honey-bee,
And live alone in the bee-loud glade.

And I shall have some peace there, for peace comes
    dropping slow,   5
Dropping from the veils of the morning to where the cricket
    sings;
There midnight's all a glimmer, and noon a purple glow,
And evening full of the linnet's wings.

I will arise and go now, for always night and day
I hear lake water lapping with low sounds by the shore;   10
While I stand on the roadway, or on the pavements grey,
I hear it in the deep heart's core.

If you had to imagine your perfect haven, your place to get away from any worries, what would it be like? List the things you would want there.

Although published in 1893, this poem is included in this section as it so beautifully expresses the twentieth-century concern of attempting to preserve a haven amidst the increasingly busy urban lives we lead. The poem was written in London at a time in the 1890s when Yeats was contemplating retiring from public life (he was to become very involved in Irish nationalist campaigns) in an idyllic search for wisdom. Innisfree is a place in Ireland (Inis Fraoigh, or Heather Island, in the middle of Lough Gill, County Silo) but what does the name also suggest? How does the fact that it is a *lake isle* add to this effect?

What tense is most of the poem in and where does this change? What effect does this have? Why do you think the poet wishes for a *small* cabin? Describe his lifestyle there, perhaps listing the phrases which describe it best. What does this suggest he is escaping from? You might like to refer to line 11.

Consider the effectiveness of the phrases: *bee-loud glade; peace … Dropping from the veils of the morning.*

Describe the rhythm of the poem – counting syllables and working out the pattern may help. Is it a regular rhythm? What do you notice about the last lines of each stanza and what effect does this have? (Perhaps compare it with Keats' 'La Belle Dame Sans Merci'.)

What sense dominates the final stanza? How does the alliteration in line 10 contribute to this? The lullaby effect of the *low sounds* seems to be a temptation which *always* haunts him *night and day*. Is this desire for peace and tranquillity perhaps a feeling that, with Keats, he is 'half in love with easeful death' or is this escapist tendency something more life-enhancing?

Compare the poem with other poetic paradises, such as Keats' 'Ode to a Nightingale', Marlowe's 'Passionate Shepherd to His Love' (noting the replies by Raleigh and Donne), or Hopkins' 'Heaven-Haven'. Note not just the contents of the paradise but what they seem to be an escape from and how the poets discuss and present the temptations. Are these temptations healthy or not? What poetic techniques do the poets use to create such havens?

*A*n Irish Airman Foresees His Death

I know that I shall meet my fate
Somewhere among the clouds above;
Those that I fight I do not hate,
Those that I guard I do not love;
My country is Kiltartan Cross,   5
My countrymen Kiltartan's poor,
No likely end could bring them loss
Or leave them happier than before.
Nor law, nor duty bade me fight,
Nor public men, nor cheering crowds,   10
A lonely impulse of delight
Drove to this tumult in the clouds;
I balanced all, brought all to mind,
The years to come seemed waste of breath,
A waste of breath the years behind   15
In balance with this life, this death.

Imagine a room full of newly signed-up soldiers during the
First World War. When they are interviewed, each gives a
different reason for joining the armed forces. Try to think of
as many as possible.

Amongst the conventional (Rupert Brooke) and the anti-
establishment (Sassoon and Owen) English responses to the
horror of the First World War, it is refreshing to have an
outsider's reaction. The Irish, as demonstrated by the Easter
Rising of 1916, in which they took advantage of the war
situation to pursue their own ends of independence from
Britain, were less than enthusiastic about the war. Which
lines in the poem show this? What might the poet mean by
likely end?

What is surprising about the airman's reasons for joining up?
He says he did not join for the normal reasons; discuss the
difference between these *public* catalysts and the *lonely
impulse* he feels.

What makes him so certain of his death?

The key word towards the end of the poem is *balanced*.
Why is this such an appropriate word? Discuss the different
ways Yeats uses it. Do you think the alternate rhyme
scheme works in the poem? Is it appropriate for such a
serious issue as foreseeing death? The poem, published
shortly after the end of the war in 1919, concerned Major
Robert Gregory, the son of Yeats' friend Lady Gregory. He
had died in 1918 over the Italian Front. How does the poem
provide consolation for those he left behind?

EDWARD THOMAS

As the Team's Head-brass

As the team's head-brass flashed out on the turn
The lovers disappeared into the wood.
I sat among the boughs of the fallen elm
That strewed the angle of the fallow, and
Watched the plough narrowing a yellow square   5
Of charlock. Every time the horses turned
Instead of treading me down, the ploughman leaned
Upon the handles to say or ask a word,
About the weather, next about the war.
Scraping the share he faced towards the wood,   10
And screwed along the furrow till the brass flashed
Once more.
       The blizzard felled the elm whose crest
I sat in, by a woodpecker's round hole,
The ploughman said. 'When will they take it away?'   15
'When the war's over.' So the talk began –
One minute and an interval of ten,
A minute more and the same interval.
'Have you been out?' 'No.' 'And don't want to, perhaps?'
'If I could only come back again, I should.   20
I could spare an arm. I shouldn't want to lose
A leg. If I should lose my head, why, so,
I should want nothing more ... . Have many gone
From here?' 'Yes.' 'Many lost?' 'Yes, a good few.
Only two teams work on the farm this year.   25
One of my mates is dead. The second day
In France they killed him. It was back in March,
The very night of the blizzard, too. Now if
He had stayed here we should have moved the tree.'
'And I should not have sat here. Everything   30
Would have been different. For it would have been
Another world.' 'Ay, and a better, though
If we could see all all might seem good.' Then
The lovers came out of the wood again:

The horses started and for the last time   35
I watched the clods crumble and topple over
After the ploughshare and the stumbling team.

Thomas, who was trying to decide whether to join up and
fight in France, had written a great deal about the English
countryside, being a keen walker as well as a professional
writer. Here, he describes stopping to admire the work of a
ploughman with his team of horses. *Fallow* is uncultivated
land whilst *charlock* is a yellow weed. Describe the position
of the poet. Why would the ploughman need to scrape the
share or blade of the plough? Describe the pace of the poem
– why is it suited to its subject matter? Why is the
conversation at intervals of ten minutes? What does the
position of the tree prove about the effect of the war? In
what sense is the ploughing and the presence of the lovers
in the background more permanent than the war? Why
might the poet especially not want to lose a leg? Explain the
phrase *If we could see all all might seem good.* Why do you
think the team is given the adjective *stumbling* in the last
line?

T.S. ELIOT

The Love Song of J. Alfred Prufrock *(extract)*

Let us go then, you and I,
When the evening is spread out against the sky
Like a patient etherised upon a table;
Let us go, through certain half-deserted streets,
The muttering retreats   5
Of restless nights in one-night cheap hotels
And sawdust restaurants with oyster-shells:
Streets that follow like a tedious argument
Of insidious intent
To lead you to an overwhelming question ...   10
Oh, do not ask, 'What is it?'
Let us go and make our visit.

In the room the women come and go
Talking of Michelangelo.

The yellow fog that rubs its back upon the
    window-panes,   15
The yellow smoke that rubs its muzzle on the window-panes
Licked its tongue into the corners of the evening,
Lingered upon the pools that stand in drains,
Let fall upon its back the soot that falls from chimneys,
Slipped by the terrace, made a sudden leap,   20
And seeing that it was a soft October night,
Curled once about the house, and fell asleep.

     ***

And indeed there will be time
To wonder, 'Do I dare?' and, 'Do I dare?'
Time to turn back and descend the stair,   25
With a bald spot in the middle of my hair –
(They will say: 'How his hair is growing thin!')
My morning coat, my collar mounting firmly to the chin,
My necktie rich and modest, but asserted by a simple pin –

(They will say: 'But how his arms and legs are thin!')   30
Do I dare
Disturb the universe?
In a minute there is time
For decisions and revisions which a minute will reverse.

For I have known them all already, known them all –   35
Have known the evenings, mornings, afternoons,
I have measured out my life with coffee spoons;
I know the voices dying with a dying fall
Beneath the music from a farther room.
    So how should I presume?   40

And I have known the eyes already, known them all –
The eyes that fix you in a formulated phrase,
And when I am formulated, sprawling on a pin,
When I am pinned and wriggling on the wall,
Then how should I begin   45
To spit out all the butt-ends of my days and ways?
  And how should I presume?

And I have known the arms already, known them all –
Arms that are braceleted and white and bare
(But in the lamplight, downed with light brown hair!)   50
Is it perfume from a dress
That makes me so digress?
Arms that lie along a table, or wrap about a shawl.
    And should I then presume?
    And how should I begin?   55

This extract from Eliot's famous exploration of English middle-class isolation and respectability explores a shallow existence, cut off from religion and any sense of purpose. The boredom and pointlessness of 'sophisticated' life, chattering about art and ideas (without any real sense of direction) is perfectly captured here. Justify the shocking simile with which the poem opens. How does it contrast with the rhythm? How does the narrator avoid the questions which really matter? List the sordid details which make the modern city world seem shabby and squalid. How is the narrator of the poem, the singer of the 'Love Song', characterised as an 'anti-hero'? Does he belong in the environment described in the poem? How does the poem capture the world of chattering? Justify the repetitions.

Contrast the poem with either one by Robert Frost or Marlowe's 'Passionate Shepherd to His Love'. Look closely at the ways the poets use repetition, figures of speech (especially simile), characterisation, description of environment and their different tones (irony, sincerity, idealism, realism) as well as their overall themes of hollow pointlessness, natural health, or amorous hope.

ROBERT FROST

Mowing

There was never a sound beside the wood but one,
And that was my long scythe whispering to the ground.
What was it it whispered? I knew not well myself;
Perhaps it was something about the heat of the sun,
Something, perhaps, about the lack of sound –   5
And that was why it whispered and did not speak.
It was no dream of the gift of idle hours
Or easy gold at the hand of fay or elf:
Anything more than the truth would have seemed too weak
To the earnest love that laid the swale in rows,   10
Not without feeble-pointed spikes of flowers
(Pale orchises), and scared a bright green snake.
The fact is the sweetest dream that labour knows.
My long scythe whispered and left the hay to make.

What conditions must there be to experience the 'joy of work'?

Swale-hay, or swamp-grass, was a common crop in moist hollows in the prairie, and is perhaps the hay which the poet is cutting here. What are the rhythmical and atmospheric conditions under which the poet is working? What does he hear? Why is the sound compared to *whispering*? Instead of tempting him with the thought of *easy gold* and imaginary winnings, the voice of the corn tells him *the truth*. What might that truth be? Does it seem to distress the poet? What kind of *gold* will the harvester be left with as he leaves *the hay to make*, to dry in the summer sun?

Compare the attitudes expressed in this poem with Lawrence's 'Last Lesson of the Afternoon' and 'Let us be men' – and with Larkin's 'Toads'.

Mending Wall

Something there is that doesn't love a wall,
That sends the frozen-ground-swell under it,
And spills the upper boulders in the sun;
And makes gaps even two can pass abreast.
The work of hunters is another thing: 5
I have come after them and made repair
Where they have left not one stone on a stone,
But they would have the rabbit out of hiding,
To please the yelping dogs. The gaps I mean,
No one has seen them made or heard them made,   10
But at spring mending-time we find them there.
I let my neighbour know beyond the hill;
And on a day we meet to walk the line
And set the wall between us once again.
We keep the wall between us as we go.   15
To each the boulders that have fallen to each.
And some are loaves and some so nearly balls
We have to use a spell to make them balance:
'Stay where you are until our backs are turned!'
We wear our fingers rough with handling them.   20
Oh, just another kind of outdoor game,
One on a side. It comes to little more:
There where it is we do not need the wall:
He is all pine and I am apple orchard.
My apple trees will never get across   25
And eat the cones under his pines, I tell him.
He only says, 'Good fences make good neighbours.'
Spring is the mischief in me, and I wonder
If I could put a notion in his head:
'Why do they make good neighbours? Isn't it   30
Where there are cows? But here there are no cows.
Before I built a wall I'd ask to know
What I was walling in or walling out,
And to whom I was like to give offence.
Something there is that doesn't love a wall,   35
That wants it down.' I could say 'Elves' to him,
But it's not elves exactly, and I'd rather
He said it for himself. I see him there

Bringing a stone grasped firmly by the top
In each hand, like an old-stone savage armed.   40
He moves in darkness as it seems to me,
Not of woods only and the shade of trees.
He will not go behind his father's saying,
And he likes having thought of it so well
He says again, 'Good fences make good neighbours.'   45

'Some traditions make no sense.' Discuss. Have you been
frustrated by people who do things because of tradition
without questioning why that tradition makes sense?

As in the previous poem, a simple seasonal task becomes
the subject of some profound questioning of the human
condition. Describe the task, saying why it needs to be done
– and why spring is the best time for it. What do you think
are the possible legal reasons to *walk the line*? Discuss the
possibility of a shifting boundary. In what way is the
procedure like a game (both in form and in importance)?

Explain the phrase *spring is the mischief in me*. What forces
are working against the wall? Describe the neighbour's
response to the new idea that Frost puts to him. Discuss the
phrase *his father's saying*. What makes the neighbour look
like a Stone Age man *armed*? What does this tell us about
his attitude towards boundaries and 'territory'? Considering
the events of the first half of the twentieth century, what is
the larger significance of such an *old-stone* attitude in the
modern age? Explain the phrase, *he moves in darkness*, in
both literal and metaphorical terms. What does the poet
mean by *he will not go behind his father's saying*? Why
behind? It is not so much the saying that the poet objects to
as the smug blindness with which it is quoted. Where is this
attitude shown most clearly?

As in Lawrence's 'Last Lesson of the Afternoon', the speaker is
trying to convey a message. Compare the pupils and the
teachers from that poem with the neighbour in this poem. Look
at how they are characterised, their success or failure and what
this tells us about mankind. What is the poet's message in
each case? Is it the same as the lesson being taught to the
neighbour/schoolchildren or does it have larger significance?

*A*fter Apple-Picking

My long two-pointed ladder's sticking through a tree
Toward heaven still,
And there's a barrel that I didn't fill
Beside it, and there may be two or three
Apples I didn't pick upon some bough.   5
But I am done with apple-picking now.
Essence of winter sleep is on the night,
The scent of apples: I am drowsing off.
I cannot rub the strangeness from my sight
I got from looking through a pane of glass   10
I skimmed this morning from the drinking trough
And held against the world of hoary grass.
It melted, and I let it fall and break.
But I was well
Upon my way to sleep before it fell,   15
And I could tell
What form my dreaming was about to take.
Magnified apples appear and disappear,
Stem end and blossom end,
And every fleck of russet showing clear.   20
My instep arch not only keeps the ache,
It keeps the pressure of a ladder-round.
I feel the ladder sway as the boughs bend.
And I keep hearing from the cellar bin
The rumbling sound   25
Of load on load of apples coming in.
For I have had too much
Of apple-picking: I am overtired
Of the great harvest I myself desired.
There were ten thousand thousand fruit to touch, 30
Cherish in hand, lift down, and not let fall.
For all
That struck the earth,
No matter if not bruised or spiked with stubble,
Went sure to the cider-apple heap   35
As of no worth.
One can see what will trouble

This sleep of mine, whatever sleep it is.
Were he not gone,
The woodchuck could say whether it's like his   40
Long sleep, as I describe its coming on,
Or just some human sleep.

'I must work harder' was Boxer's simple motto in *Animal Farm*. Do you believe that hard work makes you a better person? Think of some exceptions to this rule.

Apples were traditionally stored in barrels to be brought out at stages through the following year. A bruised apple (and bruises did not always show on the surface) was likely to rot and turn other apples rotten in the same barrel so it was generally crushed to make cider. Picking the apples (before days of mechanisation) was therefore a painstaking process. Why do you think that *the scent of apples* is the *essence of winter sleep*? What else might *winter sleep* refer to? How do we know that the poem is set early in winter? What is the pane of glass? How would it give a *strangeness* to his *sight,* a touch of the surreal? The *dreaming* is a mixture of the surreal and the mundane or ordinary. Explain this, referring to the sensual content of the dream. Are the scenes and sounds his dream will reveal realistic or do they belong to the world of fantasy? What do you notice about the tense in these lines? Compare them with the fourth stanza of Keats' 'Ode to a Nightingale'.

What is the difference between the attitude to work in this poem and in 'Mowing'? There is possibly an element of guilt in the dream – what in the first five lines has prepared us for this guilt? The Protestant work ethic, which has ensured the success of the technological advances of the previous centuries (and perhaps the American Dream itself) is perhaps a factor here. Notice where the ladder is pointing. Which lines later in the poem show the poet rejecting this idea that work is a guaranteed antidote to evil? The devil makes work for idle hands, as the proverb reminds us. What is the alternative message given by the hibernating woodchuck? How do we know the author remains unsure which message to believe?

*T*wo Look at Two

Love and forgetting might have carried them
A little further up the mountainside
With night so near, but not much further up.
They must have halted soon in any case
With thoughts of the path back, how rough it was   5
With rock and washout, and unsafe in darkness;
When they were halted by a tumbled wall
With barbed-wire binding. They stood facing this,
Spending what onward impulse they still had
In one last look the way they must not go,   10
On up the failing path, where, if a stone
Or earthslide moved at night, it moved itself;
No footstep moved it. 'This is all,' they sighed,
'Good-night to woods.' But not so; there was more.
A doe from round a spruce stood looking at them   15
Across the wall, as near the wall as they.
She saw them in their field, they her in hers.
The difficulty of seeing what stood still,
Like some up-ended boulder split in two,
Was in her clouded eyes: they saw no fear there.   20
She seemed to think that two thus they were safe.
Then, as if they were something that, though strange,
She could not trouble her mind with too long,
She sighed and passed unscared along the wall.
'*This*, then, is all. What more is there to ask?'   25
But no, not yet. A snort to bid them wait.
A buck from round the spruce stood looking at them
Across the wall as near the wall as they.
This was an antlered buck of lusty nostril,
Not the same doe come back into her place.   30
He viewed them quizzically with jerks of head,
As if to ask, 'Why don't you make some motion?
Or give some sign of life? Because you can't.
I doubt as if you're as living as you look.'
Thus till he had them almost feeling dared   35
To stretch a proffering hand – and a spell-breaking.
Then he too passed unscared along the wall.

Two had seen two, whichever side you spoke from.
'This *must* be all.' It was all. Still they stood,
A great wave from it going over them,   40
As if the earth in one unlooked-for favour
Had made them certain earth returned their love.

This simple narrative becomes an effective metaphor for
man's relations with nature, and how the natural world can
further our own intimacy with each other.

Explain the personification in the first three lines. Give the
context; who is walking up the mountain, why, and why
must they turn back? The wall where they stop is not merely
a literal boundary, but a boundary of good sense. Comment
on this in relation to the word *must* on line 10. How does
Frost emphasise how wild and deserted the landscape is
beyond this boundary at night? Why do the lovers *sigh* and
how do they use their last *onward impulse*? Consider what
would have happened if they had (a) been more sensible
and immediately turned back to civilisation; (b) marched
onward blindly ignoring the cries of good sense. It is the
pause, the balance between wild instincts and social good
sense, which makes the rest of the poem possible.

Why do the deer not immediately run? How does Frost
emphasise the deer's perspective, their field of vision – why
do they become personalities for us rather than merely
objects to look at? Look carefully at the structure of lines
16, 17 and 20. What do you notice and how does this relate
to the title of the poem?

Comment on line 29. Describe the pattern of events in the
poem in relation to the repeated phrases regarding *all* and
more. Why does Frost include a doe and a buck? In line 40,
the *it* refers back to the experience, the mystical communion
between man and beast on equal terms. What do you think
the *wave* is and why is it an effective metaphor?

Remembering what gave them the impetus to go up the
mountain (see the first lines), comment on the last line.

Compare Lawrence's 'Snake'.

*T*ree *at My Window*

Tree at my window, window tree,
My sash is lowered when night comes on;
But let there never be curtain drawn
Between you and me.

Vague dream-head lifted out of the ground,   5
And thing next most diffuse to cloud,
Not all your light tongues talking aloud
Could be profound.

But, tree, I have seen you taken and tossed,
And if you have seen me when I slept,   10
You have seen me when I was taken and swept
And all but lost.

That day she put our heads together
Fate had her imagination about her,
Your head so much concerned with outer,   15
Mine with inner, weather.

People often find comfort in familiar objects and can project many of their feelings onto these objects. Write a brief creative piece (in prose or poetry) in which a person, possibly a child, addresses such a familiar object on the subject of griefs and hopes and fears.

Like the last poem, this lyric looks at the imaginative bond man can make with nature if he does not close off the boundaries nor yet cross them. The poem is addressed to the *window tree*, as if it had become his friend over the years. The *sash* is the sliding window which must be closed at night (for the cold), but the poet refuses to close the curtains. Why?

The second stanza is very subjective. Why would the poet see the tree as *lifted out of the ground*? Think of his viewpoint and his state of mind. In what ways is the tree a *vague dream-head* and why would the poet see it like this? Why is it almost as *diffuse* as *cloud* and why does this echo his own state of mind? What would the trees' *tongues* be and how would they be *talking*? Sometimes perhaps the tongues say *profound* things and other times they merely talk in a *light* manner. Comment on this word *light*.

In the fourth stanza, how does *outer … weather* affect the tree and how does *inner weather* affect the poet? Do you find this poem an effective description of the communion of man and nature?

An Old Man's Winter Night

All out-of-doors looked darkly at him
Through the thin frost, almost in separate stars
That gathers on the pane in empty rooms.
What kept his eyes from giving back the gaze
Was the lamp tilted near them in his hand.   5
What kept him from remembering what it was
That brought him to that creaking room was age.
He stood with barrels round him – at a loss.
And having scared the cellar under him
In clomping here, he scared it once again   10
In clomping off; – and scared the outer night,
Which has its sounds, familiar, like the roar
Of trees and crack of branches, common things,
But nothing so like beating on a box.
A light he was to no one but himself   15
Where now he sat, concerned with he knew what,
A quiet light, and then not even that.
He consigned to the moon, such as she was,
So late-arising, to the broken moon
As better than the sun in any case   20
For such a charge, his snow upon the roof,
His icicles along the wall to keep;
And slept. The log that shifted with a jolt
Once in the stove, disturbed him and he shifted,
And eased his heavy breathing, but still slept.   25
One aged man – one man – can't keep a house,
A farm, a countryside, or if he can,
It's thus he does it of a winter night.

This rather sad, haunting poem uses the same Frost techniques of looking at the familiar common things in an unfamiliar light – and of finding an appropriate metaphor for that light. In previous poems it was a whispering voice, a spring-like sense of mischief and a pane of ice; here, aptly enough, it is a lamp, which is replaced by moonlight.

Explain the appearance of the frost on the windows. The phrase *separate stars* has a secondary meaning. Taken in isolation what does it suggest about the life of the old man? Why does the lamp prevent the man seeing what is outside the window? What factors in the early lines give us the impression that the man lives alone? How is this impression confirmed and emphasised at the close of the poem?

From line 15 onwards, the *light* has come to mean something quite different from the literal lamp of the fifth line. What do you think this is? Why is the moon which replaces this light described as *broken*? What does this imply? Why do you think it is a more appropriate replacement for the old man's attention than the sun? What is its task? Why do you think an old man is expected to keep *a countryside*? Does he manage?

Compare Plath's description of an old man in 'Among the Narcissi'.

The Silken Tent

She is as in a field a silken tent
At midday when a sunny summer breeze
Has dried the dew and all its ropes relent,
So that in guys it gently sways at ease,
And its supporting central cedar pole,   5
That is its pinnacle to heavenward
And signifies the sureness of the soul,
Seems to owe naught to any single cord,
But strictly held by none, is loosely bound
By countless silken ties of love and thought   10
To everything on earth the compass round,
And only by one's going slightly taut
In the capriciousness of summer air
Is of the slightest bondage made aware.

Do you find this comparison an illuminating one? Would you be flattered by a comparison to a tent? Attempt your own extended metaphysical conceit in which you compare a person to an inanimate object and list the various ways in which these two very different things are alike. Compare Shakespeare's sonnet 'Shall I compare thee?' Why is that not a metaphysical conceit? Look at Herbert's 'The Collar' or Donne's poetry for other genuine examples of the device.

This poem is a conceit in which a far-fetched, but effective, comparison is made between a woman and a *silken tent*. As in all conceits, the effectiveness depends on the number of details the author can persuade us are similar in the two, so he takes us from the feel of this tent, to its ropes, its supporting pole and the surrounding weather and compares these to various facets or aspects of the woman. What are these four features of the tent compared to in the life of the woman?

What do you notice about the grammatical structure of the whole poem? Why do you think the poet uses the adjective *silken*?

What effect would drying the dew have upon the tent's canvas? Why would this make the ropes *relent* or slacken off? Explain why the tent is *loosely bound*. Why do you think Frost makes the central pole made of wood? Why is this typical of his philosophy regarding our souls and nature? Why does *cedar* make an excellent metaphor for *sureness*? When is the soul of the woman allowed freedom and when is it reminded of its *silken ties of love and thought*? Explain the phrase *capriciousness of summer air*.

 'Profound truths found in ordinary activities.' Discuss Frost's poetry in the light of this remark.

 Discuss the ways Frost presents either man's relations with nature, or the values of work.

D.H. LAWRENCE

*P*iano

Softly, in the dusk, a woman is singing to me;
Taking me back down the vista of years, till I see
A child sitting under the piano, in the boom of the tingling
    strings
And pressing the small, poised feet of a mother who smiles
    as she sings.

In spite of myself, the insidious mastery of song   5
Betrays me back, till the heart of me weeps to belong
To the old Sunday evenings at home, with winter outside
And hymns in the cosy parlour, the tinkling piano our
    guide.

So now it is vain for the singer to burst into clamour
With the great black piano appassionato. The glamour   10
Of childish days is upon me, my manhood is cast
Down in the flood of remembrance, I weep like a child for
    the past.

Try to think of five things which remind you strongly of
when you were very young, one for each sense. What
emotions does each of these impressions bring back?

This richly evocative work uses a structure common in
poems which hark back to times of youth (compare
Heaney's 'Digging'). It begins in the present tense to
emphasise the immediacy of the impression the woman's
singing is making, before changing focus to the past and
then back to the present again. Unlike most of Lawrence's
later poetry it does not use free verse, but rhyming couplets.
However, the number of syllables varies enormously from
line to line, echoing the rhythm of the music being
described. Written in 1911, it focuses on the writer's deep
emotions for his mother and how, as a young man, he is yet
to break free of her intense love and influence. This

psychological dilemma was to form the rich background to Lawrence's first novels, *The White Peacock* and (more successfully) *Sons and Lovers*.

Where does the poet break from present to past and back to present again? What is odd about the tenses he uses? Who is the child he sees under the piano, listening to his mother playing music? How do you know? Why are the mother's feet *poised*? What impression does this perhaps suggest about her character? What does the position of the child imply? How is the whole scene made 'cosy' in the second stanza? Which is stronger, the *glamour* of the singer or the old scene? Give reasons for your answer. Why is *flood of remembrance* an appropriate expression?

Find out what the following mean and why they are appropriate in their context: *vista*, *insidious*, *appassionato*.

Examine the clever ways Lawrence uses enjambement in the poem, forcing you onwards, giving an unexpected expression, or using a very appropriate expression. As the reader's eye moves from *cast* to *down* the depression that the poet feels is perfectly recreated. Find three examples of onomatopoeia in the poem and comment on their use. Do you think the use of rhyming couplets is appropriate? Why are certain lines longer than others?

Compare the poem either with Wordsworth's 'The Prelude' or Heaney's 'Digging', showing how the poets create the scenes of their childhoods, their emotions then and their present emotions. Wordsworth's phrase 'The child is father of the man' may be worth considering as a starting point.

*L*ast Lesson of the Afternoon

When will the bell ring, and end this weariness?
How long have they tugged the leash, and strained apart
My pack of unruly hounds! I cannot start
Them again on a quarry of knowledge they hate to hunt,
I can haul them and urge them no more.   5

No longer now can I endure the brunt
Of the books that lie out on the desks; a full threescore
Of several insults of blotted pages, and scrawl
Of slovenly work that they have offered me.
I am sick, and what on earth is the good of it all?   10
What good to them or me, I cannot see!

        So, shall I take
My last dear fuel of life to heap on my soul
And kindle my will to a flame that shall consume
Their dross of indifference; and take the toll   15
Of their insults in punishment – I will not! –

I will not waste my soul and my strength for this.
What do I care for all that they do amiss!
What is the point of this teaching of mine, and of this
Learning of theirs? It all goes down the same abyss.   20

What does it matter to me, if they can write
A description of a dog, or if they can't?
What is the point? To us both, it is all my aunt!
And yet I'm supposed to care, with all my might.

I do not, and will not; they won't and they don't;
    and that's all!   25
I shall keep my strength for myself; they can keep theirs
    as well.
Why should we beat our heads against the wall
Of each other? I shall sit and wait for the bell.

Although in many ways this poem needs little preparation as it is a situation all too familiar to all of us, it is worth reading the first line in isolation before going on. Whom do you suspect is the speaker? Read the next two lines and try to work out who the speaker is now.

It seems as though Lawrence has been playing with us a little in the opening of the poem as we expect the *weariness* to belong to the pupils not the teacher. The 'lesson' here seems to be that we should enlarge our experience to envisage what it must be like to be others – even if that means empathising with teachers! The poem is not merely about the futility (or sense of hopelessness) that teachers feel sometimes but about the futility of all work. The modern disease of alienation, whereby we feel we are forced into a sort of mechanical work and cannot see the point because we are such a small part of a large workforce, is even felt by teachers. Lawrence's whole artistic drive and the essence of the message of his work was to be true to yourself, to be authentic, not to be forced by society. This is at the heart of the poem. Do you think that the attitude is selfish?

In other poems Lawrence spoke of his great joy at teaching, when he was at one with the class. Do you think he should try only when this was happening and at other times keep his *strength* for himself? Or should he persevere and do his best at all times?

Compare this poem with 'Toads' by Larkin. Which seems to be the truest picture of work, or do they, in their different ways, each contain equally authentic pictures of work in the modern world?

Intimates

Don't you care for my love? she said bitterly.

I handed her the mirror, and said:
Please address these questions to the proper person!
Please make all requests to headquarters!
In all matters of emotional importance   5
please approach the supreme authority direct!
So I handed her the mirror.

And she would have broken it over my head,
but she caught sight of her own reflection
and that held her spell-bound for two seconds   10
while I fled.

If you have arguments with people who are close to you,
discuss your own typical responses. Are you sarcastic or
submissive, vicious or prepared to compromise, vindictive
or wounded? Do you show your feelings or try to hide them?
Do you keep cool and win the argument or become more
aggressive?

In this brief witty piece, Lawrence confronts an issue which
occupied him throughout his writing career and which
continues to cause controversy: the changing roles of men
and women in twentieth-century society. In his famous essay
'Hen-sure Women and Cocksure Men', he had argued that
women's growing power and independence had left many
people of both sexes unsure as to their roles. He has since
been accused of reactionary sexism in his writings – and there
are times when he seems to uphold a strong division between
the masculine and the feminine. The poem itself, as in so
much of his work, is based in the immediacy of a personal,
rather than a general situation. His own relations with his
partner, Frieda Weekley, were fairly stormy at this time.

Who wins the argument and how? What is the significance of
the title? How much speech does the woman get in the poem
and what does this tell us? What is the tone of the poem?

Snake

A snake came to my water-trough
On a hot, hot day, and I in pyjamas for the heat,
To drink there.

In the deep, strange-scented shade of the great dark
    carob-tree
I came down the steps with my pitcher   5
And must wait, must stand and wait, for there he was at
    the trough before me.

He reached down from a fissure in the earth-wall in the
    gloom
And trailed his yellow-brown slackness soft-bellied down,
    over the edge of the stone trough
And rested his throat upon the stone bottom,
And where the water had dripped from the tap, in a
    small clearness,   10
He sipped with his straight mouth,
Softly drank through his straight gums, into his slack
    long body,
Silently.

Someone was before me at my water-trough,
And I, like a second-comer, waiting.   15

He lifted his head from his drinking, as cattle do,
And looked at me vaguely, as drinking cattle do,
And flickered his two-forked tongue from his lips, and
    mused a moment,
And stooped and drank a little more,
Being earth-brown, earth-golden from the burning
    bowels of the earth   20
On the day of Sicilian July, with Etna smoking.

The voice of my education said to me
He must be killed,
For in Sicily the black, black snakes are innocent,
    the gold are venomous.

And voices in me said, If you were a man   25
You would take a stick and break him now, and finish him off.

But must I confess how I liked him,
How glad I was he had come like a guest in quiet, to drink
        at my water-trough
And depart peaceful, pacified, and thankless,
Into the burning bowels of this earth?   30

Was it cowardice, that I dared not kill him?
Was it perversity, that I longed to talk to him?
Was it humility, to feel so honoured?
I felt so honoured.

And yet those voices: 35
If you were not afraid, you would kill him!

And truly I was afraid, I was most afraid,
But even so, honoured still more
That he should seek my hospitality
From out the dark door of the secret earth.   40

He drank enough
And lifted his head, dreamily, as one who has drunken,
And flickered his tongue like a forked night on the air,
        so black,
Seeming to lick his lips,
And looked around like a god, unseeing, into the air,   45
And slowly turned his head
And slowly, very slowly, as if thrice adream,
Proceeded to draw his slow length curving round
And climb again the broken bank of my wall-face.

And as he put his head into that dreadful hole,   50
And as he slowly drew up, snake-easing his shoulders,
        and entered farther,
A sort of horror, a sort of protest against his withdrawing
        into that horrid black hole,
Deliberately going into the blackness, and slowly drawing
        himself after,
Overcame me now his back was turned.

I looked round, I put down my pitcher,   55
I picked up a clumsy log
And threw it at the water-trough with a clatter.
I think it did not hit him,
But suddenly that part of him that was left behind
    convulsed in undignified haste,
Writhed like lightning, and was gone   60
Into the black hole, the earth-lipped fissure in the wall-
    front,
At which, in the intense still noon, I stared with
    fascination.

And immediately I regretted it.
I thought how paltry, how vulgar, what a mean act!
I despised myself and the voices of my accursed human
    education.   65

And I thought of the albatross,
And I wished he would come back, my snake.

For he seemed to me again like a king,
Like a king in exile, uncrowned in the underworld,
Now due to be crowned again.   70

And so, I missed my chance with one of the lords
Of life.
And I have something to expiate:
A pettiness.

Have you ever killed or harmed an animal and regretted it?
Under what circumstances might you need to kill an animal?
What kind of values do you associate with 'education'? Write
a list of expressions to describe a snake.

Set in Sicily, this narrative poem seems to tell a very simple
tale. The complexity lies in the ambivalent attitude of the
narrator towards the snake, with the *voices* of his *human
education* demanding that the man take charge and dominate
this beast, whilst other instincts provoke different feelings – of
admiration at the nobility of the creature, of humility in the
face of such audacious power and even, at the end, of a kind
of worship. The mention of the albatross near the end of the

poem refers to Coleridge's great poem about another act of senseless violence perpetrated by a man against nature, 'The Rime of the Ancient Mariner'. Just as the mariner killed an albatross and carried the bird as a sign of his guilt, so the narrator of 'Snake' carries the guilt of his act of *pettiness* in trying to show his superiority over the animal world, a superiority which has been undermined throughout the poem. By calling the snake a *king* of the *underworld*, Lawrence perhaps suggests that the golden creature with its black tongue symbolises not merely the natural world but the underworld within the mind of man – his primitive dark side. Ultimately the narrator is trapped by the voice of education but regrets bitterly that this should be so.

The single word *my* in the first line can be said to encapsulate the theme of the poem. In what sense is the narrator wrong to use it? In what sense is he right? What is the effect of the repetition in the second stanza (*must wait, must stand and wait*) both on the structure of the poem and on the description of the mood of the narrator? Why do you think the snake is referred to as *he* not *it*? What is the effect of the sibilant alliteration and repetition in the third stanza? Is the comparison to cattle in stanza 5 appropriate? Explain the phrase *voice of my education*. Are the values represented what you might expect? Why do you think the voices are given italics in line 36? What is the effect of the slowness of the snake's movements throughout? (Notice the way the repetition and structure slow the pace of the poem.)

 Write an extended study of the poem with reference to Ted Hughes' 'The Thought-Fox', Wilfred Owen's 'Strange Meeting' or Wordsworth's 'Nutting'.

The Mosquito

When did you start your tricks,
Monsieur?

What do you stand on such high legs for?
Why this length of shredded shank,
You exaltation?   5

Is it so that you shall lift your centre of gravity upwards
And weigh no more than air as you alight upon me,
Stand upon me weightless, you phantom?

I hear a woman call you the Winged Victory
In sluggish Venice.   10
You turn your head towards your tail, and smile.

How can you put so much devilry
Into that translucent phantom shred
Of a frail corpus?

Queer, with your thin wings and your streaming legs   15
How you sail like a heron, or a dull clot of air,
A nothingness.

Yet what an aura surrounds you;
Your evil little aura, prowling, and casting a numbness on
    my mind.

That is your trick, your bit of filthy magic: 20
Invisibility, and the anaesthetic power
To deaden my attention in your direction.

But I know your game now, streaky sorcerer.

Queer, how you stalk and prowl the air
In circles and evasions, enveloping me,   25
Ghoul on wings
Winged Victory.

Settle, and stand on long thin shanks
Eyeing me sideways, and cunningly conscious that I
    am aware,
You speck.   30

I hate the way you lurch off sideways into air
Having read my thoughts against you.

Come then, let us play at unawares,
And see who wins in this sly game of bluff,
Man or mosquito.   35

You don't know that I exist, and I don't know that you
    exist.
Now then!

It is your trump
It is your hateful little trump,
You pointed fiend,   40
Which makes my sudden blood to hatred of you:
It is your small, high, hateful bugle in my ear.

Why do you do it?
Surely it is bad policy.

They say you can't help it.   45

If that is so, then I believe a little in Providence protecting
    the innocent.
But it sounds so amazingly like a slogan,
A yell of triumph as you snatch my scalp.

Blood, red blood
Super-magical   50
Forbidden liquor.

I behold you stand
For a second enspasmed in oblivion,
Obscenely ecstasied
Sucking live blood,   55
My blood

Such silence, such suspended transport,
Such gorging,
Such obscenity of trespass.

You stagger   60
As well as you may.
Only your accursed hairy frailty,
Your own imponderable weightlessness

Saves you, wafts you away on the very draught my anger
    makes in its snatching.

Away with a paean of derision,   65
You winged blood-drop.

Can I not overtake you?
Are you one too many for me,
Winged Victory?
Am I not mosquito enough to out-mosquito you?   70

Queer, what a big stain my sucked blood makes
Beside the infinitesimal faint smear of you!
Queer, what a dim dark smudge you have disappeared into!

Like 'Snake', this poem is about man's encounter with nature, and once again Lawrence begins by emphasising the conflict before going on to discover the affinity: can he *out-mosquito* the cunning insect? Or will it show more intelligence than him? The blood-sucking allows Lawrence to suggest that man and insect are not so dissimilar after all, as one partakes (quite literally) of the other.

However, unlike 'Snake', 'The Mosquito' is in the present tense as if the poet is writing as the action occurs. Thus the reflective quality of 'Snake' is replaced by a more whimsical tone. Like the mosquito itself, the poem is lighter. This is not to say that the poem does not deal with some serious issues. Written in Italy, the poem never directly mentions, but perhaps suggests, the association of the insect with deadly malaria in that region. The reference to *sluggish Venice* describes the slow pace of life associated with that city's famous waterways – waterways which formed ideal breeding grounds for the mosquito. The Winged Victory was a statue of the Greek goddess of victory; here the association between the victorious insect and its perfect getaway vehicle is very appropriate, although the grandeur of the statue is very much at odds with the *infinitesimal* nature of the tiny foe, helping the bathetic, ironic nature of the tribute. Similarly the *trump* of victory is *hateful* and *little*, *small* and *hateful*, a *slogan* or war-cry like that of primitive peoples.

It is the paradoxical union of power and *imponderable weightlessness* which are at the heart of the poem, but the mock-heroic touch ensures a lightness of tone.

How does Lawrence convey the tiny size of the mosquito? Which are the words used to describe the mosquito at the beginning of the poem which create the associations with death? Bearing in mind that an *aura* is a mystical atmosphere surrounding, and created by, a person or creature, describe the *filthy magic* performed by the *streaky sorcerer*. How accurate is Lawrence's description of the insect's movements and flight?

The Mosquito Knows

The mosquito knows full well, small as he is
he's a beast of prey.
But after all
he only takes a bellyfull,
he doesn't put my blood in the bank.   5

Written some years later than 'The Mosquito', this poem,
like the others that follow, was first included in a volume
called *Pansies*. The poems were often brief meditations on
various aspects of commonplace life from which Lawrence
gleans a larger significance. The title of the volume was both
a punning reference to the *Pensées* (thoughts) of Blaise
Pascal, the seventeenth-century scientist and moralist, and a
recognition that the poems within Lawrence's volume were,
if small in scale, then 'organic' in their growth. 'Each little
piece is a thought ... a complete thought' wrote Lawrence in
his introduction. 'The Mosquito Knows' is fairly typical and,
being so direct, needs little explanation. The obvious larger
moral is that humans take more than they need.

'Serious issues disguised by a frivolous tone.' To what extent
would you agree with this assessment of the three poems in
this selection which deal with insects (Donne's 'The Flea'
and Lawrence's 'Mosquito' poems)?

*T*hink – !

Imagine what it must have been to have existence
in the wild days when life was sliding whirlwinds,
   blue-hot weights,
in the days called chaos, which left us rocks, and gems!
Think that the sapphire is only alumina, like kitchen pans
crushed utterly, and breathed through and through   5
with fiery weight and wild life, and coming out
clear and flowery blue!

Much of the power of this imaginative re-creation of creation
itself comes from the complex patterns of sounds as
Lawrence makes full use of alliteration, assonance and
repetition so that the final line, as simple and as beautiful as
the gem itself, has been fully prepared for, feeling the
weight, as it were, of all the sounds and concepts of the
energetic lines above it.

See if you can map out this pattern of sounds and ideas
fully, tracing the way the poet prepares us for the 'c' and the
'f' sounds, the concepts of flowers (perhaps pansies!), of
blueness and transparency, and the ingredients necessary
for this metamorphosis. Then note the unusual conjunctions
of these ideas especially in the second and sixth lines, the
different paces of the poem and the energy imparted by the
use of the imperative.

*L*et us be Men –

For God's sake, let us be men
not monkeys minding machines
or sitting with our tails curled
while the machine amuses us, the radio or film or
    gramophone.
Monkeys with a bland grin on our faces. –   5

The imperative tone is even stronger in this savage attack
on modern industrial mechanised society. Is the dramatic
beginning, an echo of Donne's 'The Canonization', to be
taken literally or as a mere figure of speech? Why do you
think there is so much alliteration in the second line? As well
as insulting modern man, the reference to monkeys
denounces our supposed evolution. If we cannot be true to
our species and our selves but must ape others and get
caught up in the machinery of our machine-driven society,
then we are not organic but mechanical. Who are the
monkeys minding machines (both in Lawrence's day and
our own)? Discuss the ideas of the *tails* and the *bland grin*.
What would you add to Lawrence's list of entertaining
machines in the light of more recent developments? Is his
message more or less relevant today? The last line is left
alone. Does the sense of incompletion add to or detract
from the poem?

Select two or three poems from the anthology and write an
essay in which you decide whether you prefer strongly
didactic poems (those preaching a strong and clear
message), detached poems (those which seem to merely
record what they see) or ambivalent poems (where the
author seems to be in two minds about what is right and
what is wrong).

W.H. AUDEN

Epitaph on a Tyrant

Perfection, of a kind, was what he was after,
And the poetry he invented was easy to understand;
He knew human folly like the back of his hand,
And was greatly interested in armies and fleets;
When he laughed, respectable senators burst
    with laughter,   5
And when he cried the little children died in the streets.

As a socialist, Auden was deeply concerned about the progress of Fascism during the middle years of the century. Unlike much of the verse contained in this anthology, Auden's is often quite directly concerned with social issues and politics. Here he attacks in a subtle manner the attitude of the all-powerful dictators who did (and still do) rule ruthlessly. Straightforward and accessible, the power of the poetry lies in its seemingly objective tone. What kind of *perfection* were Fascists *after* and what might the poet mean by *poetry* in line 2? How would the tyrant's knowledge of *folly* help him? Why is the last line so shocking?

'As patterns in society seemed to be shattering, so the old patterns in poetry (of rhyme and rhythm) seemed to be breaking up.' Discuss with detailed reference to three poems from this section, referring to structure, free verse, and any other relevant devices.

Is there a marked difference in the subject matter of the poems in this section and those of previous ages?

The Modern Age: After the Second World War

(1939–1999)

The forces which had preceded and induced the Second World War – forces of hatred, Fascism, race-related violence – have permeated our century so that it has become more apparent than ever that, as a recent novelist expressed it, 'In the past we had the barbarians. Now we have only ourselves to blame.' (*Captain Corelli's Mandolin*.) It was not only novelists who were highlighting Freud's insights into the darker side in all of us – a side depressingly apparent in the massive scale and ease with which nations have accepted and used dictatorships in order to torment one another and wield a horrific amount of power. Poets too such as Auden and his followers through the 1930s and 1940s recorded these social evils and looked into the dark psyches which make them possible.

Whilst Ted Hughes has characterised humans as animals, obeying frightening instincts even when we think ourselves most civilised, Seamus Heaney (having delved into his own psychological make-up) has explored 'the troubles' in Northern Ireland as an example of our capacity for violent division. Our tendency to blame others (barbarians) for our own problems lies at the heart of our persecution of both outsiders and the powerless – whether they be women caught in adultery (as recorded in poems by Walcott and Heaney) or those involved in mixed marriages. It is the combined recovery of voice by these groups and their efforts to forgive which perhaps give greatest hope for our future – once again justifying Shelley's claim that poets are 'the unacknowledged legislators of the world'. Paradoxically the Second World War, the greatest single confirmation of man's barbarity, gave women a greater sense of independence (they were given more jobs to do) which led, eventually, to the Feminist movement of the 1960s. Sylvia Plath became an icon of that movement after her tragic suicide. She stood on the brink of the greatest social change of our century as women broke away from their old roles as carers and housekeepers to roles in their own right as workers and earners. Her battle for independence, much of it recorded in her poetry, was constantly weighed against her own sense of duty as mother and home-maker, and this conflict within her is one of the most fascinating aspects of her work.

One of the main reasons women could reclaim some power over their own lives was the wide availability of the contraceptive pill from the early 1960s onwards. This in turn led to a sexual revolution and contributed to the Free Love and Hippy movements of the 1960s and early 1970s. There was a kind of idealism not seen since the early reaction to the French Revolution – a feeling that the world could really be made a better place by individuals living idealised lifestyles. The break away from accepted Christian and social norms, despite the backlash of a more self-centred cynicism in later decades, radically altered the way we think. Individual liberty is now far more highly prized as a result.

However the communal ways of life with which this movement experimented were soon to be replaced by an emphasis on ruthless efficiency in business not seen since Victorian times, as during the Thatcher years of the 1980s and early 1990s Britain, like America, trusted in the powers of big (and small) business to drag us out of recession. Just as Dickens, and to a lesser extent Hopkins, had bemoaned the selfishness of such a culture in the nineteenth century, so figures such as R.S. Thomas have prophesied doom from the profit culture in our own day. Meanwhile, with the further collapse of England's imperial power, new voices from the fringes began to dominate literature written in English. Thus the colonial poetry of Walcott, the Welsh verse of R.S. Thomas and the poetry of Heaney, a Catholic living in Northern Ireland, have (with the work of Ted Hughes) been amongst the most noteworthy successes in modern English.

Paradoxically, that language was not always the natural medium but often an adopted one; however each has brought an extraordinary power as well as the perspective of the outsider questioning conservative forces. The best work by these poets often combines a sense of exclusion with one of complicity with what it is to be English. They draw on the heritage of English literature whilst at the same time voicing the concerns of those on the margins, often in the idiom of the people.

Biographical Notes

Philip Larkin (1922–85)

Born in Coventry, Larkin was educated at St John's College, Oxford before becoming a librarian, eventually settling in Hull. From the late 1940s, Larkin developed a distinctive style, first modelled on Yeats, then on Hardy, before finding his own suburban voice based on new colloquial vocabulary and rhythms of speech. At once ironic and involved, he captures the mood of a whole generation of post-war, post-imperial, post-religious Britain, with its outworn values and its slightly impoverished respectability.

Ted Hughes (1930–98)

The son of a Yorkshire carpenter turned shopkeeper, Hughes won an Open Exhibition to Pembroke College, Cambridge in 1948. He did two years' National Service in the RAF before university and worked as a gardener, night-watchman and zoo-keeper afterwards before becoming a teacher. He married Sylvia Plath in 1956 and received immediate acclaim for his first collection of poetry in 1957. Hughes tended to write about the natural world rather than society, although he describes the elemental and primordial elements in mankind obliquely by referring to animals. In 1984 he was made Poet Laureate. He died in 1998 of

cancer, having published *Birthday Letters*, his poetic
account of the relationship with Plath, the previous year.

Sylvia Plath (1932–63)

Born in Boston, Massachusetts and brought up in Winthrop,
Plath lost her father, a German professor, to diabetes when
she was eight. Plath was educated at Smith College,
Massachusetts and Newnham College, Cambridge, where
she met Ted Hughes. The couple married in 1956 and
initially lived in America before returning to England and
setting up home in a remote corner of Devon. She had two
children and felt increasingly frustrated despite publishing
her first volume of poetry in 1960. Her discovery that
Hughes was having an affair contributed to her depression, a
depression which fed directly into both her poetry and her
only novel, *The Bell Jar*. She committed suicide in February
1963, during one of the coldest winters on record. Since
then she has become something of an icon for many women
who find in her suicide and some of her more disturbing
writings an image of the struggle of all women suffering
under patriarchal domination. Hughes oversaw the
publication of *Ariel*, her most successful collection of poetry,
in 1965.

Seamus Heaney (1939–)

Born and brought up a Catholic in rural County Derry,
Northern Ireland, Heaney's poetry has always explored both
the rustic and the hostile nature of his roots. The conflict in
Northern Ireland is almost always a backdrop to his work,
stated or implicit. The son of a farmer, he won a scholarship
to St Columb's College as a boarder and then to Queen's
University, Belfast, where he returned in 1966 as a lecturer
after some years as a schoolteacher. He has since lectured
on English in California, Liverpool and Harvard, and since
1989 has been Professor of Poetry at Oxford.

R. S. Thomas (1913–)

Born in Cardiff and brought up and educated in Holyhead, Thomas' parents were not Welsh-speaking and he acquired the language later, so that he never felt comfortable enough to compose poetry in any tongue other than English. This has meant an alienation from the audience closest to his heart as well as an international fame. An Anglican priest in the mainly Non-Conformist parish of Manafon in remote mid-Wales, Thomas has always faithfully recorded the struggles in a fairly bleak landscape (both the local community's and his own), and these have taken on a more universal significance. With a move to Aberdaron in north west Wales in 1967 came a slight change of perspective as his poetry became more metaphysical and philosophical, exploring that area 'somewhere between faith and doubt' which he has made his own. After his retirement from the church in 1978, Thomas has become increasingly active in Welsh nationalist politics. His *Complete Poems* were published in 1993 to coincide with his eightieth birthday.

Derek Walcott (1930–)

Born in St Lucia in the West Indies, Walcott was educated on St Georges and then Jamaica. Since his departure for the United States in 1950 he has shuttled between Boston, New York and the West Indies, and his work shows the influences of these two cultures strongly. However, the form he has always worked with, and the role-models he chose, were largely classical and British, from Shakespeare and Wordsworth to Dylan Thomas and Auden. The iambic pentameter and the sonnet, however, are given a hugely animating, quickening spur by Walcott's original handling – not least in his use of dialect. Walcott, according to Robert Graves, 'handles English with a closer understanding of its inner magic than most (if not any) of his English-born contemporaries'. He makes a virtue of being an outsider not only with regard to white Anglo-Americans but also his own people, as he is of mixed Afro-Caribbean and white race. As he says, 'And I whose ancestors were slave and Roman

soldiers have seen both sides of the imperial foam ...' This
helps give his poetry (and his drama) its sense of largeness,
earning him the Nobel Prize for Literature in 1992.

Grace Nichols (1950–)

Born in Guyana, Nichols moved to England in 1977 and
lives with her partner, the poet John Agard, and two
daughters. She was awarded the Commonwealth Poetry
Prize in 1983 for her first volume, *I is a Long-Memoried
Woman,* which explored the experience of women slaves
through the eighteenth and nineteenth centuries. She has
since come to add humour and a more up-to-date feminism
to her exploration of alienation within British society, often
assuming the voice of the outsider.

PHILIP LARKIN

*T*oads

Why should I let the toad *work*
　　Squat on my life?
Can't I use my wit as a pitchfork
　　And drive the brute off?

Six days of the week it soils　　　　　　　　　5
　　With its sickening poison –
Just for paying a few bills!
　　That's out of proportion.

Lots of folk live on their wits:
　　Lecturers, lispers,　　　　　　　　　　　10
Losels, loblolly-men, louts –
　　They don't end as paupers:

Lots of folk live up lanes
　　With fires in a bucket,
Eat windfalls and tinned sardines –　　　　　15
　　They seem to like it.

Their nippers have got bare feet,
　　Their unspeakable wives
Are skinny as whippets – and yet
　　No one actually *starves*.　　　　　　　　20

Ah, were I courageous enough
　　To shout *Stuff your pension!*
But I know, all too well, that's the stuff
　　That dreams are made on:

For something sufficiently toad-like　　　　　25
　　Squats in me, too;
Its hunkers are heavy as hard luck,
　　And cold as snow,

And will never allow me to blarney
    My way to getting   30
The fame and the girl and the money
    All at one sitting.

I don't say, one bodies the other
    One's spiritual truth;
But I do say it's hard to lose either,   35
    When you have both.

List the reasons why we work. Try to get beyond the obvious, conventional reasons. What qualities do you associate with toads?

The poem begins with two questions to which the remaining eight stanzas are an attempted answer. What do you notice about the structure of this answer? What happens halfway through it?

The toad is traditionally not only ugly but poisonous. Why do these qualities make it an appropriate metaphor for work? Which sounds does Larkin use to emphasise its relations to the snake in lines 5–6? Why does he want to achieve this? Why is *wit* compared to a *pitchfork*? Look carefully at the way work is characterised in the first two stanzas, its actions and Larkin's descriptions of it.

In stanzas 3, 4 and 5, Larkin lists some of the *lots of folk* who *live on their wits*. What does he mean by this? *Lecturers* obviously live on their wits. Does this mean they do not work? By *lispers* Larkin perhaps means those who speak a certain way because it is the fashion. A *losel* is a scoundrel or a worthless person and a *loblolly-man* is an assistant to a ship's doctor named after the loblolly or gruel he served. How can each of these be said to *live on their wits* rather than working? List the words beginning with 'l' in stanzas 4 and 5. What do you notice? Think of the poet's own name and profession: what is he trying to suggest (perhaps to convince himself)? What is Larkin telling us about his *l*ibrarian's job? Now think again why Larkin includes the obscure *losels, loblolly-men*. Had you heard of these people? What would the attraction be in living the life of a 'lout' to a responsible, sensitive man like Larkin? What is the point of saying that the tramps or gypsies described in stanza 4 *live up lanes*? What tone do you notice creeping in in stanza 5? What about the register? This register continues in stanza 6 in the colloquial cry *Stuff your pension*. The response from the responsible side of Larkin is a quotation from Shakespeare's *The Tempest,* 'the stuff/That dreams are made on'. What does he mean by it? Describe the clever pun on *stuff*. This pun is emphasised by the only full rhyme in the poem. Describe the rhyme scheme. What is the point in saying he knows his Shakespeare *all too well*? How does this disqualify him to live like a lout?

Find out what the 'work ethic' is and then work out what Larkin means by lines 25–6. The *hunkers* are the back of the thighs (particularly large on toads!) How does Larkin use the sounds of these words to emphasise the weight of the *luck* which gave him this attitude? Find out what *blarney* means.

The last stanza is slightly more difficult. Larkin is referring back to the external toad (work) and the internal toad (his own work ethic). He says that he does not know which comes first. Do you find work because you have a desire to be doing, or does work create this need so that you become dependent on it through habit? Work out the various possible meanings of the last two lines.

TED HUGHES

The Jaguar

The apes yawn and adore their fleas in the sun.
The parrots shriek as if they were on fire, or strut
Like cheap tarts to attract the stroller with the nut.
Fatigued with indolence, tiger and lion

Lie still as the sun. The boa-constrictor's coil   5
Is a fossil. Cage after cage seems empty, or
Stinks of sleepers from the breathing straw.
It might be painted on a nursery wall.

But who runs like the rest past these arrives
At a cage where the crowd stands, stares, mesmerized,   10
As a child at a dream, at a jaguar hurrying enraged
Through prison darkness after the drills of his eyes

On a short fierce fuse. Not in boredom –
The eye satisfied to be blind in fire,
By the bang of blood in the brain deaf the ear –   15
He spins from the bars, but there's no cage to him

More than to the visionary his cell:
His stride is wildernesses of freedom:
The world rolls under the long thrust of his heel.
Over the cage floor the horizons come.   20

Why do you suppose boredom is more common in our own
time than in previous centuries? What factors in our way of
life now have changed to make boredom more likely?

Hughes uses this description of a zoo to describe attitudes to
life in a manner reminiscent of D.H. Lawrence. A sense of
ennui or boredom dominates the first two stanzas. How does
Hughes emphasise that there is nothing to do? How does he
connect this boredom with human life in the twentieth
century? Justify the unexpected similes Hughes uses in the

first stanza. Why would the *sun* be *still*? In what two senses is the coiled snake like a *fossil*? When he says that the scene could be *painted on a nursery wall*, he obviously emphasises its stillness; what other qualities make this an apt description of these 'wild' animals? Which phrases make you realise that Hughes strongly disapproves of caging these creatures? How does Hughes achieve a change of pace in the third stanza? Why is this change vital to what he is trying to convey? Explain the phrase *mesmerized, /As a child at a dream.*

Why is the jaguar described as *on a short fierce fuse* at the cloths or *drills* over his eyes? What does the phrase *blind in fire* suggest? How does the poet emphasise the sound of the blood in line 15? The jaguar has in effect created his own world from his own energy. Thus the metaphors of the final stanza are not merely comparisons: there is a strong sense that the imaginary *horizons* are more real than the bars because of the intensity with which they are believed in. The decisiveness of this vision is emphasised in line 19 where the rhythm seems to add to the certainty. Work out which of the syllables should be stressed. Generally in English poetry stressed and unstressed syllables alternate. Here the poet slows the rhythm down by putting two stressed syllables together twice in the line. The whole stanza, with each line virtually independent grammatically (simplicity adding to the sure sense of grandeur) is a contrast to the spinning energy of the previous stanza where we are impelled onwards to the grammatical conclusion.

What do you think Hughes is telling us about the way we ought to live our lives and the way we actually do live them?

The Thought-Fox

I imagine this midnight moment's forest:
Something else is alive
Besides the clock's loneliness
And this blank page where my fingers move.

Through the window I see no star: 5
Something more near
Though deeper within darkness
Is entering the loneliness:

Cold, delicately as the dark snow,
A fox's nose touches twig, leaf;   10
Two eyes serve a movement, that now
And again now, and now, and now

Sets neat prints into the snow
Between trees, and warily a lame
Shadow lags by stump and in hollow   15
Of a body that is bold to come

Across clearings, an eye,
A widening deepening greenness,
Brilliantly, concentratedly,
Coming about its own business   20

Till, with a sudden sharp hot stink of fox
It enters the dark hole of the head.
The window is starless still; the clock ticks,
The page is printed.

Try to describe as accurately as you can how an idea comes to you. Is it a gradual process or sudden or a mixture of the two?

List the qualities you associate with foxes.

This poem, like many of Hughes's pieces, but perhaps to a more obvious extent, is not so much about the wild animal itself as about the human capacity to imagine, to enter the dark primitive places of the mind, reconnecting us with a more primitive human self. Just as the fox touches delicately the twigs and leaves of its surroundings, so the poet's mind is able to touch the life of an imaginary fox, fleshing it out and making it real.

What tense is the whole poem written in and what effect does this have? How would you subdivide the poem and why? Why is the time the poem is set important? What does the fact that the sky is starless emphasise? Explain the phrase *deeper within darkness* – in what sense can the fox be said to be more surrounded by darkness than a star? Remember that the fox is only part fox and part *thought*. What qualities are associated with foxes and why do these make it an appropriate symbol for thought? Take each description of the fox and try to apply it to a *thought* taking shape. Note how the images associated with the fox become more and more solid until in the final stanza the three stressed syllables *sharp hot stink* provide an almost shockingly real and fleshy feel to this fox. What happens surprisingly afterwards? How is this like a *thought*? Explain the last line.

SYLVIA PLATH

Medallion

By the gate with star and moon
Worked into the peeled orange wood
The bronze snake lay in the sun

Inert as a shoelace; dead
But pliable still, his jaw   5
Unhinged and his grin crooked,

Tongue a rose-colored arrow.
Over my hand I hung him.
His little vermilion eye

Ignited with a glassed flame   10
As I turned him in the light;
When I split a rock one time

The garnet bits burned like that.
Dust dulled his back to ochre
The way sun ruins a trout.   15

Yet his belly kept its fire
Going under the chainmail,
The old jewels smoldering there

In each opaque belly-scale:
Sunset looked at through milk glass.   20
And I saw white maggots coil

Thin as pins in the dark bruise
Where his innards bulged as if
He were digesting a mouse.

Knifelike, he was chaste enough,   25
Pure death's-metal. The yardman's
Flung brick perfected his laugh.

Like the next poem this was written in the autumn of 1959,
just before Plath and Ted Hughes returned to England. What
effect do the following descriptions of the snake create: *inert
as a shoelace, jaw/Unhinged, ignited with a glassed flame,
chaste enough*? Pick out all the details which involve colour
in the poem, and discuss how they make the scene (if not
the snake!) come alive. Consider both the individual
effectiveness of the images and their overall impact. How
does Plath use internal rhyme to emphasise the repulsive
image of the maggots? Discuss her use of enjambement
between lines and stanzas both here and throughout the
poem. Is the snake ultimately repellent or attractive? Does
the final phrase refer to the snakes *perfected* or frozen
expression, the *grin* referred to earlier, or the labourer's own
petty *laugh* at having killed this beautiful if dangerous
creature?

Compare D.H. Lawrence's 'Snake'. Look at their attitudes
towards the creatures they describe.

*M*ushrooms

Overnight, very
Whitely, discreetly,
Very quietly

Our toes, our noses
Take hold on the loam,   5
Acquire the air.

Nobody sees us,
Stops us, betrays us;
The small grains make room.

Soft fists insist on   10
Heaving the needles,
The leafy bedding,

Even the paving.
Our hammers, our rams,
Earless and eyeless,   15

Perfectly voiceless,
Widen the crannies,
Shoulder through holes. We

Diet on water,
On crumbs of shadow,   20
Bland-mannered, asking

Little or nothing.
So many of us!
So many of us!

We are shelves, we are   25
Tables, we are meek,
We are edible,

Nudgers and shovers
In spite of ourselves.
Our kind multiplies: 30

We shall by morning
Inherit the earth.
Our foot's in the door.

In this poem, Plath takes on the voice of mushrooms, quick-growing, fast multiplying and, unlike the snake of the previous poem, lacking in discernible colour. List the ways the mushrooms are described as quiet and non-aggressive. Does this harm their progress or help it? Give detailed evidence on both sides of this question before concluding. What are the other strengths of these mushrooms as they are described? Does Plath make their lot appear appealing or disagreeable or a mixture of the two? Again give detailed evidence.

How do the short lines, uncomplicated stanzas and simple grammatical units and even simpler vocabulary add to the poem? Which of the expressions might apply to the archetypal housewife of the 1950s, the 'little woman' who agreed with all her husband said?

'While Ted Hughes in his poetry chose to identify with the powerful and predatory aspects of nature … Sylvia Plath most often takes on nonhuman personae which are small, weak and unobtrusive' remarks Pamela J. Annas. To what extent is 'Mushrooms' an account of women's progress during the twentieth century? Could it apply equally to other dispossessed groups? Do you find it hopeful or depressing?

Compare and contrast this view of self with that expressed either in Plath's 'Wuthering Heights' or Hughes' 'Jaguar'.

You're

Clownlike, happiest on your hands,
Feet to the stars, and moon-skulled,
Gilled like a fish. A common-sense
Thumbs-down on the dodo's mode.
Wrapped up in yourself like a spool,   5
Trawling your dark as owls do.
Mute as a turnip from the Fourth
Of July to All Fools' Day,
O high-riser, my little loaf.

Vague as fog and looked for like mail.   10
Farther off than Australia.
Bent-backed Atlas, our traveled prawn.
Snug as a bud and at home
Like a sprat in a pickle jug
A creel of eels, all ripples.   15
Jumpy as a Mexican bean.
Right, like a well-done sum.
A clean slate, with your own face on.

Written in January 1960 whilst six months pregnant with her daughter Frieda, this poem celebrates the hopes whilst acknowledging the uncertainties of a first child – as well as merely observing the unborn child within the womb. This was a happy time for Plath; having been married to Ted Hughes for three and a half years, she had rediscovered her own poetic voice and both poets were writing prolifically after a spell at a writing school in America. They returned to England in high spirits, especially with the knowledge of the forthcoming child.

A list of metaphors and similes, the poem catalogues the various attitudes and responses of the mother. It is their sheer ingenuity and the profusion of their (sometimes contradictory) reactions which give the poem its energy. With a little thought each of these figures of speech will make sense, although it may help to know that the baby was due (and indeed was born) on All Fools' Day, April 1st, and thus was conceived at the beginning of July, American Independence Day. Why are both these days significant for Plath's view of the baby? (Turnips grow over the winter.) Why do you suppose Plath chose nine-line stanzas? Atlas was the giant (or mountain) who, in Greek myth, held up the sky. What would happen if he failed to do that and why is this a significant comparison?

What would you say was the overall mood of the poem? Do any of the ideas in the poem link with others or are they random statements of feeling?

Morning Song

Love set you going like a fat gold watch.
The midwife slapped your footsoles, and your bald cry
Took its place among the elements.

Our voices echo, magnifying your arrival. New statue.
In a drafty museum, your nakedness   5
Shadows our safety. We stand round blankly as walls.

I'm no more your mother
Than the cloud that distills a mirror to reflect its own slow
Effacement at the wind's hand.

All night your moth-breath   10
Flickers among the flat pink roses. I wake to listen:
A far sea moves in my ear.

One cry, and I stumble from bed, cow-heavy and floral
In my Victorian nightgown.
Your mouth opens clean as a cat's. The window square   15

Whitens and swallows its dull stars. And now you try
Your handful of notes;
The clear vowels rise like balloons.

Written on 19th February 1961, 'Morning Song' looks back
at the birth and infanthood of baby Frieda. It is also clouded
by depression brought on not merely by sleepless nights of
baby-minding, but the miscarriage Plath had on February
6th. During this time, Plath had, in her own view, found
herself largely left to cope with the baby whilst her husband
had been furthering his own literary career. The poem does
look at the effect of a baby on both of them, but it is notable
that it is she who goes to tend her child in the early hours of
the morning.

What is shocking about the opening simile? Notice the three
stressed syllables at the end of the line which slow the
rhythm down. Is this merely for emphasis or is there another
reason? Justify the choice of each of these words. Find
other rather surprising images for the baby and their
reaction to it in the first three stanzas. How does
enjambement in the third stanza add to this effect? Which
lines tell you how early it is and why is the metaphor
appropriate for what the baby wants at this time? What kind
of a *morning song* does the baby give and why is the final
simile an apt one for a child? Is there possibly an ironic pun
in the title?

Compare the imagery in this poem with that of 'You're'.

Wuthering Heights

The horizons ring me like faggots,
Tilted and disparate, and always unstable.
Touched by a match, they might warm me,
And their fine lines singe
The air to orange   5
Before the distances they pin evaporate,
Weighting the pale sky with a solider color.
But they only dissolve and dissolve
Like a series of promises, as I step forward.

There is no life higher than the grasstops   10
Or the hearts of sheep, and the wind
Pours by like destiny, bending
Everything in one direction.
I can feel it trying
To funnel my heat away.   15
If I pay the roots of the heather
Too close attention, they will invite me
To whiten my bones among them.

The sheep know where they are,
Browsing in their dirty wool-clouds,   20
Gray as the weather.
The black slots of their pupils take me in.
It is like being mailed into space,
A thin, silly message.
They stand about in grandmotherly disguise,   25
All wig curls and yellow teeth
And hard, marbly baas.

I come to wheel ruts, and water
Limpid as the solitudes
That flee through my fingers.   30
Hollow doorsteps go from grass to grass;
Lintel and sill have unhinged themselves.
Of people the air only
Remembers a few odd syllables.
It rehearses them moaningly: 35
Black stone, black stone.

The sky leans on me, me, the one upright
Among all horizontals.
The grass is beating its head distractedly.
It is too delicate   40
For a life in such company;
Darkness terrifies it.
Now, in valleys narrow
And black as purses, the house lights
Gleam like small change.   45

Like Brontë's novel of the same name, this poem registers
the severe impersonality of a bleak moorland landscape.
Plath and Hughes had moved to North Devon, on the edge
of Dartmoor. The landscape becomes a metaphor for Plath's
feelings of isolation as Hughes began to spend more time
away. She was now heavily pregnant with her second child
in a house which lacked many of the amenities of modern
American homes. Perhaps this explains her reference to the
bundles of firewood or *faggots* needed to light fires, in the
first line. In what ways does this opening simile work? What
time of day is described? How can horizons *dissolve and
dissolve* as she approaches? What does the following simile
say about her state of mind, her faith in those around her? If
the first stanza implies a coldness in her life, how does the
second intensify this sense of despondency? If the *sheep
know where they are* what does this imply about her own
sense of belonging? In the fourth stanza she comes across a
ruined cottage and imagines ghosts. The sheer sense of
solitude given by these ghosts should be compared to
Brontë's novel. Compare the image which opens the final
stanza with that concerning Atlas in 'You're'. What does this
one emphasise and how is it different? A sense of strength
suddenly becomes apparent as she strides back towards,
but not yet in, the community of society. How does the last
brilliant image emphasise the insignificance (and cowardice)
of the valley-based communities, which seem to stand for
the rest of mankind?

*B*lackberrying

Nobody in the lane, and nothing, nothing but blackberries,
Blackberries on either side, though on the right mainly,
A blackberry alley, going down in hooks, and a sea
Somewhere at the end of it, heaving. Blackberries
Big as the ball of my thumb, and dumb as eyes   5
Ebon in the hedges, fat
With blue-red juices. These they squander on my fingers.
I had not asked for such a blood sisterhood; they must
    love me.
They accommodate themselves to my milkbottle,
    flattening their sides.

Overhead go the choughs in black, cacophonous flocks – 10
Bits of burnt paper wheeling in a blown sky.
Theirs is the only voice, protesting, protesting.
I do not think the sea will appear at all.
The high, green meadows are glowing, as if lit from
    within.
I come to one bush of berries so ripe it is a bush of flies, 15
Hanging their bluegreen bellies and their wing
    panes in a Chinese screen.
The honey-feast of the berries has stunned them; they
    believe in heaven.
One more hook, and the berries and bushes end.

The only thing to come now is the sea.
From between two hills a sudden wind funnels at me,   20
Slapping its phantom laundry in my face.
These hills are too green and sweet to have tasted salt.
I follow the sheep path between them. A last hook
    brings me
To the hills' northern face, and the face is orange rock
That looks out on nothing, nothing but a great space   25
Of white and pewter lights, and a din like silversmiths
Beating and beating at an intractable metal.

In its simplest terms, an account of picking blackberries (which are stored in a milkbottle) on a walk towards the coast, this poem seems to contain a metaphor for life. On a literal level, explain the ideas involved in the following phrases: *a blackberry alley, going down in hooks, dumb as eyes, blood sisterhood*. Examine the descriptions of the choughs or red-legged crows, the flies, the wind and the sea. Compare the end of the second stanza with similar ideas in Keats' 'To Autumn' (lines 8–11, 17–18) – a poem written at just the same time of year. There seems to be a pun on *hook* in Plath's poem, referring not merely to the last corner of the *blackberry alley* but the sickle employed by the harvester – or by the grim reaper, Death himself.

Life as a journey is a common motif in literature. This one begins and ends in *nothing* – appropriately enough for a poet who had denied God's existence at the age of eight, after the sudden death of her father. Try to work out whether the three stanzas (each, like 'You're', of nine lines) might stand for the three phases of female life: youth, middle age and old age.

Compare the poem either with Heaney's 'Blackberry-Picking' or with any poem by Frost. To what extent is description given for its own sake in each poem and to what extent is there a more profound meaning or message in each?

*M*irror

I am silver and exact. I have no preconceptions.
Whatever I see I swallow immediately
Just as it is, unmisted by love or dislike.
I am not cruel, only truthful –
The eye of a little god, four-cornered.   5
Most of the time I meditate on the opposite wall.
It is pink, with speckles. I have looked at it so long
I think it is a part of my heart. But it flickers.
Faces and darkness separate us over and over.

Now I am a lake. A woman bends over me,   10
Searching my reaches for what she really is.
Then she turns to those liars, the candles or the moon.
I see her back, and reflect it faithfully.
She rewards me with tears and an agitation of hands.
I am important to her. She comes and goes.   15
Each morning it is her face that replaces the darkness.
In me she has drowned a young girl, and in me an old
    woman
Rises toward her day after day, like a terrible fish.

What are the various reasons and occasions people might look at mirrors?

Written about a month later than 'Blackberrying', this is a fairly bleak description of Plath's life and the lives of women in general, spoken as if by a mirror. Mirrors have long been a symbol for women and were central to Plath's imagery, though used in fairly complex ways.

In what way is the mirror more accepting of faults, more objective, than human beings? Why is it also extremely demanding on women and able to dominate their lives? How does the mirror become a metaphor for relationships towards the end of the first stanza? Why do you think the poem is in two equal nine-line stanzas? Does the second stanza begin with a pretend game on the part of the mirror, like some of the pretend games we demand of women? In various parts of the poem, the mirror seems to be like a lover, a child, a pet, a friend, a powerful presence. Identify and discuss these phases in the poem. In what ways does Plath show her need for a reliable friend in this poem? Explain the power of the last two lines.

Among the Narcissi

Spry, wry, and gray as these March sticks,
Percy bows, in his blue peajacket, among the narcissi.
He is recuperating from something on the lung.

The narcissi, too, are bowing to some big thing:
It rattles their stars on the green hill where Percy   5
Nurses the hardship of his stitches, and walks and walks.

There is a dignity to this; there is a formality –
The flowers vivid as bandages, and the man mending.
They bow and stand: they suffer such attacks!

And the octogenarian loves the little flocks.   10
He is quite blue; the terrible wind tries his breathing.
The narcissi look up like children, quickly and whitely.

Written about the poet's Devon neighbour, Percy Key, who was recovering after an operation for lung cancer, this poem contrasts the health and vitality of the flowers with images of illness and decay. *Narcissi* are small, white, daffodil-like flowers which, because they grow alongside ponds and lakes, gave rise to the myth of the narcissist, the person obsessed by himself, especially his appearance. The term *wry* here means bent. How does it contrast and yet connect with the first word of the poem? What relationship does it have to the opening of the second stanza? Discuss the use of colour in the poem. Why is it difficult to distinguish man and plant in the imagery of the poem? What do you think Plath is suggesting? How does she use the caesura in the third stanza to suggest a balance between the two, as though one is the reflection of the other? The simile in this stanza seems more at home in T.S. Eliot than Wordsworth at first sight (compare the latter's 'Daffodils'); why however is it very fitting? Explain the last line and relate it to line 10.

To what extent is Plath's poetry the cry of a victim? Consider patriarchy, depression and the subservience of women in your answer.

SEAMUS HEANEY

Mid-term Break

I sat all morning in the college sick bay
Counting bells knelling classes to a close.
At two o'clock our neighbours drove me home.

In the porch I met my father crying –
He had always taken funerals in his stride –   5
And Big Jim Evans saying it was a hard blow.

The baby cooed and laughed and rocked the pram
When I came in, and I was embarrassed
By old men standing up to shake my hand

And tell me they were 'sorry for my trouble',   10
Whispers informed strangers I was the eldest,
Away at school, as my mother held my hand

In hers and coughed out angry tearless sighs.
At ten o'clock the ambulance arrived
With the corpse, stanched and bandaged by the nurses.   15

Next morning I went up into the room. Snowdrops
And candles soothed the bedside; I saw him
For the first time in six weeks. Paler now,

Wearing a poppy bruise on his left temple,
He lay in the four foot box as in his cot.   20
No gaudy scars, the bumper knocked him clear.

A four foot box, a foot for every year.

 The poem needs to be read once for the sense of mystery
and then again for the details. When reading the poem the
first time, jot down your thoughts and expectations after
each stage: what associations does the title bring, positive or
negative? How does the opening stanza upset these

expectations? What do you suppose is wrong? Continue this process of asking yourself questions throughout the poem.

Much of the power in this poem, based on the true story of the loss of his brother, comes from the sense of mystery as the tragedy is only gradually revealed. This seems to be a deliberate attempt by the poet to convey his own young mind floundering to come to terms with this strange, alien experience. The numbness also finds an echo in the tone of the poem which objectively observes and resists all sentimentalising.

Why do you think the sounds of the words are important in the second line? What figures of speech are used? Why do you think the poet emphasises the bells going off at regular intervals whilst the boy counts them? Which two words give a faint suggestion of death in the line? Why is the behaviour of the men throughout the poem difficult for the boy to deal with? How does the poet emphasise the contrast between the reactions of father and mother? Why are these unexpected and therefore more confusing for the boy? How do we find out that the boy is at boarding school and what effect does this have on his relations with his family? The most shocking reaction to the death is, perhaps, the baby's. Why do you think the poet includes it when he does? What is ironic about its laughter, which *rocked the pram*?

When the corpse arrives it is *stanched* to prevent the flow of blood. What else in the stanza has been *stanched*? Explain the phrase *soothed the bedside*. What does the fact that *candles* are there tell us about the religion of the household? Which two facts in this stanza tell us that the accident happened about halfway through the Easter term?

The poet emphasises the brightness of the bruise by colour and contrast. Explain this. The poppy is also a flower which traditionally symbolises sleep and death, perhaps because it is the source of the strong narcotic drug opium. Describe how the boy died. How is this scene very different from the arrival of the *bandaged* corpse the day before?

Why is the last stanza so brief and so shocking?

Digging

Between my finger and my thumb
The squat pen rests; snug as a gun.

Under my window, a clean rasping sound
When the spade sinks into gravelly ground:
My father, digging. I look down   5

Till his straining rump among the flowerbeds
Bends low, comes up twenty years away
Stooping in rhythm through potato drills
Where he was digging.

The coarse boot nestled on the lug, the shaft   10
Against the inside knee was levered firmly.
He rooted out tall tops, buried the bright edge deep
To scatter new potatoes that we picked
Loving their cool hardness in our hands.

By God, the old man could handle a spade.   15
Just like his old man.

My grandfather cut more turf in a day
Than any other man on Toner's bog.
Once I carried him milk in a bottle
Corked sloppily with paper. He straightened up   20
To drink it, then fell to right away
Nicking and slicing neatly, heaving sods
Over his shoulder, going down and down
For the good turf. Digging.

The cold smell of potato mould, the squelch and slap   25
Of soggy peat, the curt cuts of an edge
Through living roots awaken in my head.
But I've no spade to follow men like them.

Between my finger and my thumb
The squat pen rests.   30
I'll dig with it.

Describe a piece of handiwork, a skill, which a boy might traditionally learn by watching his father. Describe the movements of the hands in this operation in detail. Is the skill one which is dying out? Will it be useful in the future?

Peat digging is a traditional economic activity of Ireland, the peat being dark soil formed from the remains of vegetable matter and making excellent fuel. For Heaney, the peat bogs formed a complex metaphor of the connections between Ireland's past and its present. Here it is much more personal as his grandfather's peat-digging is replaced by his father's vegetable gardening. In the first two lines of the second stanza, the poet emphasises the sounds carefully. Identify the figures of speech and say why they are effective and evocative (strongly bringing back memories). Describe how and why the poem changes tenses. Compare Lawrence's 'Piano'.

List the various ways hands are used in the poem. How far is the poem about continuity and how far is it about change? Compare the digging of the father in the fourth stanza with the digging of the grandfather in the sixth. Which would you say is the more expert? What are the 'fruits' of their labours? You will notice that as he goes further back, each generation seems to be digging deeper. In the seventh stanza Heaney brings together the efforts of father and grandfather. What does he mean by the phrase *awaken in my head*? What does this phrase have to do with the creation of the poem? Why does the poet have *no spade to follow men like them*? What do you think has separated him from his forebears? What replaces the spade for Heaney the poet? How can he be said to *dig with it*? What are the fruits of his labours and what *living roots* is he in danger of cutting? Look again at the stanzas describing the digging of the two men. Are there any phrases which could be used to describe Heaney's new type of digging, the creation of poems?

Follower

My father worked with a horse-plough,
His shoulders globed like a full sail strung
Between the shafts and the furrow.
The horses strained at his clicking tongue.

An expert. He would set the wing.   5
And fit the bright steep-pointed sock.
The sod rolled over without breaking.
At the headrig, with a single pluck

Of reins, the sweating team turned round
And back into the land. His eye   10
Narrowed and angled at the ground,
Mapping the furrow exactly.

I stumbled in his hob-nailed wake,
Fell sometimes on the polished sod;
Sometimes he rode me on his back   15
Dipping and rising to his plod.

I wanted to grow up and plough,
To close one eye, stiffen my arm.
All I ever did was follow
In his broad shadow round the farm.   20

I was a nuisance, tripping, falling,
Yapping always. But today
It is my father who keeps stumbling
Behind me and will not go away.

Once again, the poet is digging in the peat-layers of his past to discover his roots, his sense of identity. Here he also looks at the startling changes which come over competent people as they grow older. Ploughing, his father's profession, used to be even more specialised than it remains today, because of the added difficulty of dealing with live creatures, the horses. The principles had changed little for centuries until the advent of the tractor. The *team* of horses, harnessed between two bars or *shafts*, would pull the plough which would turn the earth or *sod* over, leaving a trench or *furrow*. The *wing* would cut the bottom of the furrow whilst the *sock* turned the earth. The difficulties came in lining up furrows, handling the horses and turning at the end of each furrow, the *headrig*. The ploughmen would wear hob-nailed boots to prevent them slipping on the mud.

How do we know that both horses and ploughman are working hard? What does the phrase *shoulders globed* mean? What does it suggest about the size of the father and the boy's perspective? Connect it with an image in the fifth stanza. Describe in detail how Heaney gives the impression that his father is *an expert*.

There is a change of emphasis in the poem exactly halfway through. Describe it. Why is the last stanza so shocking?

With reference to both these poems, discuss to what extent Heaney was a follower.

Blackberry-Picking

Late August, given heavy rain and sun
For a full week, the blackberries would ripen.
At first, just one, a glossy purple clot
Among others, red, green, hard as a knot.
You ate that first one and its flesh was sweet   5
Like thickened wine: summer's blood was in it
Leaving stains upon the tongue and lust for
Picking. Then red ones inked up and that hunger
Sent us out with milk-cans, pea-tins, jam-pots
Where briars scratched and wet grass bleached
    our boots.   10
Round hayfields, cornfields and potato-drills
We trekked and picked until the cans were full,
Until the tinkling bottom had been covered
With green ones, and on top big dark blobs burned
Like a plate of eyes. Our hands were peppered   15
With thorn pricks, our palms sticky as Bluebeard's.

We hoarded the fresh berries in the byre.
But when the bath was filled we found a fur,
A rat-grey fungus, glutting on our cache.
The juice was stinking too. Once off the bush   20
The fruit fermented, the sweet flesh would turn sour.
I always felt like crying. It wasn't fair
That all the lovely canfulls smelt of rot.
Each year I hoped they'd keep, knew they would not.

Like many of Heaney's poems this begins simply, only to take on a more profound meaning at the end. Why does the poet break the poem into two stanzas as he does? Pick out the various similes in the poem and justify each one. Which phrases in the poem: make the blackberries seem more like meat than fruit; are taken from ordinary domestic life (especially kitchens); suggest the world and viewpoint of the child? As always in Heaney's poems the sounds of the words are magical. Look at the assonance in lines 6–7 and the alliteration at the beginning of the second stanza, which suggest hunger and horror respectively. Why is there full rhyme in the last two lines and before that only imperfect rhyme? Considering especially the phrase *the sweet flesh would turn sour*, discuss what the poem suggests about the disillusionment of childhood.

Compare Plath's 'Blackberrying'.

*O*ld Smoothing Iron

Often I watched her lift it
from where its compact wedge
rode the back of the stove
like a tug at anchor.

To test its heat she'd stare   5
and spit in its iron face
or hold it up next her cheek
to divine the stored danger.

Soft thumps on the ironing board.
Her dimpled angled elbow   10
and intent stoop
as she aimed the smoothing iron

like a plane into linen,
like the resentment of women.
To work, her dumb lunge says,   15
is to move a certain mass

through a certain distance,
is to pull your weight and feel
exact and equal to it.
Feel dragged upon. And buoyant.   20

What are the main ways women's lives have changed since
the Second World War?

Old-fashioned irons were heated not by electricity but by
being left on top of stoves. This simple poem begins by
describing the way Heaney's mother ironed before going on
to describe her attitude to this work. In what ways is the first
stanza obviously a child's perspective? What good would
spitting on the iron do? What does the phrase *spit in its iron
face* imply about her attitudes to this task? Comment on the
phrase *soft thumps*. The third stanza seems more loving and
more evocative in its tone. Why is this? Compare it with
Lawrence's 'Piano'.

Suddenly in the fourth stanza the poem takes on a different tone. Describe that change. Which image in this stanza reminds you of the tug boat of stanza one? Why is this one different (comment on the phrase *at anchor*)? In what ways is the movement of the iron *like the resentment of women*? Think of its shape, its effect, and perhaps the phrase *soft thumps*. What would women have had to resent?

How can her *dumb lunge*, her silent movement, say anything? What figure of speech is involved here? What do the next lines (16–17) remind you of in the way they are phrased? Why is such technical phrasing ironic for this housewife's *dumb lunge*? Do you feel you *pull your weight* in the household? *To work*, her movement implies, is to tug, to pull a weight, and to *feel / exact and equal to it*. Are modern women feeling less and less *equal to it* or more? Why is the last line surprising? What is the effect of the full stop? Link the line with the transport images of stanzas one and four.

Compare the attitudes to and definitions of work in this poem with Heaney's 'Follower', Frost's 'After Apple-Picking', Larkin's 'Toads' and Lawrence's 'Last Lesson of the Afternoon'. Which seems to you most appropriate to modern life? Explain fully the effectiveness of the metaphors they choose for the type of work they are describing.

*P*unishment

I can feel the tug
of the halter at the nape
of her neck, the wind
on her naked front.

It blows her nipples   5
to amber beads,
it shakes the frail rigging
of her ribs.

I can see her drowned
body in the bog,   10
the weighing stone,
the floating rods and boughs.

Under which at first
she was a barked sapling
that is dug up   15
oak-bone, brain-firkin:

her shaved head
like a stubble of black corn,
her blindfold a soiled bandage,
her noose a ring   20

to store
the memories of love.
Little adulteress,
before they punished you

you were flaxen-haired,   25
undernourished, and your
tar-black face was beautiful.
My poor scapegoat,

I almost love you
but would have cast, I know,   30
the stones of silence.
I am the artful voyeur

of your brain's exposed
and darkened combs,
your muscles webbing   35
and all your numbered bones:

I who have stood dumb
when your betraying sisters,
cauled in tar,
wept by the railings,   40

who would connive
in civilized outrage
yet understand the exact
and tribal, intimate revenge.

Are women still judged differently from men in terms of their
sexual relationships? Why has this traditionally been the
case? Discuss the ways we judge and compare the names
we give to women and men who 'sleep around'.

Heaney became fascinated by the discoveries of bodies
preserved for two thousand years in the peat bogs of
Europe. Living in an area famous for its boglands, he saw
the remains of these Iron Age people as a strong link with
the past of the region and an appropriate metaphor for our
own present-day instincts and attitudes. The girl he
describes in this poem was found in Denmark and seems to
have been a sacrificial victim. The historians of this period
record that such victims were often women found guilty of
adultery.

The opening stanzas are an exercise in historical empathy
as the poet tries to feel what it was to be the woman being
drowned and then the crowd watching. How does he achieve
this and make us feel sympathy for the woman, and an
immediacy as if we were there? List the expressions which
achieve these things. Explain the phrase which describes the
noose around her neck as *a ring / to store / the memories of*

love. Look up the Biblical reference 'let he who is without sin cast the first stone' in John, chapter 8. Why does Heaney say he would have cast *stones of silence*? How might silence be just as effective a punishment for adultery as direct condemnation?

In the tenth stanza the poet refers to a gruesome practice in modern-day Northern Ireland: if a local Catholic girl was found to be sleeping with one of the British army stationed in the province, she would be ceremonially tarred and feathered as an example to others. Relate this practice to what happened to the Danish girl. What does the fact that Heaney, a Catholic, stood mute whilst this may have happened say about him? Which two tribes is Heaney referring to in the last stanza, and what does this imply about human progress and civilisation since the Iron Age?

Relate the poem to Robert Frost's 'Mending Wall'.

In 'Digging', Heaney updated the phrase 'the pen is mightier than the sword'. How does his pen deal with such dangerous subject matter as death, change and conflict?

R.S. THOMAS

The Evacuee

She woke up under a loose quilt
Of leaf patterns, woven by the light
At the small window, busy with the boughs
Of a young cherry; but wearily she lay,
Waiting for the siren, slow to trust   5
Nature's deceptive peace, and then afraid
Of the long silence, she would have crept
Uneasily from the bedroom with its frieze
Of fresh sunlight, had not a cock crowed,
Shattering the surface of that limpid pool   10
Of stillness, and before the ripples died
One by one in the field's shallows,
The farm woke with uninhibited din.

And now the noise and not the silence drew her
Down the bare stairs at great speed.   15
The sounds and voices were a rough sheet
Waiting to catch her, as though she leaped
From a scorched storey of the charred past.
And there the table and the gallery
Of farm faces trying to be kind   20
Beckoned her nearer, and she sat down
Under an awning of salt hams.

And so she grew, a small bird in the nest
Of welcome that was built about her,
Home now after so long away   25
In the flowerless streets of the drab town.
The men watched her busy with the hens,
The soft flesh ripening warm as corn
On the sticks of limbs, the grey eyes clear,
Rinsed with dew of their long dread.   30
The men watched her, and, nodding, smiled
With earth's charity, patient and strong.

This beautiful tale of the nourishing power of the countryside is the most lyrical or graceful of the poems included in this selection of Thomas' work. Like 'Farm Child' and 'Cynddylan on a Tractor', it was published in 1952 in a collection called *An Acre of Land*. All three focus on rural issues, but with varying attitudes displayed by the poet. Whereas 'Cynddylan' is cynical and 'Farm Child' objective, 'The Evacuee' is positively warm in its depiction of rural charm and its effect on a child evacuated from a city during the bombing blitz of the Second World War. As Rector of Manafon from 1942, Thomas would have experienced first-hand the effects of evacuation on a number of city children to rural mid-Wales. Here, of course, he idealises the situation whilst emphasising by way of contrast both the harshness of the bombed world in the cities at that time and the dull *drab* quality of city life in general. Describe the way Thomas uses enjambement in the first two lines to trick the reader momentarily. How would a *loose quilt* feel? Why is it an appropriate metaphor for the effects of the lights? Trace Thomas' own beautiful *patterns*, not of light but of sound, throughout this stanza, noting particularly his use of alliteration to add lyricism. Do hard or soft sounds predominate? Why is there an exception to this pattern on line 9? Explain why she is *slow to trust* the silence. She feels more at home in the *uninhibited din* of the daytime farm: explain carefully the extended metaphor of lines 16–18. An *awning* is a roof, here made (metaphorically) of the *salt hams* hanging on hooks from the simple farm kitchen. Pick out other details which would have made the house seem strange and unsophisticated to the girl. Why is the metaphor *rinsed with dew* appropriate when describing the washing away of the girl's fears and cares?

*F*arm Child

Look at this village boy, his head is stuffed
With all the nests he knows, his pockets with flowers,
Snail-shells and bits of glass, the fruit of hours
Spent in the fields by thorn and thistle tuft.
Look at his eyes, see the harebell hiding there;   5
Mark how the sun has freckled his smooth face
Like a finch's egg under that bush of hair
That dares the wind, and in the mixen now
Notice his poise; from such unconscious grace
Earth breeds and beckons to the stubborn plough.   10

The boy is held up like an exhibit in a museum, or the
subject of a wildlife documentary. How does the poet
achieve these effects? List the metaphors and similes in the
poem which are drawn from nature. Explain how each one
is an appropriate description of the boy. How does Thomas
capture the sheer energy and fun of the boy's life? The
mixen is the dunghill, where muck or slurry is kept before
spreading on the fields as fertiliser. What is paradoxical
about the way the boy stands with such *grace* in such a
setting? Why is it actually very fitting that he should almost
pose there for us? What will happen to this fun-filled boy in
future? What are the two meanings of *poise* and why do they
both apply to this 'Farm Child'?

Compare 'The Evacuee'.

Cynddylan

Ah, you should see Cynddylan on a tractor.
Gone the old look that yoked him to the soil;
He's a new man now, part of the machine,
His nerves of metal and his blood oil.
The clutch curses, but the gears obey   5
His least bidding, and lo, he's away
Out of the farmyard, scattering hens.
Riding to work now as a great man should,
He is the knight at arms breaking the fields'
Mirror of silence, emptying the wood   10
Of foxes and squirrels and bright jays.
The sun comes over the tall trees
Kindling all the hedges, but not for him
Who runs his engine on a different fuel.
And all the birds are singing, bills wide in vain,   15
As Cynddylan passes proudly up the lane.

This fiercely ironic satire on man's 'progress' in the
twentieth century might be compared with some of
Lawrence's work. What makes this less generalised than
other condemnations is the closely observed detail, the
dramatic quality of the poetry. Like all drama it needs a
central character and a conflict of sorts. Work out the
qualities of Cynddylan as hero. Who are his enemies? What
is ironic about these enemies? Why is *yoked* such an
appropriate expression? Why do you suppose the poet
chooses to rhyme *soil* with *oil*? There are two rhyming
couplets in the poem which coincide with the most savage
pieces of criticism. Why do you think the poet uses rhyme
in this way? Comment on the use of the word *lo* in line 6.
How does the poet make the scene (missed by Cynddylan)
beautiful in lines 12–13? Bearing in mind the next line, why
is *kindling* an appropriate metaphor? Why do the birds open
their beaks *wide in vain*?

Children's Song

We live in our own world,
A world that is too small
For you to stoop and enter
Even on hands and knees,
The adult subterfuge.   5
And though you probe and pry
With analytic eye,
And eavesdrop all our talk
With an amused look,
You cannot find the centre   10
Where we dance, where we play,
Where life is still asleep
Under the closed flower,
Under the smooth shell
Of eggs in the cupped nest   15
That mock the faded blue
Of your remoter heaven.

The poem begins very simply as a way of expressing the
differences between adult and childish worlds and ends in a
complicated metaphor which takes time to work out.
Despite all patronising efforts to get involved, the adult
remains too *analytic* to really belong in this small world, too
aware that he is playing. In the last five lines the *centre* of
the child's imaginative world is described as an enclosed
space with its own *heaven*. Why are *flowers* and *eggs*
appropriate comparisons for this closed space? What colour
must the eggs be? What makes the child's heaven less
remote than the adult one, both in terms of the metaphor
chosen and their own access to heavenly worlds?

A Blackbird Singing

It seems wrong that out of this bird,
Black, bold, a suggestion of dark
Places about it, there yet should come
Such rich music, as though the notes'
Ore were changed to a rare metal   5
At one touch of that bright bill.

You have heard it often, alone at your desk
In green April, your mind drawn
Away from its work by sweet disturbance
Of the mild evening outside your room.   10

A slow singer, but loading each phrase
With history's overtones, love, joy
And grief learned by his dark tribe
In other orchards and passed on
Instinctively as they are now,   15
But fresh always with new tears.

Like the previous poem, this was first published in 1955 in
the volume *Song at the Year's Turning*. Both are obviously
concerned with song but this one more specifically. What is
there about the bird's appearance which contrasts with its
song? What figure of speech is involved in the expression
sweet disturbance? Compare the last stanza with both
Keats' 'Ode to a Nightingale' and Hardy's 'Darkling Thrush'.
There is perhaps a touch of symbolism here as the bird
seems to stand for other types of singers who *instinctively*
pass on the grief and joy of previous generations. Given
Thomas' dual profession, what other kinds of *dark tribe*
might the poet have in mind?

*L*ore

Job Davies, eighty-five
Winters old, and still alive
After the slow poison
And treachery of the seasons.

Miserable? Kick my arse!   5
It needs more than the rain's hearse,
Wind-drawn, to pull me off
The great perch of my laugh.

What's living but courage?
Paunch full of hot porridge,   10
Nerves strengthened with tea,
Peat-black, dawn found me

Mowing where the grass grew,
Bearded with golden dew.
Rhythm of the long scythe   15
Kept this tall frame lithe.

What to do? Stay green.
Never mind the machine,
Whose fuel is human souls.
Live large, man, and dream small.   20

What activities would you expect to be appropriate for an eighty-five-year-old man? Imagine such a character and invent a monologue for him describing his day and giving advice to the young.

Describe the sudden change in tone between stanzas one and two. What does the poet mean by the *treachery of the seasons*? How is this continued into the second stanza? A *hearse* would, in Job Davies' youth, have been *drawn* or pulled by horses. Bearing this in mind explain the metaphor in lines 6–8. Why is a *perch* appropriate for a *laugh*? Describe, in your own words, Job's attitude to life. What effect does his unexpected activity of stanza three have and how does it fit in with Job's views of the world? How does the poet capture the rhythm of Job's mowing? Stanzas two and five begin with similar questions. What do these imply about the poem? To stay *green* is to stay young rather than the modern meaning of ecological care; Job's message however is similar to many of the 'eco-warriors' of more recent times. What makes it different (less practical, more romantic) is his reference to *souls*. Explain the last line. How would a *small* dream be better for the soul (and the planet) than a large one?

Find out who the biblical Job was. Why might this be an appropriate name for the hero of the poem? Do you agree with the *lore* or wisdom he gives?

'Never mind the machine.' Compare and contrast the presentation of Job Davies with the hero of 'Cynddylan on a Tractor' in the light of this remark.

The Window

Say he is any man
anywhere set before the shop window
of life, full of comestibles
and jewels; to put out his hand
is to come up against   5
glass; to break it is
to injure himself.
            Shall he turn
poet and acquire them
in the imagination, gospeller   10
and extol himself for his abstention
from them?
            What if he is not
called? I would put the manufacturers
there. Let them see the eyes   15
staring in, be splashed with the blood
of the shop-breakers; let them live
on the poet's diet, on the pocket-money
of the priest.
            I see the blinds   20
going down in Europe, over the
whole world: the rich with everything to
sell, the poor with nothing to buy it with.

The remainder of the poems in this selection are from Thomas' 1986 volume, *Experimenting with an Amen*. In some ways, as the poet has grown older, moved further west and become more withdrawn, his poetry has become bleaker. At the same time it can be said to grapple perhaps more intensely with the issues of modern life as well as Thomas' own perennial doubts as to the existence and nature of God.

In this poem Thomas shows most clearly the 'mantle of an Old Testament prophet' that one critic claims that he has chosen for himself. Living in a remote corner of Wales, Thomas has retreated from and, to a certain extent, rejected many aspects of modern life. From his hermit-like vantage point he is free to comment on the world around him and the growing indifference of the profiteers and fat-cats to the plight of those in relative and absolute poverty. Of the latter type of poverty there has been a huge increase since the late 1970s; find out why this was. 'The Window' depends for its power on the ambiguity of the symbol which hovers between a physical picture and a representative one.

How does Thomas use enjambement in the first three lines to emphasise this ambiguity between the literal and metaphorical? What are the three solutions to the problem of the man outside the window in the first two stanzas? What might the positive and negative results of each solution be, both for the man and society as a whole? In the third stanza, Thomas suggests another solution, which is to let the 'haves' see the lives of the 'have-nots' first hand. However, the final stanza is a bleak one. There is perhaps a reference to 'fortress Europe' here with its policies of protecting its own trade against the cheaper products made in the Third World. There has always been a gap between rich and poor in the world. Which modern developments might make the *window* between these two worlds much more transparent?

Moorland

It is beautiful and still;
    the air rarefied
as the interior of a cathedral

expecting a presence. It is where, also,
    the harrier occurs,   5
materialising from nothing, snow-

soft, but with claws of fire,
    quartering the bare earth
for the prey that escapes it;

hovering over the incipient   10
    scream, here a moment, then
not here, like my belief in God.

Thomas has edited collections of religious poetry and more specifically of George Herbert's work. However, despite Thomas' dual roles of priest and poet, one critic has claimed that his work reads more like a 'hymn to doubt' than a hymn to God. Certainly, like Herbert in 'The Collar', Thomas wrestles vigorously with that doubt. He presents it here starkly and unflinchingly with an element drawn from the poetry of Ted Hughes – the brutal world of the animal kingdom. How is the moorland scene like a *cathedral*? Why would a cathedral be *expecting a presence*? Instead of that supernatural presence Thomas is given a natural one. Why is the hawk *materialising from nothing*? Which bit of it would be *snow-soft*? To *quarter* the earth is to separate it into portions which can then be scoured for prey, before swooping down. *Incipient* here means expected. Why is the last line so shocking? How has the poet prepared us in the first stanza?

Discuss the ways Thomas presents either country life or 'progress' in his poetry.

DEREK WALCOTT

A Country Club Romance

The summer slams the tropic sun
Around all year, and Miss Gautier
Made, as her many friends had done,
Of tennis, her deuxième-métier.

Her breathless bosom rose   5
As proud as Dunlop balls;
She smelled of the fresh rose
On which the white dew falls.

Laburnum-bright her hair,
Her eyes were blue as ponds,   10
Her thighs, so tanned and bare,
Sounder than Government bonds.

She'd drive to the Country Club
For a set, a drink, and a tan;
She smoked, but swore never to stub   15
Herself out on any young man.

The club was as carefree as Paris,
Its lawns Arcadian;
Until at one tournament, Harris
Met her, a black Barbadian.   20

He worked in the Civil Service,
She had this job at the Bank;
When she praised his forearm swerve, his
Brain went completely blank.

O love has its revenges,   25
Love whom man has devised;
They married and lay down like Slazengers
Together. She was ostracized.

Yet she bore her husband a fine set
Of doubles, twins. And her thanks   30
Went up to her God that
Her children would not work in banks.

She took an occasional whisky;
Mr Harris could not understand.
He said, 'Since you so damn frisky,   35
Answer this backhand!'

Next she took pills for sleeping,
And murmured lost names in the night;
She could not hear him weeping:
'Be Jeez, it serve us right.'   40

Her fleet life ended anno
domini 1947,
From Barclay's D.C. & O.
Her soul ascends to heaven.

To Anglo Catholic prayers   45
Heaven will be pervious,
Now may Archdeacon Mayers
Send her a powerful service.

Now every afternoon
When tennis soothes our hates,   50
Mr Harris and his sons,
Drive past the C.C. gates.

While the almonds yellow the beaches,
And the breezes pleat the lake,
And the blondes pray God to 'teach us   55
To profit from her mistake'.

Are there any problems associated with mixed marriages?
If so, does this mean they should never go ahead?

Does sport help bring down the barriers of race?

Originally published in *In a Green Night*, 1962, though
written some ten years earlier, this poem shows the
influence of W.H. Auden's suburban ballads ('Miss Gee' and

'Victor') with their matter-of-fact language and dry humour, distancing the teller from the tale. The restrained artfulness allows Walcott to control and channel his genuine anger. As the product of a mixed marriage himself (his paternal grandfather was white), Walcott was well placed to comment on society's attitudes towards this 'bridge' between the cutlures. Here he dexterously satirises white colonial superiority and does so in a humorous way through the use of an extended series of puns, metaphors and similes based on a game of tennis. List these references to the sport, commenting on their appropriateness and humour. How does the rhythm of the poem and its use of feminine rhymes contribute to the light tone? Compare Sassoon's 'The General'. Comment on the suddenness achieved in line 28, mentioning the enjambement and the previous rhyme. Why does the poet say *her God*? Who do you think *ostracized* her and why? What effects does this have on their marriage?

Why will *Heaven ... be pervious* to *Anglo Catholic prayers*? What tone is Walcott employing here? What does *C.C.* stand for and why does Harris drive by? Comment on the last two lines of the poem.

Tales of the Islands

Chapter III
la belle qui fut

Miss Rossignol lived in the lazaretto
For Roman Catholic crones; she had white skin,
And underneath it, fine, old-fashioned bones;
She flew like bats to vespers every twilight,
The living Magdalen of Donatello;   5
And tipsy as a bottle when she stalked
On stilted legs to fetch the morning milk,
In a black shawl harnessed by rusty brooches.
My mother warned us how that flesh knew silk
Coursing a green estate in gilded coaches.   10
While Miss Rossignol, in the cathedral loft
Sang to her one dead child, a tattered saint
Whose pride had paupered beauty to this witch
Who was so fine once, whose hands were so soft.

This is one of a sequence of sonnets each giving a different picture or tale of life in the islands of the West Indies. Here we have the beautiful woman who has fallen (*la belle qui fut*) and the poet's memories of not just her, but the reaction of his family (and perhaps the local population as a whole) to her. St Lucia, where Walcott grew up, had been French long before it was a British colony, and Walcott was brought up as a Methodist surrounded by Roman Catholics. He describes his background as a 'genteel, self-denying Methodist poverty'. A *lazaretto* is a hospital for the diseased poor, especially lepers. In what two senses is she a leper? Donatello was an Italian sculptor of the Renaissance; his 'Magdalen', a sculpture of Mary Magdalene the repentant prostitute whom Christ forgave, is a thin spidery creation. What clues have we got in the poem that Miss Rossignol: is old; is perhaps diseased; is religious; drinks; wears high heels; is in mourning; has had sex without being married; is not as rich as she once was; is thought to be evil by the local population? There may be more than one clue for each feature. Discuss the effectiveness of each image. Are there any indications that the poet who looks back on his youth is less critical than he had been? How can we deduce that his mother is 'self-denying' and unforgiving? Although there is no rhyme scheme the poem retains the distinction, as in a Petrarchan sonnet, between octet and sestet. How? One critic (Wayne Brown) remarks that this poem 'should be read in a tone of exaggerated wonder ... the tone of a parent reading a bedtime story to a small enthralled child'. What do you think such a reading adds to the poem?

Compare Heaney's 'Punishment'.

Chapter V
'moeurs anciennes'

The fête took place one morning in the heights
For the approval of some anthropologist.
The priest objected to such savage rites
In a Catholic country; but there was a twist
As one of the fathers was himself a student   5
Of black customs; it was quite ironic.
They lead sheep to the rivulet with a drum,
Dancing with absolutely natural grace
Remembered from the dark past whence we come.
The whole thing was more like a bloody picnic.   10
Bottles of white rum and a brawling booth.
They tie the lamb up, then chop off the head,
And ritualists take turns drinking the blood.
Great stuff, old boy; sacrifice, moments of truth.

Chapter VI

Poopa, da' was a fête! I mean it had
Free rum free whisky and some fellars beating
Pan from one of them band in Trinidad
And everywhere you turn was people eating
And drinking and don't name me but I think   5
They catch his wife with two tests up the beach
While he drunk quoting Shelley with 'Each
Generation has its *angst*, but we has none'
And wouldn't let a comma in edgewise.
(Black writer chap, one of them Oxbridge guys.)   10
And it was round this part once that the heart
Of a young child was torn from it alive
By two practitioners of native art,
But that was long before this jump and jive.

These two poems should be read in conjunction, each giving different angles on the same event. What features are common to both? How can we guess who is speaking in each sonnet? Who is speaking the last line of 'Chapter VI'? Why do you suppose that Walcott uses rhyme in these poems? Describe the events as seen by the various speakers, the anthropologist, the uneducated local and Walcott himself. What is the attitude of the speaker in 'Chapter VI' towards the *black writer chap*? What is ironic about the fact that this *chap* is saying that we have no *angst*? Find out what *angst* means. What is the significance of the last four lines of 'Chapter VI'?

Chapter X
'adieu foulard ...'

I watched the island narrowing the fine
Writing of foam around the precipices, then
The roads as small and casual as twine
Thrown on its mountains; I watched till the plane
Turned to the final north and turned above   5
The open channel with the grey sea between
The fishermen's islets until all that I love
Folded in cloud; I watched the shallow green
That broke in places where there would be reef,
The silver glinting on the fuselage, each mile   10
Dividing us and all fidelity strained
Till space would snap it. Then, after a while
I thought of nothing; nothing, I prayed, would change;
When we set down at Seawell it had rained.

Unlike many of the sonnets in this sequence, this, the last
one, uses a full rhyme scheme to suggest finality and
completion. The repeated refrain or pattern of *I watched*
tells of the young man's sadness at leaving his home. List
the details in the poem which show how carefully the poet is
looking at his landscape from the departing plane. What
would he mean by *all fidelity strained / Till space would
snap it*? One critic has written of the 'peculiarly cathartic
effect of the final line'. What do you think the critic means
by this comment? Refer to the fact that, grammatically, the
line stands alone. Why do you think this is?

Which chapter of 'Tales of the Islands' do you find most
effective, and why?

*M*idsummer, Tobago

Broad sun-stoned beaches.

White heat.
A green river.

A bridge,
scorched yellow palms   5

from the summer-sleeping house
drowsing through August.

Days I have held,
days I have lost,

days that outgrow, like daughters,   10
my harbouring arms.

Like a Haiku, this seemingly simple collection of descriptive
phrases gains its power from the associations between
words. Walcott lived in Tobago whilst working for the
Trinidad Guardian but this poem was published a few years
later in 1976. He had two daughters by his second marriage
of 1962. How does the poet sketch, evocatively, the summer
in Tobago? Discuss particularly his use of colour and how
he evokes the sleepiness of hot days. How is *palms*
ambiguous? Why does the *bridge* become a metaphor for
memory? Discuss the rhythm of the last two stanzas. What
does the poet mean by *harbouring arms*? Why is the simile
of the last stanza so effective?

Walcott once wrote, 'There are homecomings without
home.' Discuss with reference to this and the previous
poem. Compare and contrast Grace Nichols' work.

The Virgins

Down the dead streets of sun-stoned Frederiksted,
the first freeport to die for tourism,
strolling at funeral pace, I am reminded
of life not lost to the American dream;
but my small-islander's simplicities   5
can't better our new empire's civilized
exchange of cameras, watches, perfumes, brandies
for the good life, so cheaply underpriced
that only the crime rate is on the rise
in streets blighted with sun, stone arches   10
and plazas blown dry by the hysteria
of rumour. A condominium drowns
in vacancy; its bargains are dusted,
but only jewelled housefly drones
over the bargains. The roulettes spin   15
rustily to the wind; the vigorous trade
that every morning would begin afresh
by revving up green water round the pierhead
heading for where the banks of silver thresh.

Frederiksted is a town in the Virgin islands, a *freeport*, where taxes are reduced to encourage tourists to come and buy cheap goods. In this poem Walcott laments the old simple life of the island which has been lost because of more and more 'trade' and tourism, the *American dream* of commercial enterprise. The American Virgin Islands were bought by the United States from Denmark in 1917 to become part of what Walcott terms the *new empire*; however, the term can be used to describe the new cultural dominance of the United States throughout the world in the twentieth century. Whilst America's territory may not be as large as the British Empire of the previous century, its global domination, based on trade and cultural imperialism, is vast and still growing.

Why is the title an ironic comment on these once-innocent islands? What pattern of images dominates the first three lines? Why is each image appropriate? Comment on the word *civilized* which ends line 6, both in terms of its tone and with regard to the enjambement. In lines 8–9, Walcott claims that the island sells its *good life* (the beaches, the climate which are its assets) too cheaply so that unemployment remains high; why would this mean that the crime rate is on the rise? Pick out the images of a dying, soulless island in the lines which follow. How does Walcott make it seem a ghost town? Why is *jewelled* such a clever image for the *housefly* both in its appearance and the suggestion of wealth? The image in the last lines concerns the ferrying of tourists to casinos and banks. However, on the last line, there is also the first positive reference to the old life of *simplicities* before tourism came to dominate. Identify the old trade referred to. Why do you think Walcott ends triumphantly on a full rhyme where there had been (at most) imperfect or half-rhyme before?

The Bright Field

My nerves steeled against the power of London,
I hurried home that evening, with the sense
we all have, of the crowd's hypocrisy,
to feel my rage, turned on in self-defence,
bear mercy for the anonymity   5
of every self humbled by massive places,
and I, who moved against a bitter sea,
was moved by the light on Underground-bound faces.

Their sun that would not set was going down
on their flushed faces, brickwork like a kiln,   10
on pillar-box bright buses between trees,
with the compassion of calendar art;
like walking sheaves of harvest, the quick crowd
thickened in separate blades of cane or wheat
from factories and office doors conveyed   15
to one end by the loud belt of the street.
And that end brings its sadness, going in
by Underground by cab, by bullock-cart,
and lances us with punctual, maudlin
pity down lanes or cane-fields, till the heart,   20
seeing, like dark canes, the river-spires sharpen,
feels an involuntary bell begin
to toll for everything, even in London,
heart of our history, original sin.

The vision that brought Samuel Palmer peace,   25
that stoked Blake's fury at her furnaces,
flashes from doormen's buttons and the rocks
around Balandra. These slow belfry-strokes
cast in the pool of London, from which swallows
rise in wide rings, and from their bright field, rooks,   30
mark the same beat by which a pelican goes
across Salybia as the tide lowers.

List the things which all people, black or white, from whatever background, have in common.

What would an outsider first notice about London? What are its most typical sights?

This complex, difficult poem rewards close study and careful re-reading. The basic premise, which we only understand fully towards the end of the poem, is that the black St Lucian poet, feeling intimidated by the streets of London, constantly refers in his imagination to the people and fields of his own home, drawing the conclusion that, since we are all human and all must die, then even the imperial colonisers deserve our compassion. Why would the streets of London have a particular source of *power* for a black writer? Why is their power fairly intimidating for most of us? How does Walcott make his appeal in the poem a general one (rather than merely provincial) in lines 2–3? Why do members of a crowd display *hypocrisy* in their dislike of crowds? In lines 7–8, Walcott feels his rage (he has been moved, like Hamlet, to turn against a *bitter sea* of troubles – in this case the crowd) turning to pity as he is *moved* in sympathy, realising that these are not his enemies but his fellow-sufferers. What clever pun is involved in *Underground-bound*? Where will these faces ultimately end up?

The British used to claim that the sun would never set on the British Empire, meaning both that some of its territories would always be in daylight and there would be no end to that dominance. How does Walcott sympathise with the end or death of empire in the second stanza? How does he suggest, in line 12, that the *compassion* will not last very long and has a limited shelf-life? List the images which belong more to the Caribbean than London in the rest of the poem. With which London image are they connected in each case? Bells toll in London to mark the hour – but they also toll to show that *the quick*, or the living, have come to an *end*, the passing-bell of death. What does Walcott convey to us about death in these very different worlds as we pass along the crowded conveyor belt of life? London is the source of our *original sin* because, just as Adam and Eve lost paradise, so the British spoiled the paradise islands of the Caribbean by colonising them. Samuel Palmer was an eighteenth-century engraver and Blake's poems can be found in this volume.

 Walcott, who was born of mixed race (his father's father was white), claimed in a different poem that 'I whose ancestors were slave and Roman / have seen both sides of the imperial foam ...' Do you find evidence of this ambivalent view in this poem?

 Compare these images of Britain's capital with Blake's 'London' and Wordsworth's 'Composed on Westminster Bridge'.

 Walcott has been described as 'a magnificent descriptive poet' and a poet 'whose power extends far beyond the islands'. Discuss either or both of these comments (by George Szirtes) in relation to the above selection.

GRACE NICHOLS

Those Women

Cut and contriving women
hauling fresh shrimps
up in their seines

standing waist deep
in the brown voluptuous   5
water of their own element

how I remember those women
sweeping in the childish rivers
of my eyes

and the fish slipping   10
like eels
through their laughing thighs

A memory of the Caribbean island of Guyana, where Grace
Nichols grew up, this poem describes the women fishing
with *seines* or large nets *sweeping* the mouths of rivers for
shrimps. How might the women be said to be *cut* in two
(refer to the second stanza)? How is this a child's
perspective? What does the poet mean by *contriving*? Why
is the *brown voluptuous / water ... their own element*?
Explain the way the metaphor works in the third stanza.
Why are the eyes (and the memory) of the young poet like
the nets of the women? Describe the mood of the action
described – especially with regard to the transferred epithet
laughing thighs.

Compare 'Midsummer, Tobago' by Walcott.

*T*ropical Death

The fat black woman want
a brilliant tropical death
not a cold sojourn
in some North Europe far / forlorn

The fat black woman want   5
some heat / hibiscus at her feet
blue sea dress
to wrap her neat

The fat black woman want
some bawl   10
no quiet jerk tear wiping
a polite hearse withdrawal

The fat black woman want
all her dead rights
first night   15
third night
nine night
all the sleepless droning
red-eyed wake nights

In the heart of her mother's sweetbreast   20
In the shade
of the sun leaf's cool bless
In the bloom
of her people's bloodrest

the fat black woman want   25
a brilliant tropical death yes

One of a series of poems in which Grace Nichols gives voice to the figure of the West Indian mother figure, trapped in England, a land of cold, after the immigrations of the fifties and sixties. Having been encouraged to the 'motherland' when England needed cheap labour after the war, many of these black people were ostracized and home-sick, but unable to afford to return to the sunny, if poor, lands they had left. Nevertheless the dream of return remained. Why do you suppose the poet breaks off when she does at the end of the first line? Why is this an important, independent line – a somewhat surprising statement in modern Britain? Can you find any other examples of West Indian dialect in the poem? Why is *brilliant* such an effective adjective? To appreciate the significance of the two imperfectly rhyming end-words of lines three and four, it is perhaps wise to look at Keats' poems 'La Belle Dame Sans Merci' and 'Ode to a Nightingale'. *Forlorn*, as Keats stressed, is a word which even sounds mournful and seems to belong to the 'fairy-lands' of escapism. To *sojourn* is what the knight did in a pale and sickly manner in 'La Belle Dame Sans Merci'. Discuss the poet's use of the forward slash (/) in the first two stanzas. What does she mean by *blue sea dress*? Why is the rhyme scheme effective in the second and third stanzas? What does Nichols mean by *bawl* at a funeral? With what *cold* customs does she contrast this in the next two lines? There is a pun in the fourth stanza on *rights* and *rites*. Explain this. What is a *wake* and why would it be *red-eyed*? Discuss the rhythm of the fifth stanza and explain the phrases *mother's sweetbreast*, *leaf's cool bless* and *people's bloodrest*. Comment on the final word. What does the lack of punctuation add to the poem, especially the last line?

GLOSSARY
OF LITERARY TERMS

alliteration – the repetition of consonant sounds, generally but not always at the beginning of words, e.g. *f*lying *f*orward e*ff*ortlessly, *Ph*yllis *f*ell.

allusion – when a writer deliberately tries to echo either the phrasing or the ideas of another poet, and wants the reader to be aware of the reference.

antithesis – most simply, a strong contrast, but used more technically, the balanced opposition of two qualities or things in the same line. Pope uses it most effectively.

assonance – the repetition of similar or identical vowel sounds when there is not a full rhyme, e.g. she l*ea*pt up to f*e*tch h*e*lp. Notice that it is the *sound* that matters not the letter as it appears on the page. Thus the 'e' in 'she' is not a similar sound to that in 'fetch'.

ballad-form – generally a simple song-like structure made up of repeated regular stanza forms, typically four lines per stanza and eight syllables per line. There is often repetition, as the ballad form was originally sung as a folk song.

bathos – a writer may build as if towards a climax and then undermine that climax comically. For instance, R.S. Thomas, in 'Cynddylan', describes the mighty farmer as a knight in shining armour scattering ... hens(!). The adjective is 'bathetic'.

blank verse – iambic pentameter with no rhyme.

caesura – a break in the rhythm midway through a line used to create balance or contrast.

catharsis – the purging or cleansing of powerful emotions by experiencing literature. Thus we feel a form of fear or horror when watching tragedy but this is a positive rather than a negative experience because we have purged our minds not in a real-life situation but because of the imagined suffering of others. The adjective is 'cathartic'.

conceit (Metaphysical) – see **metaphor**.

couplet – see **rhyme**.

didactic – a form of literature which primarily teaches or preaches.

dramatic monologue – all dramatic poetry involves the dramatic devices of conflict and of implied dialogue. The monologue asks the reader to envisage one speaker giving their version of events, often with an implied audience. Such a monologue reveals personality, thoughts, desires, etc. – often more than the speaker might want to reveal.

end-stopping – see **enjambement**

enjambement – a French word which describes the running on of one line of poetry into another, providing a sense of continuity. The opposite to this is **end-stopping** where the sense of a sentence comes to a full (or reasonably full) stop at the end of each line or couplet. **End-stopping** is much more structured whereas enjambement provides a sense of natural spontaneity.

epic – a heroic, extended narrative poem dealing with serious themes (often involving the gods or legendary heroes) in an exalted style.

free verse – that poetry which seems to have very little formal structure, with little regularity in terms of patterns of syllables, rhyme etc. Favoured in the twentieth century, partially as a reflection of the breakdown in society's structures and a new uncertainty about our place in the world due to the falling away of religious authority.

haiku – a Japanese form of poetry, sometimes imitated in English, consisting of three lines which together comprise seventeen syllables. Often these short poems contain seemingly unconnected ideas which on closer inspection actually relate to each other.

heroic couplet – a pair of rhymed lines of **iambic pentameter**, generally containing a complete thought and an element of balance or **antithesis**. See also **enjambement**.

hyperbole – exaggeration for effect.

iamb / iambic – see **rhythm**.

iambic pentameter – the most common rhythm in English poetry. Made up of ten syllables (decasyllabic), five of which are stressed.

lyric – a short poem exploring the poet's thoughts and feelings in a personal manner.

metaphor – the opposite of the literal. A comparison which instead of stating outright that something is 'like' another thing (as a **simile** does), implies the comparison by identifying the two things. Many clichés (or dead metaphors) began life as ordinary metaphors before becoming stale through overuse. For example the expression 'we were over the moon' is obviously not to be taken literally but metaphorically. When Keats claims that he sees a lily on the brow of a lovesick knight, he is expressing both metaphorically and creatively the death-pale quality associated with the knight's autumnal surroundings and his mortal sickness. Metaphors and similes can be **extended** over several lines – this is particularly common in **epic** poetry. When they are particularly far-fetched they are known as **conceits**, often used by the Metaphysicals.

motif – a recurring theme or repeated image.

narrative – storytelling; the way a story is told.

ode – a long lyrical poem often addressed to (and celebrating the qualities of) a person or an emotion – e.g. Tennyson wrote an ode on the death of the Duke of Wellington, whilst Keats wrote one addressed to a mood, melancholy.

onomatopoeia – words where the sound echoes the meaning, e.g. 'twittering' 'creak' 'hiccup' and less straightforwardly 'whisper' or 'murmur'.

oxymoron – see **paradox**.

paradox – a statement which seems illogical, or self-contradictory, but which contains an underlying truth. **Oxymoron** is similar but uses only two words which juxtapose the two opposing qualities, e.g. 'falsely true', 'darkness visible'.

personification – a type of metaphor in which either a dead thing or quality is given the qualities of something animate, or something non-human is given human qualities, e.g. 'the sullen wind', 'Joy, whose hand is ever at his lips, bidding adieu'.

Poet Laureate – a semi-official role which began at the end of the seventeenth century. One poet is chosen by the monarch and awarded a nominal 'pension' in return for which they compose odes and poems on suitable occasions and act as a sort of spokesperson for poetry.

pun – a play on words in which two meanings are meant – e.g. 'Thou hast not done' wrote Donne to God, meaning both 'you have not finished' and 'you have not got me (Donne)'.

quatrain – see **sonnet**.

refrain – occasionally used to describe a 'chorus' or repeated phrase, giving the effect of music. Tennyson uses this device widely.

register – the chosen level of language, ranging from the colloquial (associated with conversation, often chatty and informal) to the grand and formal. A comparison between Larkin and Milton will give the two extremes. Register also has to do with class. A low register often involves slang and dialect terms and less sophisticated vocabulary and sentence structure.

rhyme – an echo of sound between two or more words, extending from the last fully stressed vowel to the end of the word, e.g. 'hill' 'kill'; 'follow' 'hollow'. These are examples of **full rhyme**. **Imperfect rhyme** is also used by poets e.g. 'soul' and 'wall', where there is just enough similarity to suggest a link but the imperfection suggests an atmosphere of disharmony. Similarly **half-rhyme** or **consonance** suggests discordance; here there is a repetition of similar or identical consonant sounds with a change in the intervening vowel, e.g. 'grained' and 'groyned'; 'feather' and 'father'. Generally poets use **end-rhyme** to link two lines together, suggesting order, harmony or a link between two concepts. Rhyming **couplets** form a pattern whereby two consecutive lines rhyme (*aabbcc* etc.); an **alternate** rhyme scheme is a pattern of rhyming every other line (*ababcdcd* etc.). **Internal** rhyme can link ideas or sounds which are not at the end of lines. **Feminine rhyme** rhymes over two rather than one syllable (e.g. 'father', 'rather'). Unlike **masculine rhyme** (on one syllable, e.g. 'far', 'star'), feminine rhyme is often used to lighten the tone, sometimes for comic effect.

rhythm, metre – generally in English poetry, iambs (the iambic rhythm or metre) are used for flowing natural rhythms, trochées (trochaic) for tripping, often childish or comic rhythms. Speech of course is a mixture of the two and often poets deliberately follow the natural rhythms of speech (or thought) rather than the seemingly artificial, ordered regular rhythms of traditional poetry. Other effects can be achieved by deliberately breaking a pattern for emphasis or to suggest disorder, putting many unstressed syllables in a line to speed the rhythm, or putting many stressed syllables together to slow the rhythm down for emphasis. A line of poetry is generally divided into **feet**, where a **foot** of verse is a unit consisting of one stressed syllable and any number of unstressed. A line made up of five feet, the most common in English, is a **pentameter**; a line of four feet is a **tetrameter**.

roundelay – a medieval form of poetry, since imitated in more modern verse, which is a short simple song with a recurring 'refrain' or chorus.

simile – a comparison using 'as' or 'like'; see **metaphor**.

sonnet – a poem of fourteen lines, generally with a regular rhyme scheme and using the **iambic pentameter**. The **Petrarchan** or **Italian** sonnet is made up of an **octet** (eight lines, rhyming *abba abba*) followed by a **sestet** (six lines rhyming *cde cde*). This is generally divided by a **volta**, or a change in subject matter or argument (accompanied by a change in rhyme scheme). The **Elizabethan** or **Shakespearian** sonnet has three **quatrains** (four lines, rhyming *abab cdcd efef*) followed by a **couplet** (*gg*), often a witty change of direction or summing up of the poem.

stanza – a verse or section of poetry, generally separated by a gap. The stanza is used to divide different sections or to structure the poem just as paragraphs are used in prose.

stress – consider the two words 'falling' and 'enough'. 'Falling' is a **trochée** since the first syllable is stressed (there is more emphasis on 'fall' than 'ing' – try emphasising 'ing' and seeing what it sounds like). 'Enough' is an **iamb** since there is more emphasis on the second syllable, whereas the first is unstressed.

structure (or form) – the number of syllables per line, the rhythm established, the number of lines per stanza, the number of stanzas etc. all give an idea of the way a poet structures a poem. Regularity or pattern may often be contrasted with irregularity, which perhaps suggests spontaneity, as in free verse, a less structured form.

tone – consider what effect the poem is meant to have on you. Is the writer being sarcastic, more mildly ironic, ambivalent, heartfelt or sincere, amusing, or detached? This is the tone.

transferred epithet – this is seen when a quality which actually applies to one thing is given, or transferred, to another – for example when Owen describes the 'clumsy helmets' which the floundering soldiers put on, when it is the soldiers and not the helmets that are made clumsy by the difficulty of the task and the panic induced by the gas.

volta – see **sonnet**, above.

Acknowledgements

The publishers are grateful to all copyright holders for permission to reproduce poems. Whilst every effort has been made to trace copyright holders, if any acknowledgement has been inadvertently omitted, the publishers will be pleased to make the necessary arrangements at the first opportunity.

Siegfried Sassoon 'The General' copyright Siegfried Sassoon by permission of George Sassoon.

T S Eliot 'The Love Song of J Alfred Prufrock' from *Collected Poems 1909–1962* by TS Eliot, reprinted by permission of Faber & Faber and Harcourt Brace Jovanovich.

Robert Frost 'Mowing', 'Mending Wall', 'After Apple-Picking', 'Two Look at Two', 'Tree at My Window', 'An Old Man's Winter Night', 'The Silken Tent' by permission of Jonathan Cape.

D H Lawrence 'Piano', 'Last Lesson of the Afternoon', 'Intimates', 'Snake', 'The Mosquito', 'The Mosqito Knows', 'Think–!', 'Let us be Men' from *The Complete Poems of DH Lawrence*, by permission of Laurence Pollinger Limited and the Estate of Frieda Lawrence Ravagli and Viking Penguin Inc.

W H Auden 'Epitaph on a Tyrant' from *Collected Poems* by WH Auden, reprinted by permission of Faber & Faber and Curtis Brown.

Philip Larkin 'Toads' from *The Less Deceived* by Philip Larkin, by permission of The Marvell Press.

Ted Hughes 'The Jaguar', 'The Thought-Fox' reprinted by permission of Faber & Faber.

Sylvia Plath 'Medallion', 'Mushrooms, 'You're', 'Morning Song', 'Wuthering Heights', 'Blackberrying', 'Mirror', 'Among the Narcissi' from *Collected Poems* by Sylvia Plath, reprinted by permission of Faber & Faber and HarperCollins.

Seamus Heaney 'Mid-term Break', 'Digging', 'Follower', 'Blackberry-picking', 'Old Smoothing Iron', 'Punishment', from *New Selected Poems 1966–1987* by Seamus Heaney, reprinted by permission of Faber & Faber and Farrar, Straus & Giroux.

R S Thomas 'The Evacuee', 'Farm Child','Cynddylan' from RS Thomas, *Collected Poems*, JM Dent and Sons. 'Children's Song', 'Lore' from RS Thomas, *Selected Poems 1964–68* (Bloodaxe Books, 1986) 'A Blackbird Singing', 'The Window', 'Moorland', by permision of Macmillan Press.

Derek Walcott 'A Country Club Romance' from *In a Green Night: Poems 1948–60* by Derek Walcott, by permission of Jonathan Cape. 'Tales of the Islands', 'Midsummer Tobago', 'The Virgins', 'The Bright Field' from *Collected Poems 1948–1984*, by Derek Walcott, reprinted by permission of Faber & Faber and Farrar, Straus & Giroux.

Grace Nichols 'Those women', 'Tropical Death' from *Fat Black Women's Poems* by Grace Nichols, Virago.